Stanley P. Chase

THE POEMS AND PLAYS OF
JOHN MASEFIELD

PLAYS

THE MACMILLAN COMPANY
NEW YORK · BOSTON · CHICAGO · DALLAS
ATLANTA · SAN FRANCISCO

MACMILLAN & CO., Limited
LONDON · BOMBAY · CALCUTTA
MELBOURNE

THE MACMILLAN CO. OF CANADA, Ltd.
TORONTO

THE
POEMS AND PLAYS OF
JOHN MASEFIELD

VOLUME TWO
PLAYS

New York

THE MACMILLAN COMPANY

1918

PREFACE

THE first of the plays in this volume, *The Campden Wonder*, was written at Greenwich, near London, at the end of 1905 and beginning of 1906. I had heard the fable of it, The Campden Wonder, in Chipping Campden, in Gloucestershire (where the events happened, or are said to have happened) some years before, while staying there with friends. I had wished, at that time, to write a play upon the subject, and to have it acted in Campden, with other plays founded on the events in that countryside. This scheme came to nothing. In those years many people were dramatizing the events of their cities and districts. There were pageants at Romsey, Winchester, Oxford, Bury and other places. I had hoped that the larger villages might follow the example of the towns. *The Campden Wonder* was produced at the Court Theatre in London in 1907.

Mrs. Harrison, *The Sweeps of Ninety-Eight* and *The Locked Chest* were written at Greenwich in 1906. The fable of *Mrs. Harrison* is a part of the fable of *The Campden Wonder*. It can be found in one of the two pamphlets which preserve the story of the Wonder. *The Sweeps* is an invention, though some of the characters, Major Sirr, and Thomas Judkin Fitzpatrick once lived, and used some of the words allotted to them. The fable of *The Locked Chest* is taken from the Laxdale Saga. All these plays have been acted, the second and third many times.

After I had finished *The Locked Chest*, I wished to try a longer play. A friend in London told me of a case of miscarriage of justice which had happened in Kent early in the last century. I took this as the groundwork of my fable for *The Tragedy of Nan*. I added some inventions to the fable, such as an unhappy love affair, and the characters of the household. I began the play in January and finished it in September, 1907, at Greenwich.

When I was finishing *Nan* I worked at a one-act play upon *The Death of Pompey the Great*, as described in the life of Pompey in North's *Plutarch*. The tragedy of Pompey seemed to be too big a subject for a one-act play, so I left the draft and began anew on fuller lines. I wrote the first act of the play in 1908 in London and the second and third acts in 1909 at Great Hampden.

My next play was *The Faithful*, a pageant showing the tragedy of the 47 Ronin of Japan. This play was begun at Hampstead in January and finished at Great Hampden in May, 1913. I had known the story of The Ronin for many years, and had long hoped to make a play of it, but could not see a dramatic form for it. I planned it and began to write it (in 1912) as a tale in verse, but changed my mind on seeing Mr. Granville Barker's productions of *Twelfth Night* and *The Winter's Tale*. They shewed me more clearly than any stage productions known to me the power and sweep of Shakespeare's construction of "scene undivided and passion unlimited." They helped me to construct *The Faithful* as a play with "continuous performance" for a double or platform stage.

After finishing *The Faithful*, I began the verse play, in one act, of *Philip the King*, about January, 1914. Soon afterwards I began a second one-act play in verse, on the subject of Good Friday. Both of these plays were begun at Hampstead. *Philip* was finished at Lollingdon in May of that fatal year. *Good Friday* was interrupted by the war and never completed. I had hoped in a rewriting to make the play a clash between Christ and the High Priest. This was one of the many millions of human hopes destroyed in that year.

I was a playwright, according to my power, for ten years, during which the theatre in England was the main interest of my fellows and myself. We did not do what we hoped to do (the war stopped that), but we had good fun in trying, and the sport of the effort, mixed up, as it was, with the beauty of youth and the depth of friendship, seems now some of the salt of my life. These plays belong to the days of before the war. What may come after the war is still unsure; but while we are men we have hope, that what comes after us will be better. I hope still to see in England a theatre where playwrights will be doing easily and well, and as a matter of course, the plays which we saw in our dreams, in those old days when we thought the censor a hardship.

JOHN MASEFIELD.

CONTENTS

		PAGE
THE CAMPDEN WONDER		1
MRS. HARRISON		41
THE LOCKED CHEST		61
THE SWEEPS OF NINETY-EIGHT		119
THE TRAGEDY OF NAN		143
THE TRAGEDY OF POMPEY THE GREAT		261
THE FAITHFUL		377
PHILIP THE KING		529
GOOD FRIDAY		581

[ix]

THE·CAMPDEN WONDER

THE CAMPDEN WONDER

PERSONS

	PLAYED BY
JOHN PERRY	.Mr. Norman McKinnel
DICK PERRY	Mr. H. R. Hignett
PARSON	. Mr. Edmund Gurney
TOM CONSTABLE.	. Mr. Norman Page
MRS. PERRY	. Miss Carlotta Addison
MRS. HARRISON. . . .	Miss Dolores Drummond

This play was produced at the Court Theatre, in London, on the 8th of January, 1907, under the direction of Mr. H. Granville Barker.

THE CAMPDEN WONDER

Scene I

Scene. *Harrison's Kitchen in Campden.*

JOAN

Be the master come home from Charringworth yet?

RICH:

I an't heard him, I an't.

JOAN

He be gone a great while. It's near ten.

RICH

[*Going to the door*]. Be you there, Master?—No, a ben't come home yet, Mother.

JOAN

Why, whatever have a kept 'en. If that ben't ten a striking!

RICH

Old Mr. Curtis, he've a harvest feast to-night. Her'll have stopped with old Mr. Curtis, Mother. Her'll sleep there after veast, in the barn, I do think.

JOAN

[*Laughing.*] He be a good one, he be. Seventy year old he be—And her do drink, her do, and her do sing. Law! how a do sing, to be sure; and a do like a's ale.

[3]

Rich

Her be a good old soul—A old ram, he be. Lor, now, to think on the merry deeds of him, the old sinful soul. Only last year now—him away so sly now, like a old fox. They said a was killed for sure; and there a were to Gloucester surely, a drinking, a drinking merry, and him his three-score and ten!

Joan

Her be a merry old soul. Her be a trusty good soul—And a be a good master. Her've done right by thee, Dick.

Rich

Her did say this noon, I should have twelve shillin' a week after Michaelmas. That's more than brother John gets.

Joan

Ah, to think of that now! More than thy brother John! Thy brother John—he be a strange one, he be. I do fear I'll live to see thy brother John hanged! He be earnin' nine shillin' a week, and he drink that, he do.—And he be a handsome lad, Dick, a fine grown lad, John be. He be like his feyther was.

Rich

I do think as how a should do summat for you, Mother, and not go a-drinking all he do earn.

John

He be a handsome lad, Dick, thy brother John. A dear, a dear, he be the very spit of his poor feyther, and he be a sad one, he be; and he do drink all his nine shillin'

[4]

[*Enter* JOHN]

JOHN

Who do drink all his nine shillin'?

JOAN

Ah, John! there thou be, lad. You be late out, John.

JOHN

You were talking about me, you were. You were saying as
I drank—you and Dick there. He be a godly one, brother
Dick be. [*To Dick*]. You keep your tongue shut about me,
and about my nine shillin'. If I do drink it, I drink it open.
I ben't one to go knucklin' to pa'son, I ben't. Nor I dont' go
knucklin' to my lord, like some I know.

JOAN

There, there, John. Don't 'ee take on, now!

RICH

It would be better, I do think, if as how you did go knucklin',
as you call it, stead of swillin' like a beast up to beerhouse.

JOAN

There, there, Dick, lad, don't 'ee go for to mad him. Speak
un fair, lad— thy elder brother he be.

JOHN

[*Mimicking.*] Ah! speak un fair—You shut your head,
Mother. I be good enough to stand up to Dick, I be. Who
goes swillin' like a beast?

[5]

RICH

You do. They be fair shamed to speak to us, neighbours be. They be a drunken lot, them Perrys, they say—'Ah,' they say, " I see John Perry over to Aston. He were asleep in the ditch, the drunken sot!"

JOHN

Who say?

RICH

Parson say, and Farmer Hill say, and thy poor Mother say, and I say too, if they ben't good enough.

JOHN

Let un say! You be a lot of old puts, all on you— You leave I, I advise thee. I won't take no preachin' from you. You be a old put, and Mother be.

RICH

Rather be a old put, than rotten fruit, you drunken dog, you!

JOHN

I ben't no drunken dog.

RICH

You be.

JOAN

Ah! Don't 'ee mad un now, Dick.

JOHN

Better be a drunken dog than a knuckler to Pa'son. You was always the good one, you was. You was like the good boy in the Bible, you always was. You was born to tread on my corns, you was, you closhy put.

[6]

RICH

I ben't no closhy put.

JOHN

You've crossed I long enough, Master Dick. You cross I no more, or I'll give you a cross 'll set thee i' the muck.

RICH

I don't cross thee, John, nor I never done.

JOHN

You be a liar! Wan't you a gettin' sixpence when I were a gettin' nought? Wan't it you got the hat give you? Wan't it you got Master's coat with the red trimmings? And I got nought. You with your pretty face, you grinning pinkanye! Wan't you a gettin' eight shillin' when I were a gettin' but seven? And I your elder, and your better.

DICK

You be my elder, but you ben't my better. If I got eight shillin' an' you seven, it's because I didn't go swillin' over to Aston. I didn't get drunk, I didn't.

JOHN

No, nor you hadn't got the soul in you, you mean. Then you comes a sucking and a trucking to Master Harrison—"Ah!" you says, "ben't I a godly one? Ben't I proper and godly?" "Ah!" you says—So you get took to be his servant. Wan't that a cross to me? Wan't I enough servant to him? I didn't want no knucklin' sniveller helping me. You call that not crossing, don't you? Ah!

[7]

Joan

Now ha' done, John, ha' done. Don't 'ee mind thy brother Dick, John.

John

But I will mind him, I tell 'ee. He have crossed me since we weren't that high. Ah! you dog, you. I be a drunken one, be I? You must get more than I get, must you? And my lady'll speak to you. "Good mornin', Perry," she'll say, "Oh! what beautiful weather." "Good evenin', Dick," she'll say, "You ben't no sot, you ben't. You ben't like your brother John."— No, no, you be a innocent lamb, you be; but you be warned! You have done of your crossing me—you dear sweet suckin' innocent lamb. You was him got sore knees from praying, you was, you dog of dogtown!

Joan

Ah! John dear, do a done!

Rich

Now, don't you go calling names, John Perry. I'll tell you what you are. You're a disgrace; you'll come to a bad end. I never crossed you, and you know it. It's true I'm getting more than you. After Michaelmas I'll be getting more still. I'll be getting twelve shilling a week. If you'd do more, and drink less, you'd be getting the same.

John

If I'd do more! Don't you preach to me. What's the good of doing more, with you stepping in over my head. Twelve shilling a week you're going to have, are you? You are not. You think yourself high in the world. You think you're a

clever one. You think you'll do better than your brother.
You will not. Not with me here. High in the world you think
yourself with your twelve shilling. I'll bring you low—I'll bring
you lower than the lowest.

RICH

It'll take a soberer man than you to do it.

JOHN

What'll it take?

JOAN

A dear! A dear! That ever I should see the day! Go home,
Dick lad, you're only angering your brother.

JOHN

Lower than the lowest, I'll bring you. You shall drag in the
dirt, you and your twelve shillin'!

RICH

I tell you it'll take a soberer man than you. Go home, man.
Get someone to pump on you. You need sobering. I wonder
you're not ashamed to talk that way afore your mother!

JOHN

Don't learn me my duty, you Noll Crumwell's man, you
Dicky Kill King!

RICH

What am I?

JOHN

A canting put. That's what you are—and a dog—A dirty

[9]

twelve shilling sneck up of a Ledbury lawyer; but you mark me, I'll bring you down!

RICH

Go home and sleep it off, man. I'm sick of hearing you.

JOHN

What? What? Sick, are you? I'll make you sicker.
[*He flies at Rich: and grapples with him.*]

JOAN

[*Running to door.*] Help! Help! Mrs. Harrison!

[*Enter* MRS. HARRISON]

MRS. H:

Lord save us, and spare us! Good God, be good to us! Why, what's all this? Lord God's my mercy; why, Dick, why, John! John, what are you doing here? I thought I forbid you my kitchen. Dick, I'm ashamed of you! As for you, John, a gaol's the best place for you. Dick, I'm ashamed of you, fighting in your Master's kitchen, and with your own brother! You'd ought to be ashamed of yourself! It was enough to turn all the beer in the cellar, the noise you were making.

RICH

He began it, mum!

JOHN

You be a liar.

JOAN

Remember your duty.

[10]

Mrs. H.

Now say a word more, John Perry, and I'll have you bound over. As for you, Dick, I'll tell your Master. Has your Master come in yet?

Dick

No 'm. Us haven't heard him.

Mrs. H.

Lord God, be good to a sinful woman. If I haven't enough to bear! It's not enough that I have my house made a common bawdy house. Like a den of thieves it was, the noise you were making; and my man must go boozing till I don't know what hour.—It'll be another of this gallivaunts—I'll give him harvesting when comes in. Go saddle the mare, one of you, and go to Charringworth and bring him back with you.

John

[*Rising.*] I'll go, give me the lantern, Mother.

Dick

You set down, John Perry. You ain't fit to bring any one home.

John

Give I the lantern. [*To* Dick] I'll give you a bloody head if you orders me.

Dick

Set down, when you're told. Give me that light.

JOHN

No, you don't! Stand back. Would you? Take that! [*he hits him*].

JOAN

Ah, Lord! Ah, Lord! Don't 'ee, Dick, lad.

MRS. H.

Now, John John Perry—Lord God's my hope and mercy. There'll be bloody adultery done. What, John, I say!

JOHN

I'll learn 'ee.

DICK

Let go of my throat, or I'll hit'ee one.

JOAN

Ah dear! Ah dear! Oh, do 'ee.

MRS. H.

[*Snatching a cider mug and dashing cider into* JOHN's *face— the fighters separate.*] Lord God's my hope and mercy! If I'm not all of a tremble—all of a tremble you've made me. And the cider all over my new taffety! Lord God's my witness, there might have been murder done. Get you of out this, John Perry. I do believe, John, as you'd do murder. Get you out of this. Never you darken these doors again. I believe as you'd cut my husband's throat—Lord Jesus have mercy! for what he had on him. Saddle the mare, Dick. You're the only one of the two I can trust. Saddle the mare, Dick. Where's my bottle of cordials?

[*Exit*]

DICK

I knowed how it would be—and I get disgraced because you
go swilling beer, and come here drunk. Give us the lantern.
[*He lights it. John glowers at him*].

JOAN

Ah dear! ah dear! Ah, Dick, I do wish thee wouldn't mad
thy brother. Ah dear! Ah dear! He be that like his poor
feyther.

DICK

[*Taking harness down.*] You're a disgrace, you are. You're a
disgrace to Campden—you're a disgrace to your mother. You
make us shamed. Ugh, you drunkard!
[*Exit Dick with Harness and Lantern:* JOHN *glowers after him.*]

JOAN

[*In a quavering voice.*] Ah dear, ah dear. I be getting old.
It ben't like it were. There be none to comfort me now my man
is taken. If thy poor feyther were alive now! Ah, John dear,
don't 'ee mind thy brother Dick. Ah dear, he do mad thee,
that he do. He do vex thee sore. Ah dear! I must be getting
home.—It be late. Don't 'ee mind thy brother Dick, John.

JOHN

I'll mind my brother Dick.
[*She goes out slowly after waiting a moment.* JOHN *glowers
after her.*]

JOHN

[*Slowly.*] Old Harrison be out late. They think he be gone
away boozing, but he ben't. Only I know where old Harrison

be gone. [*A pause.*] Twelve shillin' a week you be gettin'. Twelve shillin' a week, and I nought but nine. [*The mare's hoofs sound outside.*] Ah, ha, ha! I'll do it—That's what I'll do.

[*Re-Enter* JOAN]

JOHN

I'll drag him lower than the low, him and his twelve shillin'.

JOAN

Do 'ee come, John. I be all of a shake.

JOHN

[*Going*]. Lower than the dirt, I'll drag him.

CURTAIN

[*The Curtain rises again immediately*]

SCENE II

SCENE: *The same.* MRS. HARRISON AND THE PARSON. (DICK PERRY, *within, singing, and* JOAN *joining in the chorus, heard faintly.*)

PARSON

Come, come, Mrs. Harrison, bear a good heart! Come, don't take on so. Your husband's only—only gone to see a friend. He'll be back to dinner, I daresay.

MRS. H.

Not with the friends he goes to see, no. Oh, if I haven't much to bear.

[14]

PARSON

O, but, Mrs. Harrison, come now, go in and take some breakfast. Why, your husband's well enough. Think, think of last
year, what a turn he gave us. No one would hurt Mr. Harrison.
It's absurd. Anyone would think he had been murdered.

MRS. H.

Murdered—ah! There's some comfort in a corpse. There's
satisfaction in a body. I was saying that to Mrs. Murrell. "If
one has the body," I said, "one knows one has done one's duty
by it." One knows that it's all for the best, and then there's
the funeral. O dear, O dear—my man lying drunk in a ditch!
It's his beer again—Beer, beer, beer. It's his ruin. O, if I had
you here, William Harrison! O, a corpse would be a mercy com-
pared to this. And half of my lady's corn not cut, and the
reapers saying they must have another penny a day. O, William Harrison! Man is a trial, and a rod of affliction. It's a
gnashing of teeth you've been to me.

PARSON

Why, my good Mrs. Harrison, this'll never do. Why, here's
John Perry back. Come, John, you've brought good news, I'm
sure. Come, Mrs. Harrison, here's John back. Well, John,
have you found Mr. Harrison? Where was he?

JOHN

No, nor won't find him—Neither you nor no one.

PARSON

John!

[15]

JOHN

Neither you nor no one.

MRS. H.

There, now! If he hasn't been at the drink again. I smell it on him from here—like an empty cider cask. I think I've enough to bear without you getting drunk, John Perry.

JOHN

You have enough to bear—that's true.

PARSON

What do you mean, John, man? He's not drunk, Mrs Harrison. What is it? What has happened?

MRS. H.

You don't mean to say he was seen with Mrs. Emsworth? I'm—

PARSON

Hush, Mrs. Harrison—we are all in God's hand. Speak John. Tell us! Speak, man, can't you?

JOHN

I want my words took down.

[THE PARSON *looks hard at him*]

MRS. H.

Is it as bad as that? He's been seen with the scarlet woman! He's been sitting on the seven hills. I know it. O dear, O dear, drinking the wine of wrath.

[16]

PARSON

Hush, Mrs. Harrison. [*He sits down to ink and paper.*] Now, John, tell us all you have to say. Mrs. Harrison, we are but children, we must submit to Providence. We are here to declare the glory of God, not to cry over our little hurts. If Providence has taken your husband, you should rejoice. Now, John, speak, tell us everything. Come, Mrs. Harrison.

[*The voices of* DICK *and* JOAN *within, singing*]

JOHN

I ben't going to tell my words, till there be witnesses. I want Tom Constable, and I want Mother here, and brother Dick. I got Tom Constable, outside. I brought 'en special.

PARSON

[*Going to door.*] Mrs. Perry! Dick! Is Tom Constable, outside there still, or has he gone home?

DICK

[*Within.*] He be here, sir.

PARSON

Just ask him to step inside, and will you come in too, both of you?

[*Enter* DICK, JOAN AND TOM CONSTABLE]

Stand at the door, Tom, and attend to what is said.

TOM

I will, sir.

PARSON

[*Aside.*] Mrs. Perry, just get out the cordials, and set them

[17]

by Mrs. Harrison, I'm afraid she may swoon. [*She does so.*] I want you all to attend to what John, there, has to say. Now, John, tell all you know.

JOHN

I ben't going to tell my words, not till I had my book-oath took.

PARSON

Lay your hand on this testament.

JOHN

[*Putting hand on testament.*] I be going to testify.

[*A pause*]

JOHN

I be going to testify. [*Glowering at* MRS. HARRISON.] Mrs. Harrison, thee'd best drink a drop—I got awful news. I got awful news. Mr. Harrison be dead.

PARSON

Be patient, Mrs. Harrison, hear all. How dead?

JOHN

Murdered dead.

ALL

What?

JOHN

Murdered dead!

PARSON

[*Standing up.*] We are but children, Mrs. Harrison. Whom God loveth he chasteneth. How was he murdered, John?

[18]

JOHN

I be going to testify. I want my words took down. [PARSON
takes pen.]—It was us murdered Mr. Harrison.

ALL

What, what, what d'ye mean?

JOHN

It was I, and Mother, and Dick there, murdered Mr. Harrison.

DICK

You—liar!

JOAN

Be you gone mad, John?

PARSON

Have a care what you say, John Perry.

JOHN

For his gold we murdered him.

MRS. H.

I don't believe a word you're saying—[Weeps.]

JOHN

For his gold we murdered him.

DICK

I wonder God don't strike thee dead, John.

JOAN

John have gone crazed, sir. It be the sun—he were in the sun afore he took food this morning. Do 'ee sit, John. Us'll bathe thy poor head for'ee.

JOHN

We murdered en dead for his gold. For his gold we murdered en—didn't us, Dick?

DICK

Mr. . . . Sir! God have afflicted my poor brother—He don't know what he say.

JOHN

I know what I say, I do. And you do. It lie black on my breast—It was your bloody mind planned it.

MRS. H.

You be a-lying, John Perry. You always was a liar! I was saying what a liar you was only yesterday, to Mrs. Murrell I said it—"that John Perry be a liar," I said. Where did you murder him? Where's the body?

JOHN

We murdered en dead for his gold.

DICK

Shall us put leeches to en's head, Sir? He be mazed. It be the blood. Shall I go fetch Doctor?

PARSON

[*In a hard voice.*] Stay where you are, Richard Perry. Come here to the table—and you, Mrs. Perry. Will you lay your hands to this testament and swear you are innocent of this crime? This crime John accuses you of?

DICK

Sir, you don't surely—sir, you don't go for to believe him?
Sir, you don't go for to believe him?

JOAN

My poor boy be crazed, sir. Make 'en set, sir. He don't
know what he do say.

PARSON

I ask you to put you hands to this testament, and swear you
are innocent of this crime. This crime John here accuses you of.

DICK

Sir, you ben't thinking—O! God, sir, you ben't thinking
that?

JOAN

I do swear it, Sir. I swear it purely. Do 'ee let me bathe
his head now, Sir. It be only a wammering-like.

JOHN

It ben't no wammering. It lie black on my breast.

PARSON

Come here to the table, Dick Perry. I want you to swear—
Put your hand on this testament.

DICK

[*Aloud.*] What be I to say, sir?

JOHN

Say how we killed en, Dick. Say how we laid en dead.

[21]

DICK

I say you be a wicked liar, John, a liar afore God. I say as I be false accused, and as Mother is. And I say you be a wicked liar, John, or you be smit mad.

JOHN

You come to me last night, you did. And Mother come—"Let's kill en," you said—And you'd said it afore. "Let's kill en," you said—and Mother said it.

DICK

Parson, do believe en! [*A pause.*]—God help my poor wife! [*He goes to testament.*]—I do swear as I be false accused. As I be innocent—And as Mother be.

MRS. H.

And I believe thee, Dick. Thy brother John be a liar: to Mrs. Murrell I said it. If he ben't swooning, now.
[DICK *puts his hand to his head, and sways a moment. He takes out a handkerchief, as he takes it out he drops some twine.*]

JOHN

[*Pouncing on the twine.*] Now what d'ye say, Dick Perry? 'Ee don't know this, do 'ee, now. What be this string, Dick? What be this, Mother?

DICK

It be my poor wife's hair net.

JOAN

Why, so it be. It be a hair net, to be sure.

[22]

PARSON

What do you know of this hair-string, John Perry? Do you know it?

JOHN

I know it, I do. And Mother know it, and Dick. To our cost we know it. It be the cord we murdered en with.

JOAN AND DICK

Oh, John Perry!

PARSON

Where was this? This that you say?

JOHN

Below Battle Ridge. At the foot o'hill it were. By the brook, where they found ens collar.

JOAN

Us was never nigh the place.

DICK

John, have done with thy sport. Say you be fooling. Parson —Do 'ee think what 'ee be saying.

JOHN

I *do* think, I do. And *you* think. I confessed, I have. I made a clean breast—our sin be black—black it be—to kill poor Mr. Harrison.

PARSON

Be calm, Mrs. Harrison, hear all. [*He writes.*] Now tell us how you killed him. Listen Tom, you will have to give evidence at the trial.

DICK AND JOAN

Sir, don't you believe en. Sir, you ben't goin' to believe en. He be lying, sir. Mrs. Harrison knows he be lying. He be smit mad, sir.

PARSON

Keep silence, please. You will be heard in due course. Now, John.

JOHN

So brother Dick he says, "Let's kill en," "For ens gold," says Mother. Often they'd said it. So us goes out—

PARSON

What time was this?

JOHN

It were—it were twelve. So us goes out, and we see old Mr. Harrison coming, singing. In the moonlight we seed en, and Dick and Mother and I, we strangles un—with this cord. O, it were a black deed!

MRS. H.

[*Interrupting.*] John Perry, you be lying—where's the body? I don't believe as my poor man be dead. Nor I won't. Not till I touch his cold corpse—there now.

PARSON

Where is the body, John?

JOHN

Mother and Dick took ens body. They were hardened uns, they were. I were that shook by our black deed! O, a black deed it were. Where did 'ee put ens corpse, Mother? Hey, Dick?

DICK

[*To Parson.*] Sir, he be play-acting. You see he be play-acting.

JOAN

If my poor man were alive, us wouldn't be like this, us wouldn't. Do 'ee not damn thy soul black, John. Thou knows us be innocent.

JOHN

A proper hardened un, you was; and Dick was.

PARSON

Richard Perry, can you now, in the sight of God, put your hand on this testament, and swear yourself innocent, after what John here has said? Can you Mrs. Perry?

MRS. P.

I be a poor old widow woman, I be. I an't got no man, I an't, not since my poor man were took. Seventy year have I lived in Campden, and some time it have been hard, and some time it have been not so hard; and us have had our little home, us have, though us were poor. I have brought my sons up in the fear of the Lord. I wasn't never questioned like this afore. Us have borne a good name, us have, though us were poor. I be innocent, Sir. God forgive my poor lying boy.

JOHN

God forgive thee leading I to murder.

PARSON

Now, Richard Perry.

MRS. H

Dick be fainting. [*To* PARSON.] It be a cruel shame, it be, sir, to vex us so. For shame, Sir.

DICK

I be innocent, I be. John knows I be innocent. My poor wife knows I be, and Mother knows. [*He touches book and sways.*]

PARSON

His nose is bleeding. It is the hand of God. God hath spoken, Tom.

TOM

Ess, sir.

PARSON

Call thy men.

[TOM *goes to door and whistles.*]

DICK

What be 'ee going to do, please, sir. Us have sworn.

[*Enter* MEN]

PARSON

Tom Constable, take John here, and Dick, and Mrs. Perry, to the lock-up.

DICK

Sir, do 'ee now!

TOM

Thee'd best come quiet, Dick. Us won't hurt 'ee.

DICK

But I be innocent. It be a lie. I ben't no murderer.

[26]

PARSON

You will be able to prove that at your trial. Remove them,
Tom.

JOHN

Our blood be due for our black deed—Us shall all hang.

JOAN

Give me thy arm, Tom. I be a old woman. I ain't got no
man, I an't. Book says us must be patient. [*She goes to* JOHN
and strokes his face.] John, boy, thee be that like thy dad, John.
Us must get Doctor to un, mustn't us, Dick? [*She makes her
reverence to* PARSON.]

TOM

Come, mother, lean on my arm.

DICK

Bear on me, Mother. [*They support her to door.*]

JOAN

[*Turning at door.*] Mrs. Harrison, us be poor folk, false accused. Do 'ee get Doctor to look to my poor boy.

JOHN

Us shall be like Staffordshire—three hung in one knot.

PARSON

Do your office, Tom.

[*Exeunt* CONSTABLES, ETC.]

[MANENT PARSON & MRS. HARRISON]

Bear up, Mrs. Harrison. We are like old lanterns in the hall—

we are dark—we are broken. And anon God takes us, and sets us on the walls of Heaven, amid unspeakable beauty, to light His Courts. Your husband—

Mrs. H.

Mr. Parson, sir. You be a man of God, and you be a scholard. It don't beseem the likes of me to talk plain to the likes of you. You'd ought to go down on your knees and ask forgiveness. You be swift to shed innocent blood. *You* talk of lanterns, and such. Down on your knees, you ought to go. You've been and committed them Perrys on the word of a liar and a dog. My man ben't murdered—my man ben't murdered. That John Perry'd hang his mother for a sup of drink.

Parson

Mrs. Harrison, John Perry would not accuse himself; you forget yourself.

Mrs. H.

Forget myself, do I! In my own house—quotha! Ladida indeed—so I forget myself! You be a sneck up of a covetuous Levite, a creeping into widows' houses. That's what you be. Ladida indeed! But I ben't no widow. When my man comes home he shall reckon with thee, he shall. And the Perrys shall. They'll teach 'ee to shed innocent blood on the word of a dog and a liar. Marry, come up!

[*Exit* Parson]

O, Willy Harrison, Willy Harrison! You and your beer will be my death.

Curtain

[28]

Scene III

[*A room in the lock-up at Broad Campden.* Mrs. Perry, Dick, John, *secured by wrists and ankles to chains. They are in different corners. A table in front.*]

Joan

Us be to die, Dick. Do 'ee bear up, lad. Thou, knows John, as us be innocent. And God he knows it. Us shall have mercy, Dick. Us shall walk the gold streets and that—forever, Amen.

Dick

It be easy for you to talk, Mother. I do think of my poor wife, I do, and of my poor babes. " There goes his wife," they'll say. That's what neighbours'll say. " Him as killed poor Mr. Harrison."

John

" As killed him for uns gold."

Dick

John, do 'ee now speak. Say as us be innocent. Don't 'ee see us hanged, boy. There be my poor wife, and my poor babes. Do 'ee speak, John, speak. Her'll be but a tramp, and my little Nan and all. Her were saying so pretty—And I shan't see un again. Lord, never again! And her'll want bread to eat, and go to bed crying. Do 'ee speak, John. For God's sake, John, say as us be innocent.

John

Us'll have ballads sung—and I shouldn't wonder. Us'll

[29]

all be in a ballad. "The bloody Perrys, they was hanged—O, grief!" And there'll be drums, and the sun a-shining—on Broadway Hill and all. And there'll be neighbours. Sure to be. And us'll go in a cart, like high up folk. "There they go"; neighbours'll say, " as killed un for ens gold. They was always bad ones, them Perrys," they'll say.

JOAN

John, thou be going afore thy Maker, thou be. Us be going to die to-day. It be a sad thing for a old woman to die with her sons—her two boys, as she's been that proud of. To be hanged up on a hill with neighbours calling her a old witch. And then, there be Dick's little maids. O, John, do 'ee speak, lad! And us won't be put in churchyard. I shan't lie with my poor man, a dear! Whatever will I do, a dear! I shan't lie with my poor man!

JOHN

I ben't going to speak, I ben't. I said my say. To Judge I said it. Her were all in her red gownd. "Ah, you Perry," he said: " you be a notable rogue." Her had a sword afore her. Now us be going to be hanged. I wonder will us have ale give us. Old Cop of Aston, they give *him* ale.

[*Enter* TOM CONSTABLE]

TOM

Master Parson, sir.

JOAN

He ben't here—yet—Tom.

TOM

Can I do aught for 'ee, Mrs. Perry?

JOAN

Us be past it, Tom, I do thank 'ee. It be my boy, John, and my boy, Dick, as I be grieved for. And them little maids of Dick's. Us be false accused, us be, my poor mad boy knows. And God knows. And them little ones'll want bread when us be gone!

TOM

Mrs. Harrison have took Dick's little ones. God save 'ee, Mother. Us knows as you be innocent. And neighbours says it. God bless ee, Dick, if I don't see ee again.

DICK

God bless 'ee for thy kind words. 'Ee comfort poor Nan, Tom. Don't 'ee let folk say as her Daddy were hung. God comfort my poor Nan.

TOM

God bless 'ee, Dick, lad, and comfort 'ee. God forgive 'ee, John. Thy hands be red of blood, John; God forgive 'ee. [*To* PARSON.] Saving your presence, sir.

PARSON

Go, Tom.

[*Exit* TOM]

JOAN

I be ready, sir. I be ready to go in the cart.

PARSON

Ah, Mrs. Perry! In a few moments you will be before God's Judgment Seat, a trembling bird on God's hand. How will

[31]

you ask mercy of Him, when you have hardened your heart here on earth; denying the guilt for which you suffer!

JOAN

I ben't afeard to meet my God, sir. God have pity upon the poor and on the widows. I be innocent of blood, I be. I've been a great sinner, and I be punished for it. I set my boy John afore my boy Dick. Parson, I be dying. Will 'ee let I lie in Chrisom ground? Let I lie near my man, Parson, along of my poor husband?

[*Enter* TOM]

TOM

[*In a choking voice.*] It be the Sheriff, sir.

PARSON

Come, Mrs. Perry. You are about to walk in Paradise, among the holy ones. You are about to stand before God, in the glory unspeakable. Lean on me—lean on Tom here.

JOAN

John, won't 'ee say now as we be false accused? 'Ee won't see thy old mother hanged? Do 'ee speak. Say as you spoke lies, John. Thee knows 'ee did.

DICK

For God's sake, John.

JOHN

I confessed to Parson, and I confessed to Judge, I ben't bound to confess to you.

[32]

JOAN

God have mercy on us all then. May He have mercy on you, John—And on you, Dick—and on me, thy mother—and on all poor souls. May us meet glorified in God's golden courts, Amen.

PARSON

Amen. Come, Mrs. Perry.

JOAN

God be with 'ee, Dick. I've put 'ee to bed, Dick, a many times. But now I be going to bed afore you.

DICK

God be with 'ee, Mother. God comfort 'ee.

JOAN

God be with 'ee, too, John. For all your sins. [*She turns to go.*] 'Ee be that like thy poor feyther, John. I be going to God's holy house.

TOM

Lean on me Mother. [*They go out at door—the drums beat up.*]

JOHN

O, us be going to have drums.

DICK

Thou be a dog, John, thou be. O, John, say as us be innocent, say it out, now. It'll save Mother. It'll save my little Nan. . . Call, John; call! O, John, thou be a dog!

[33]

JOHN

Call, Dick. That be right. Call, Dick. Shout! Thy throat it won't call much longer.

DICK

Ah, God!

JOHN

O! It be "Ah, God" now, be it! It were "I be a proper godly one," it's not so long since. How about thy twelve shillin' a week, Dick? You that was to be that high in the world? Eh, Dick? Thy twelve shillin'? Lower than the dirt I've dragged 'ee. Like I said I'd do. Lower than the dirt, thou and thy twelve shillin'.

DICK

Then thee ben't mad. Thee've sworn our lives away!

JOHN

You be a clever one, you be!

[*Re-enter* PARSON, *very white and sick, and* TOM]

DICK

Parson, John have confessed. He've confessed he have sworn false. O! Parson, do 'ee save Mother. He have confessed, sir.

JOHN

He be mazed, sir. Give un a cordial, Parson. He be clean mazed.

DICK

O, Sir, hear en. Do 'ee save Mother. Her said he'd done it a purpose to cross I. Do 'ee listen, sir.

[34]

PARSON

Come, Richard Perry. Compose yourself. We are poor
flames blowing in the wind, now one way, now another. In
the peace of God's house our light will burn steadily. Come,
Richard Perry.

[TOM *undoes chains*]

DICK

God help my poor wife. God help all dying men as folk
won't listen to! I've lived honest, and I've worked honest,
and this be the end.

PARSON

It is but the beginning. There is no end to the glory and the
peace of God.

DICK

[*To* JOHN.] And no end to the fire for such as thee, John.
May the red hot worms gnaw thy body, John. You dog, you
dog!

PARSON

Come, Dick. Help him, Tom.

DICK

O Parson, do 'ee make John speak. He have confessed, sir.
O! sir, he have confessed. Indeed, sir, he've confessed. Make
un speak, Parson. It'll save my Nan.

PARSON

Come, Dick. It is but a step. Do not seek to stay longer
in this wicked world.

[35]

DICK

But he've confessed, Parson. He've said as he were lying. O! sir, do 'ee.

JOHN

Give un a cordial, Parson. He be fair mazed. Help en, Tom.

TOM

Come, be a man, Dick!

[Exeunt—The drums again]

JOHN

There he do go, him and his twelve shillin'. Ah, you godly one! Ha, you godly one! They got you. Lower than the dirt, like as I said I'd do. Afore all Campden! You and your twelve shillin'! Make un a speech, Dick. Make thy speech and confession. O! if I might see thee. O! if only door were open. Thee be looking pale, you and your twelve shillin'. You that thought to be high in the world. Aha! Aha!

[A cry without and drums]

There he do go! Aha! Aha!

[A pause]

[Re-Enter PARSON and TOM]

PARSON

O! the pity of it, the pity of it! O! Lord strengthen me.

JOHN

Mr. Parson, Sir, might I speak to 'ee, sir?

PARSON

In a minute. In a minute, John. O! Lord, have pity.

John

I be a dying man, Parson. I got summat to say to 'ee.

[PARSON *stands*]

Parsons, will 'ee give I comfort? I been a great sinner, I have. I been drunk, and I stole; and I been poaching, and I gone with women. And I kill poor Mr. Harrison. O! I been a black one, I have. Shall I have mercy, Parson? Be I doomed to the fire?

Parson

There is joy, John, over one sinner that repenteth. God's mercy is infinite. Put your trust in Him, John.

John

Ah, sir. I do feel it in my heart. It be a glow, like.

Parson

Come, John Perry.

[TOM *undoes chains*]

There is yet one thing, John. Where is Mr. Harrison's body? You are about to die, John. Tell us this, that he may have Christian burial.

John

It were Dick and Mother took his body, sir. I don't know where it be, I don't. But perhaps one day you'll find en. You'll be wiser on that day, Parson.

Parson

You talk strangely, John.

John

A dying man have a right to talk strange. I be ready, Sir. Will you say a prayer for me, Sir? "Our Father" or summat.

[37]

PARSON

Repeat it after me, John. Come.

[*Exeunt: Drums again*]

[*A pause, during which the drums beat. Then a march as the troops pass away.*]

[*Enter* MRS. HARRISON, *panting*]

MRS. H.

Are you there, Dick? Ah! Ah! If I'm not near my death. Are you there, Dick? Mrs. Perry!

[*Enter* PARSON. MRS. H. *fans herself.* PARSON *mops his brow.*]

PARSON

The wages of sin is death. [*He mops and sits down.*] The wages of sin is death. He talked strangely. And the old woman —Ah, God, her gray hairs—and then the frantic one, about his child. Ah, have pity, O Father! The wages of sin is death, death. It has been a terrible day. A terrible day.

MRS. H.

What's terrible? How has it been terrible? What ails you, man?

PARSON

[*Looking at her.*] O, Mrs Harrison—

MRS. H.

Oh? Well, he's come home, like I said he would.

PARSON

Who?

MRS. H.

Who? Why, William Harrison, my husband.

PARSON

Come home?

MRS. H.

Yes, come home, like I said he would.

PARSON

Come home?

MRS. H.

If you don't vex a sinful woman's flesh! Yes, he has come home—boozing—That's where he's been.

[PARSON *covers his eyes and moans*]

[*Aloud.*] Now, don't set there moaning—You've got to set them Perrys free.

[*She goes to him and shakes him*]

Go and find 'em, and set 'em free. Come, come, now, don't 'ee take it to heart. We all make mistakes. That John Perry, he might have had 'em all hanged.

PARSON

[*Weakly.*] They are—all hanged.

MRS. H

What?

PARSON

Hanged. This morning.

MRS. H.

But it was to-morrow.

PARSON

No, to-day.

MRS. H.

But this be the sixteenth? This be Tuesday?

PARSON

No. [*A long pause.*]

MRS. H.

So that's why the town was empty. That's why the prison's got no—[*Fiercely.*] Be you telling the truth?

PARSON

O, don't, don't!

[*A pause*]

MRS. H.

May God be good to a sinful woman.

PARSON

Amen.

MRS. H.

They be happy to be out of such a world.

PARSON

"O, Father, Now is my soul troubled, and what shall I say?"

MRS. H.

Us be two poor souls, Parson.

[*Crying and laying her hand on his*]

CURTAIN

[40]

MRS. HARRISON

MRS. HARRISON

PERSONS

WILL HARRISON
PARSON
TOM CONSTABLE
MRS. HARRISON

MRS. HARRISON

SCENE: *A Room in* MRS. HARRISON'S *House.*

MRS. H.

There's your cider. Take it; there's a toast in it. Take it.
And now, you and I will have a reckoning.

WILL H.

Huh!

MRS. H.

[*Rapping table.*] You may groan and you may grunt, but
you'll listen to me. And you'll answer me. You'll answer me,
before you leave this room.

WILL H.

Gerr yer.

MRS. H.

I want to know about you, William Harrison. A nice husband you've been to me. And now I want to know about you,
and you'll answer me. Where've you been all this long while?
Where've you been, I say? What Dolly Draggletails have you
been with?

WILL H.

Ah, put your head in a bag!

MRS. H.

Put my head in a bag! Put my head in a bag! You low
dog, you. There's a way to talk to a woman. There's a way

to talk to a wife. How dare you tell me put my head in a bag. How dare you, after what's past? How dare you? After leaving me alone this long while. Is this a world to leave a woman alone in? Is this a world to leave a nice, comely, decent, fine-grown woman alone in? Let alone your wife!

WILL H.

Huh! I run no risks leaving you.

MRS. H.

No. So you ran no risks, didn't you? There's some would have said different. There's some set a higher price on beauty than what you do. A comely woman's something to them, it is.

WILL H.

It is, is it? They're welcome!

MRS. H.

When you've done with your insults, we'll talk. Where've you been all this long while?—You've been with your beer and your dollymops!—I'm sick to think I've kissed you.

WILL H.

And I am.

MRS. H.

Thank you. Thank you for nothing. And now I want an answer. When you've done with your sneers and your jeers I want an answer. D'ye know what you've done by going away? D'ye know what your beer and your trollopsing have been the cause of?

WILL H.

I know what your naggin's 'll be the cause of. Here—[*he bangs mug*]—Cider.

MRS. H.

You'll answer me first.

WILL H.

Cider, I say.

MRS. H.

You have been the cause of three folk being hanged;—John Perry, and Dick Perry and poor old Mrs. Perry;—Hanged. Hanged by the neck! That's a fine thing, isn't it, for beer and trulls to do? Where've you been, you tank, you dog, you low thing. Where've you been? What can you say for yourself?

WILL H.

Gimme my cider. Gimme my cider when I tell you!

MRS. H.

[*Snatching cider mug.*] Here! [*She smashes it on floor and stamps on fragments.*] There! That's all the cider you'll get. Now, answer.

WILL H.

[*Getting up and snatching her wrists.*] Be that the game? Well, I'll answer. Sit down there. And you say another word, and you'll get a knock'll give you sense! I'll tell you where I've been; and keep it dark. You'd better. You speak a word of it, and you'll be missed. The first dark night as comes, you'll be missed.

MRS. H.

That means you'll murder me.

[45]

Will H.

Listen! I went away acos I was paid to go away. D'ye understand that? Paid.

Mrs. H.

Who paid you?

Will H.

Ah! Wouldn't you? And I was paid three hundred golden pound to go away. And my going away was worth that to the man as paid it.

Mrs. H.

Where did 'ee go to?

Will H.

I weren't never more'n twenty mile away.

Mrs. H.

Then 'ee knew. 'Ee knew of what—'ee knew of the Perrys?

Will H.

I knowed all about the Perrys.

Mrs. H.

You knowed about the Perrys?

Will H.

And glad to.

Mrs. H.

You knowed they was to be hanged?

Will H.

And glad to.

[46]

Mrs. H.

And 'ee could have saved 'en.

Will H.

I knowed one worth two of that. You listen to I and keep your mouth shut. John Perry knew where I were. And why I'd gone. Think I'd let 'en live when he were that crazy to go and get hanged? Think I'd stop 'en hanging when he knew my secret? Gerr yer; talk sense!

Mrs. H.

Then you let them poor souls be hanged, knowing they was innocent.

Will H.

Ah, talk sense.

Mrs. H.

You set by and let them all be hanged?

Will H.

Didn't I tell you I got three hundred pound? What's the Perrys to me? I know my duty, I hope. Hark you to me, missus. It was my Lord give me that £300. It was to my Lord's advantage I should be away awhile. What's three Perrys, or six Perrys, or a churchful of Perrys to my Lord? Hark you to me! [*He gets up and goes to her.*] And you breathe so much as a shuddering, wee glimmer of a whisper,— you just raise your little dove-like voice—you just dare to! [*He snaps his fingers.*] And it'll be your last.

Mrs. H.

[*Slowly.*] And—I'm—to—live—with—a—murderer? I've

had a murderer to bed with me, and held 'en in my arms! [*To* WILL H.] And what tale will you tell the neighbours? What tale am I to tell the neighbours when they ask? Lord God! if it ben't pitiful!

WILL H.

Damn the neighbours! Gimme my cider.

MRS. H.

There's footsteps coming up the walk. It'll be parson. O God, Will, what be I to tell en?

[A knock at the door]

WILL H.

Why, tell 'en—tell 'en—Tell 'en something; you'd better. Say I was kidnapped. And bear me out, now. Bear me out in that. I was kidnapped. [*Another knock.*] Set down there, [*she sits*] and now, remember. You say a word of the truth, [*he snaps his fingers*]—your neck'll go like that!—Come in! Who be there?

[Enter TOM CONSTABLE *and* PARSON]

Why, if it bain't you, parson. Come in. Come in! Why now, if this ben't strange. What wonders I have to tell 'ee.

PARSON

O Harrison. There have been wonders indeed. To think of you coming home safely, after all. Your wife is looking quite white, even now. I don't wonder.

WILL H.

They do say, as joy kills quicker'n grief, parson.

Parson

You must look after Mrs. Harrison. It has been a terrible time for her.

Tom

Ah! it has.

Will H.

[*Recognising* Tom.] Why, Tom. Tom Constable. And how be you, Tom? Why, what joy it be to meet all the old folk agen.

Tom

Thank 'ee, sir. I be doing kindly, sir.

Parson

Yes, I brought Tom as a witness. I have to write to my Lord and tell him everything. Ah me, it is a terrible tale! And so you've come back?

Will H.

They do say as seein' is believin'.

Parson

Just to think, Mrs. Harrison. Ah, Mrs. Harrison! And so you've come back. O! if you had but come a day sooner. No, not a day; an hour; twenty minutes.

Will H.

We be in God's hands, parson.

Parson

It is the truth. And where've you been? Tell me now. Tell me everything. *Everything!*

[49]

Will H.

Well, you'll think there's still miracles.

Mrs. H.

He was kidnapped, parson; think of that, kidnapped.

Will H.

By a man on horseback.

Mrs. H.

By two men on horseback.

Parson

Where was this? Was this where they found the collar?

Mrs. H.

Yes, by Battle Ridge. They wore masks, and they seized him.

Tom

Why didn't 'ee welt their nags? I'd a welted en, afore they'd seized I.

Mrs. H.

How could an old man fight agenst two?

Parson

Yes,—and then?

Will H.

Why then. . . . Why. . . . Let me see. Yes. So they said. . . . No a said nothing. . . . They up and . . . . How were it now? [*Aside to* Mrs. H.] Help me out or I'll hit 'ee one.

Mrs. H.

They up and set you afore one of them. You told me just now.

Will H.

Ah, they did. Afore one of them they set me.

Mrs. H.

And he'd been eating onions, parson. Think of that. The one he set afore had been eating onions. Think of him noticing that. Think of a man noticing that.

Parson

Go on, go on.

Will H.

So they set me afore one of them. And he'd been eating onions. I could never abide the smell. No. I never could abide onions. Did you ever know me abide the smell of onions?

Mrs. H.

No, you never did. You never could abide onions.

Will H.

They do say as one man's meat be another's poison—

Parson

So then?

Will H.

Why, all in good time. . . . So then. . . . Where was I?
So then. . . . You be in such a hurry. . . . Why. . . .
So then. . . . I wish 'ee'd not interrupt.

[51]

Mrs. H.

Here, William Harrison. If you aren't a trial and a torment. Do for goodness' sake let me tell the story!

Tom

Ah, do 'ee.

Parson

Go on, Mrs. Harrison.

Mrs. H.

So they rode him off, oh, for miles. And then they came to a house, and they locked him in a room for all the next day. And at night they rode him off agen. And so on for a day or two. And then they came to a ship. And there he heard 'em selling his body for a slave. Selling his body for a slave—a slave to the Turk!

Parson

How much did they give for you, William?

Will H.

I heard one of them say thirty shillin'.

Parson

But that couldn't have been for you. That'd never have paid taking you across England.

Mrs. H.

It'd be more like thirty pound.

Will H.

Well, it might a been pound. Thirty pound then.

Mrs. H.

And then the ship was at sea, and at last they come to the Turks' country, where they sold him for a slave.

Parson

To think of that now! A Campden man a slave to the Turk!

Tom

O Lord! thy wonders!

Will H.

I was a slave to the Turk.

Parson

What work did you do, William?

Will H.

Why hard work.   Hard work it was.

Mrs. H.

He was a slave to a doctor, parson,—digging in the herb beds.

Will H.

I dug 'em with a spade.

Tom

I'd a liked to a seen 'ee dig, master.

Parson

And how did you get away, William?

Will H.

Well, I got away, didn't I,—though I be old.

Tom

Old and bold as the saying is.

Parson

Ah, but how?

Mrs. H.

His master sent him to an English merchant with a bottle
of elixir. The merchant was sick. And William said he was
an Englishman as had been stole away. And the merchant
put 'en in a ship. And so he came home.

Parson

What port did you land at?

Will H.

[*Puzzled.*] It was Norfolk, I do think.

Mrs. H.

Norfolk my grandmother! *Portsmouth* don't I keep telling
you. [*To* Parson.] I think my man would make a saint cross.
Portsmouth, Will. Norfolk's in France.

Will H.

Ah, *Portsmouth*. I ben't no learned astronomer. One place
be like another to me. I don't hold with these new fangled
towns. I been a slave to the Turk. Give I Campden.

Tom

O, the wonders of the Lord!

Parson

Well, Will; you ought to write a book.

Will H.

I don't know about any book. The Christian religion's book enough. There's a book. All else is sin, books is.

Tom

Ah!

Parson

Now, Will. I want you to come up to the church with me to return thanks for your restoration, and ask His mercy for our sins, and for the deaths of his innocents, the Perrys.

Will H.

Ah, that I will, Parson. [*They turn to go.*]

Parson

Come, Mrs. Harrison.

Mrs. H.

I be feeling overcome, Parson, I'll stay here and read the Bible, while you prays.

Parson

You must take care of yourself, Mrs. Harrison. You must look after your wife, William. She has had a grievous trial.

Will H.

She'll pull round, you'll find. Joy cometh in the morning.

Mrs. H.

Have I been a good wife to you, Will?

Parson

She's been overwrought, William.

Mrs. H.

Have I been a good wife to you, Will?

Will H.

Now don't 'ee fuss. Set quiet. She'll be all right; she just needs letting alone a while. Come, parson, us'll just step to church. [*Exit* Parson *and* Will H. Tom *holds door for them.*]

Mrs. H.

[*As* Tom *goes.*] Tom!

Tom

Yes, Mrs. Harrison?

Mrs. H.

Come here, Tom. [Tom *goes to table.*]

Mrs. H.

Reach me the Bible.

Tom

Here it be, miss.

Mrs. H.

Now, Tom.

Tom

Yes, Mrs. Harrison.

Mrs. H.

You know them little girls of Dick Perry's?

Tom

Ay!

Mrs. H.

You'll look after them little girls, Tom?

TOM

I said I'd do. And I will do.

MRS. H.

You'll not let folk say as their daddy were hung?

TOM

I'll break their heads as says it. They'll not say it twice, if they says it once.

MRS. H.

You'll swear that, Tom, swear it on the Bible.

TOM

There be'n't no call to swear, mum. You knows me, I hope.

MRS. H.

Swear it. Swear you'll look after 'em. Whatever happens. . . .

TOM

What I can do I'll do.

MRS. H.

[*Going to a drawer.*] This be for you, Tom, to spend for them little girls. It be what I got by my hens. It be near five pound in silver.

TOM

I don't ask no money, I be glad to do a kindness. I don't ask no money.

MRS. H.

Take it. Take it, I say! And may the Lord prosper you for all you do for them poor little maids. Look after 'em, Tom.

[57]

Tom

I'll look after 'em, mum.

Mrs. H.

Now go, Tom. I be all-to frushed and of a frammock.

Tom

Can I get 'ee anything?

Mrs. H.

No, Tom. Now 'ee go.

Tom

Good day to 'ee, mum.

Mrs. H.

God save 'ee, Tom.

[*Exit* Tom]

Mrs. H.

I been wife to a murderer. . . . I been wife to a murderer. . . . I've been to bed with a man as done murder; and I've helped un clear after. . . . [*She rocks in her chair; then gets up and goes to cupboard.*] But never no more, William Harrison, you've had your last of me. . . . [*She opens cupboard.*] I be the lowest of the low. O Lord, I be the lowest of the low. . . . I feel as I'd been spat on. [*She rummages among bottles.*] But never no more, William Harrison. . . . God have mercy on a sinful woman. . . . You've had your last of me, William Harrison. You can go to your Jennies, you can. . . . [*She takes out a paper.*] This is it. This is it,—is the cure. I bought it for the rattens as ate my chicks. What'll kill rattens'll kill folk. Where be my thimble? [*She pours powder into thimble and drinks.*] Ugh! it be bitter! [*She pours again and drinks.*] Ugh! [*She*

puts thimble and paper into fire. The fire spurts up.] Ah, pretty
it be! [*She goes to table and begins to read the Bible: she spells
it out slowly.*]

"But when Jesus saw it, he was much displeased, and said
unto them: Suffer the little children to come unto me. Suffer
the little children to come unto me." Us be little children—
"And forbid them not.". . . It be a long road for poor
folk. . . . It be a cold road for us, poor children. . . . [*dies*].

THE END

THE LOCKED CHEST
A PLAY IN ONE ACT
(From a Tale in the Laxdaelasaga)

PERSONS

THORD GODDI	. . . .	*A Farmer*
THOROLF	. . . . .	
INGIALD	. . . . .	*A Lord*
SOLDIERS	. . . . .	*Adherents of Ingiald*
VIGDIS GODDI	. . . . .	*Wife of Thord*

SCENE

Iceland

THE LOCKED CHEST

SCENE: *A room.   A chest used as a bench.   A table, etc.* VIGDIS *embroidering a cloth.*

VIGDIS
[*Singing.*]

> My love is drowned in the Lowlands,
>   Away.   Heigho.
> My love is drowned in the Lowlands,
>   Lowlands no more.

[*Enter* THORD GODDI]

Well, Thord.   I hope you had a good market.
[*Sings.*]

> His hair is cold with the seaweed,
>   Away.   Heigho.
> His hair is cold with the seaweed,
>   Lowlands no more.

Come and sit down by the fire, won't you?
[*Sings.*]

> O my love is drowned in the Lowlands,
>   Away——

THORD
For heaven's sake, stop it.

VIGDIS
Stop what?

THORD
That caterwauling.

[63]

VIGDIS

Caterwauling?

THORD

I'm not going to have that howling when I've got a headache——

VIGDIS

I'm sorry I sang when you had a headache.   I didn't know.

THORD

I've always got a headache.

VIGDIS

I'm sorry, Thord.

THORD

O, don't "sorry" me.   If you're so sorry as all that there'd
have been a nice supper ready.   But there.   It's always the way.

VIGDIS

Let me get you your supper.

THORD

O, I don't want it now, thanks.   I couldn't eat it.   Why
wasn't it ready for me, the moment I came in?

VIGDIS

But, Thord.   My dear man.

THORD

How many more times am I to tell you I won't be "my
deared" when I've a headache?

VIGDIS

I'm sorry, Thord.

THORD

If you knew how much it aggravated. But there. You only do it to drive me mad.

VIGDIS

I don't, Thord.

THORD

Contradict me. Do. That's right. Contradict me. I suppose you'll say next—— But there, it's always the way.

VIGDIS

Thord!

THORD

Now, why wasn't supper ready the moment I came in?

VIGDIS

You said you'd be home late, Thord, and that supper wasn't to be till half-past seven.

THORD

You might have known the fair would be a bad one.

VIGDIS

Was the fair a bad one?

THORD

O, use your sense. Use your sense, woman.

VIDGIS

But I do, Thord.

[65]

THORD

Would I be here at this time if the fair had been a good one?
You know perfectly well I shouldn't.

VIGDIS

I'm so sorry, Thord.

THORD

[*Growling.*] Yes, so that you might have more money to
spend on jewellery. [*He sits down.*] I'm tired.

VIGDIS

Let me help you pull your boots off. [*She pulls a boot and
drops it.*]

THORD

O, for Heaven's sake.
Didn't I tell you I'd got a headache? But there. No, I'll
take off the other myself. I'm tired to death.

VIGDIS

Let me give you a nip of brandy.

THORD

Brandy? With a headache? You know brandy nearly kills
me. Now do for Heaven's sake leave me alone.

VIGDIS

You're tired, Thord. You're tired. Lie down on the chest,
and rest till supper. You're tired to death.

THORD

I wouldn't be tired if I wasn't driven half mad by your tongue.
A plague take all wives and all fairs.

[66]

VIGDIS

Tell me about the fair, Thord, if you're not too tired.

THORD

I've already told you about the fair.

VIGDIS

Were there many people?

THORD

Enough to fill a graveyard. I'd be glad to have the burying of some of them.

VIGDIS

What's the news?

THORD

News? What d'ye want with news?

VIGDIS

But I like to hear what's going on. What were they talking of?

THORD

What were who talking of?

VIGDIS

The people at the fair.

THORD

None of their business. That's what they were talking of. They were talking of a murder.

VIGDIS

A murder!

THORD

[*Shouting.*] A murder. Can't you pay attention when I'm talking to you? I said a murder. Why don't you listen?

VIGDIS

Who has been murdered?

THORD

I didn't say anyone had been murdered.

VIGDIS

But you said——

THORD

But I said nothing of the sort. There was a fight down on the beach and a man was killed.

VIGDIS

What man?

THORD

That big swaggering fellow Hall.

VIGDIS

Hall? Brother of Ingiald?

THORD

Yes. Brother of Ingiald. A lout he was, too.

VIGDIS

Who killed him?

THORD

Does it matter to you who killed him?

VIGDIS

No. Only I would like to know.

THORD

You're always wanting to know. You want to know too
much. What was Hall to you?

VIGDIS

Nothing. My cousin was his partner. That's all I know
about him. And they used to quarrel all day, as though they
were man and wife.

THORD

I suppose that's meant for me. Well, I don't know who killed
him. But I know this.

VIGDIS

What?

THORD

I pity the man who did it.

VIGDIS

Why?

THORD

Have you any sense at all, woman?

VIGDIS

I don't see why he should be pitied.

THORD

Well, I do. D'you suppose a great man like Ingiald will
let his brother's murderer escape?

[69]

VIGDIS

But you said it was a fight on the beach.

THORD

I said. I said. I said. Nag. Nag. Nag. Even if it were,
d'you suppose a man like Ingiald would let the man escape?
Ingiald'll hunt him down. That murderer's a doomed man.

VIGDIS

Poor fellow, I say.

THORD

Serve him right, I say. Serve him right.

VIGDIS

I wonder who it was.

THORD

It isn't known who it was. Two or three are suspected.

VIGDIS

I hope it wasn't cousin Thorolf.

THORD

Well, if it was he must take the consequences.

VIGDIS

That man Hall was a sad man to work with. I hate to speak
ill of a dead man; but he had a bad name.

THORD

He was a drunken boor.

VIGDIS

He went for Thorolf with an axe once.

THORD

Well, I pity the man who went for *him* with an axe. Is supper ever going to come at all? Or am I to stay talking here all night?

VIGDIS

Won't you go in and lie down, Thord? Supper will be ready in a moment.

THORD

How can I go in and lie down? You know perfectly well I've got to see to the chores. I can't trust the hired men.

VIGDIS

I'll run out and see to the chores, Thord.

THORD

You? I can't trust you to get supper, let alone do the chores. No. I must sacrifice myself. I've got a headache and I'm half dead. But there, it's always the way. I must do a thing myself if I want it done. Give me my boots.

VIGDIS

Let me go, Thord. I'll see the cows driven in and milked.

THORD

Give—me—my—boots. Don't I tell you? Don't tell me what you'll do and what you'll not do. There [*puts on boots*], I thought when I came in I'd have time to rest myself. But

[71]

there. It's always the way. [*Turns to go out.*] What are you glowering there for? Go—and—get—the supper ready. When you've worn me to my grave I suppose you'll be glad. You do make me so mad.

VIGDIS

I'll have supper directly, Thord.

THORD

You do make me so mad. But there. It's always the way. [*He goes out.*]

VIGDIS

It's a pity we've no child, Thord and I. They say a child is a great sweetener in a house. If we'd a child, perhaps he wouldn't take on so. Ah well. It wasn't like this when we were courting. I must get this table clear. If I'd had a child now, he'd have been different. That's what a wife must expect. Nothing but "O my headache," and "O if I'm not tired." I only wanted to hear about the murder. It's not so often we get a murder to talk about. The way he talks you'd think we had one every day. So Hall is murdered. I never liked that man. I wonder who killed him. Well. There's one comfort. My cousin Thorolf wouldn't go for to kill a man. Not even Hall, he wouldn't. He wouldn't kill a fly, my cousin Thorolf wouldn't. He's like a blessed babe. [*The door at the back is knocked violently.*] Bless us and save us.

VOICE

Let me in. Let me in. Vigdis. Thord.

VIGDIS

Who's there?

VOICE

Open. Open. For God's sake let me in.

VIGDIS

Enter. If you be of God.

VOICE

Open.

VIGDIS

[*Running to door.*] Come in. Who's there?

[*Enter* THOROLF]

Thorolf. Cousin Thorolf. How are you?

THOROLF

Stand back. Don't kiss me.

VIGDIS

What's the matter, Thorolf?

THOROLF

Stand back. You keep your hands off.

VIGDIS

But I'm your cousin, Thorolf.

THOROLF

Yes. But perhaps you won't be quite so glad to be my cousin when you hear the news.

VIGDIS

What news, Thorolf?

THOROLF

About Hall.

VIGDIS

He's dead. What d'ye mean, Thorolf?

THOROLF

I killed him, Vigdis.

VIGDIS

You, Thorolf?

THOROLF

He cheated me. O, but I can't go into that. So we fought, and I killed him. It was a fair fight. I didn't want to kill him, God knows.

VIGDIS

Men have no sense when they have swords in their hands.

THOROLF

It was a fair fight.

VIGDIS

I'm not blaming you, Thorolf. It seems men must kill each other from time to time. But what are you going to do now?

THOROLF

What indeed?

VIGDIS

You know what it means. You must know what it means. Do they know you did it?

THOROLF

Ingiald will know by this.

[74]

VIGDIS

But you know what Ingiald is. He'll be after you to-night, now. Now. What will you do? What will you do, Thorolf?

THOROLF

You're my cousin, Vigdis?

VIGDIS

Of course I'm your cousin.

THOROLF

You wouldn't cast me off. You don't think worse of me. I mean, it was a fair fight. It was fair and square.

VIGDIS

Of course I won't cast you off. You're my cousin. Men have no sense at any time. But when they have swords in their hands—it might happen to anyone.

THOROLF

Vigdis. Will you stand by me?

VIGDIS

You're my cousin, Thorolf. There's my hand. But don't waste time like this. Where will you hide? Who can shelter you against Ingiald? The King himself could hardly do it. It's death to shelter you. Where will you go? Think. Think. Where will you go?

THOROLF

I was thinking perhaps you would shelter me.

VIGDIS

I, Thorolf?

THOROLF

You and Thord.

VIGDIS

And Thord?

THOROLF

I was thinking perhaps you would.

VIGDIS

Against Ingiald?

THOROLF

Until I could get a ship. Only till I could get a ship.

VIGDIS

Against a man like Ingiald?

THOROLF

I know it's a risk, dear. I know it's a risk.

VIGDIS

You know, Thorolf, my man Thord isn't much of a warrior.

THOROLF

It wouldn't be for long, dear. If I could lie low a night or two——

VIGDIS

What should we be, against Ingiald?

THOROLF

If we could just put him off the track, dear, then I could

[76]

slip down to Broadfirth and get a ship. It would only be a night or two.

VIGDIS

Thord is Thord. And I'm only a woman, and women aren't much good in a case of this sort.

THOROLF

Let me stay, Vigdis. Will you?

VIGDIS

I wish I could think of a plan.

THOROLF

Where else can I go?

VIGDIS

Go? You won't go anywhere. You'll just stay here, where you are. Don't worry yourself about that. It's Ingiald and Thord I'm thinking of.

THOROLF

My God, Vigdis, you're good. I'll kiss you for that.

VIGDIS

Oh, none of your nonsense, now. This is no kissing matter. No, you can't stay in here. Let go my hand, or I'll box your ears. Come this way, now. I'll shut you up in the sheepfold. Quickly, now, before my husband comes. [*Goes out at side door.*]

THOROLF

I've only got to put Ingiald off the track, dear. Old Hrut will get me a ship.

[77]

VIGDIS

Put Ingiald off the track first, my friend. We'll think of the ship later. Come along. [*Exeunt.*]

[*The other side door opens, and re-enter* THORD.]

THORD

Vigdis. Vigdis. Is supper ready yet? Now if that isn't too bad. What's the woman thinking of? Vigdis, I say. It's not enough that I have a headache, and get fairly fratted to death, but I'm to be kept waiting for my supper. Vigdis. Vigdis, I say. [*Enter* VIGDIS.]

VIGDIS

What is it, Thord?

THORD

What is it? Supper. Where's supper? Why on earth isn't supper ready?

VIGDIS

I've had a visitor, Thord. A guest.

THORD

A guest, eh. Who invited him?

VIGDIS

No one invited him. He's a sort of a relation of mine.

THORD

So it is a he. How long am I to be tortured with him?

VIGDIS

I'd like him to stay for some time. If you don't mind, Thord.

THORD

You know I mind. You know as well as I do I can't abide strangers in the house. They make this house just like an inn. Except that they never pay for what they have. I will not put up with it. It's enough that I'm half mad with headache, but I must have a stranger in the house. But there. It's always the way. Who is this stranger? Is he respectable?

VIGDIS

He's a sort of relation of mine. I told you just now.

THORD

A relation. If it had been a stranger I wouldn't have minded; but to have a relation. And I shall have to be civil to him. Vigdis, I do think you might have had a little thought of me. But there. You think of no one but yourself. It's always the way with you women.

VIGDIS

It won't be for long, Thord.

THORD

I tell you what it is, Vigdis. If he's respectable he may stay the night and go on before breakfast. If he's one of these rowdy fellows, or if he's in trouble, I'll not have him near the place. I'll put the dogs on him myself.

VIGDIS

You cannot, Thord. I've already taken him in. I can't go back on my word. I've promised him shelter now.

THORD

Shelter?

VIGDIS

You see he's in trouble.

THORD

What trouble? Who is he, once for all?

VIGDIS

Cousin Thorolf.

THORD

Thorolf! What's he been doing? He's an idle blackguard, Thorolf.

VIGDIS

He's not.

THORD

He is, I say. Don't contradict. What's he been doing?

VIGDIS

There was. . . . It was. . . . It was a fair fight, Thord.

THORD

A—fair—fight. You—don't—mean——

VIGDIS

Down on the beach.

THORD

Not. . . . No. . . . Not Hall?

VIGDIS

Yes. He killed Hall.

THORD

Ingiald's brother.

VIGDIS

Ingialds' brother.

THORD

And you've been such a fool as to take him in. To take in Hall's murderer. Ingiald's brother's murderer.

VIGDIS

It was a fair fight, Thord.

THORD

It—was—a—fair fight. A—fair—fight. Ingiald's brother. A fair fight.

VIGDIS

They fought with swords.

THORD

In my house. Here. Ingiald's brother's murderer. And you've let him in. Where is he?

VIGDIS

In the sheep-fold at the back of the house, for the present. That's a good place. They'd never look among the sheep.

THORD

My head is like the seven mills of Milltown. In my house. O, my head. O miserable man. It'll be my death. It's not enough that I must have a headache, and come home tired out, but I must have Ingiald down on me. He'll burn the house. He will. He will. I know Ingiald. He'll burn the

house. He's sure to find out. And if he doesn't burn the
house he'll put a blood-fine on me. He'll fine me a flock of
sheep. It's not enough that I'm fratted to death and find no
supper ready, but I must lose my cattle and be murdered in
my bed. But there, it's always the way.

VIGDIS

You'll be nothing of the sort. Have pity on poor Thorolf.

THORD

Pity. Let poor Thorolf show a little pity on me. I'm a ruined
man. Ingiald will drag me up and down by the hair. He'll hit
me in the ribs with his great fists. He will. He will. I know
Ingiald. And you go and take in a murderer. A murderer. If
it had been a murderer of some common man I wouldn't have
minded. But the murderer of Ingiald's brother.

VIGDIS

I tell you it was not a murder. Thorolf's no murderer. He's
like a woman in most things, Thorolf is. I tell you it was not a
murder. It was a fair fight.

THORD

So Ingiald'll say. Yes, he'll say. I'll take your sheep, he'll
say. And them nice cows too, Thord, he'll say. It was a nice
fair fight, he'll say, so now I'll burn you in your bed. I know
Ingiald. Ahoo. Ahoo.

VIGDIS

Well. I wouldn't be a cry baby. There's worse things than
being burned in our beds. Come. Be a man, Thord. One
would think you were afraid of dying.

THORD

O, hold your nagging tongue, for God's sake. Ahoo. Ahoo.

VIGDIS

It will all come right, Thord. Look. I'll get you some nice supper.

THORD

You'll drive me mad in another minute. Supper, Ingiald's knife'll be the only supper I shall have. Hold your nagging tongue, and let me die in peace.

VIGDIS

It's very likely that we'll have Ingiald here before long. He's not a man to wait on the road. He comes like an eagle, Ingiald does.

THORD

O what shall I do? What shall I do?

VIGDIS

Do? Put a bold face on it. There's no danger where there's no fear. Look him in the face and tell him to walk out of here.

THORD

He may be coming now. Look out at the door, Vigdis. Is he coming?

VIGDIS

There's someone coming. It's a party of men. A dozen, quite.

THORD

O, I'm not fit to die. I'm not.

VIGDIS

Be a man. They're coming quickly. They'll be here in a minute. Yes. It's Ingiald. There's his red cloak. He's walking ahead of the rest. Be a man now, Thord. It'll be all right.

THORD

O! O!

VIGDIS

Can you think of any better plan than the sheep-fold?

THORD

O!

VIGDIS

O, why didn't I marry a man? You don't think he'd look in the sheep-fold, with all the sheep in it? I'm sure he wouldn't.

THORD

O, Thorolf's all right. It's myself I'm thinking of. It's myself. O!

VIGDIS

I wonder you aren't ashamed.

THORD

I was getting on so well. I'd have been able to buy Rapp's field next year——

VIGDIS

Think of poor Thorolf. Brace up, man. Ingiald'll suspect at once if he sees you like that. What's your life? What's my life? It's our guest's life that matters.

THORD

An idle vagrant's life better than mine? If it had been the King, now.

VIGDIS

Thord, brace yourself. Thorolf's safe in the sheep-fold. Ingiald can prove nothing. Your guest's life depends on the way you look. Don't flop there like a done-out old gather-up of a bachelor. Swell your chest out. Put a scowl on, like a Viking. That's better. Here they are.

[*A knock at the door.*]

THORD

O, I'm a dead man.

VIGDIS

O, I could shake you. For Thorolf's sake, perk yourself.

[*A knock.*]

Come in. Go and open the door, Thord.

THORD

I can't. How can you ask me to open the door?

[*A knock.*]

VIGDIS

Go on, Thord. Go. Open, man.

THORD

Vigdis. You don't mind. You open. Your nerves aren't like mine.

VIGDIS

Quick, Thord. It's for the host to open.

[85]

VOICES

Open within there. Open in the name of the law.

VIGDIS

I must open, then. [*Goes to the door.*] Come in, come in.

[*Enter* INGIALD *and* MEN-AT-ARMS]

INGIALD

God save all here. Thank you, Vigdis.

VIGDIS

My man's not quite himself, to-night, Lord Ingiald.

INGIALD

I'm sorrry to hear that. What pin pricks now, Thord?

THORD

Ah. Oh.

INGIALD

[*Looking keenly at both of them.*] I should have thought life was pretty quiet up here. No fighting. No gambling. No anxiety——

VIGDIS

My man gets run down, Lord Ingiald. It's going to these fairs that does it. I've known him come home in a way of speaking, and he'd be all cold, like a dead man. It's the nerves and that on the brain. [*A pause.*] What could I do for you, Lord Ingiald? Will you not sit down? Is there anything you would like to take? It's not often we see you up here. Why, I don't think I've seen you, not since last October twelve month.

INGIALD

No. I daresay not. [*He goes over to* THORD *and bangs him on the shoulder.*]

THORD

Ow. What is it, Ingiald? Don't.

INGIALD

I want to have a talk with you, my friend.

THORD

A—a talk. O yes. Yes, that. Yes. Very nice.

INGIALD

[*To his men.*] Go out and stand by the door. Don't budge till I tell you.

MEN

Ay, ay, sir.

[*Exeunt*]

VIGDIS

Wouldn't your men be pleased to take a drop of something? You've surely not come all the way from Sheep Isles. What is it we could do for you, Lord Ingiald? Perhaps you would let me hear it. My man's not himself to-night. Were you wanting any hands to help get your harvest in? Tell me what it is.

INGIALD

Thank you, Vigdis. I want to have a talk with Thord, here.

THORD

I—I'm so ill, Ingiald. It's the weather. Vigdis will do any

business. My head. My head is bad. I'm a martyr to my head in wet weather.

INGIALD

I know what it is. My own head gives me tortures. But I must have a talk with you. Perhaps you would ask your wife to mull me a little ale?

VIGDIS

You must let me mull it in here, then. The kitchen fire's out.

INGIALD

I should be delighted; but my nerves can't bear the smell of ale being mulled. It always upsets me. [*To* THORD.] Perhaps you would ask your wife to—to look at the sunset. Most beautiful sunset, outside.

VIGDIS

Yes, we were looking at it this last half hour.

INGIALD

I see. Well. Vigdis. I must talk to Thord here privately. Will you go into the next room? I won't keep you long.

VIGDIS

Certainly, Lord Ingiald. Now, I won't have you telling my man about any of those naughty baggages at Reykjavik. He knows quite enough, already.

INGIALD

I won't mention a single baggage. [*He calls to a* SOLDIER.] Erik, just atttend the lady for a moment. [*Aside to* SOLDIER.] See she doesn't leave the room.

Vigdis

I know you men. [*She tries to catch* Thord's *eye*.] I'll make him repeat every word you say. [*She goes out unconcernedly*.]

Ingiald

[*Aside*.] Well. If you're not a wonder. [*Sharply*.] Now, Thord, my friend, I've got only one thing to say to you. Where's Thorolf?

Thord

Thorolf.

Ingiald

Well?

Thord

Which Thorolf would that be?

Ingiald

You know quite well which Thorolf.

Thord

O, you mean old Thorolf of the Ridge? Ah yes. A fat man. He——

Ingiald

Now, Thord. [*Glares at him*.]

Thord

O, young Thorolf. Koll o' Dales' lad. He goes to school, now.

Ingiald

[*Rapping the table*.] Thord.

Thord

Don't, Ingiald. You put a fellow out so.

[89]

INGIALD

Where's Thorolf? Vigdis's cousin. Your cousin, Thorolf.

THORD

Ha, ha, ha! *That* Thorolf. Yes. An idle blackguard. Yes.

INGIALD

Yes. That Thorolf. Where is he?

THORD

I've not seen him, Ingiald.

INGIALD

I suppose you've not heard about him, either?

THORD

No.

INGIALD

Not? Sure?

THORD

No. I mean yes. Of course I've heard about him.

INGIALD

About what he has done to-day?

THORD

I didn't know he did anything to-day.

INGIALD

You heard about my brother?

THORD

Your poor brother, Hall? Yes, I was truly grieved. I was quite upset.

INGIALD

That's what Thorolf did.

THORD

Thorolf?

INGIALD

Now where is he?

THORD

Your brother?

INGIALD

I see. You won't answer.

THORD

Now don't be hasty, Ingiald. You're so hasty. You don't give me a chance. What is it you want to know?

INGIALD

Where is Thorolf?

THORD

I've not seen him, Ingiald. How should I know where Thorolf is?

INGIALD

He was seen coming towards this house.

THORD

Towards this house?

INGIALD

Only an hour ago.

THORD

Thorolf?

INGIALD

No more talk, my friend. Where is he?

THORD

I don't know, Ingiald. I don't know.

INGIALD

You lying knave.   You creeping worm.   You dog of——.
I'll ram this scabbard down your throat. You say you don't
know. Where is he? Any more of your lies and I'll squeeze
your lying tongue off.

THORD

Don't, Ingiald. Don't. You're hurting. Don't, man.

INGIALD

Well. No more of your lies, then.

THORD

Now you've hurt me. I shall have a sore throat for a week.

INGIALD

Do you good. [*A pause.*] Now then, Thorolf's here. Isn't
he? Hey?

THORD

Yes, Ingiald.

INGIALD

I thought we should come to it sooner or later. See what
comes of being patient. So he's here. Hidden somewhere?

THORD

Yes, Ingiald.

INGIALD

Where is he hidden?

THORD

O, but I couldn't tell you that. If I told you that I'd have to leave the country. No one would speak to me, if I told you that.

INGIALD

That's nothing to do with me. Now then. Where is he?

THORD

O, I couldn't.

INGIALD

Hey?

THORD

I'd have to leave this farm. Have mercy, Ingiald.

INGIALD

Mercy, eh?

THORD

I couldn't bear it. I'm not strong, Ingiald. My head.

INGIALD

D'ye see this little knife of mine?

THORD

O, don't, Ingiald. Ingiald, you don't mean. Ingiald, I'd have to leave the country if I told you.

INGIALD

Look here, Thord. I'm going to get Thorolf before I go. Let's understand each other.

THORD

O, yes, Ingiald. I'll do anything. I'll say anything. But I can't tell you where he is. I can't. I'd have to leave the country.

INGIALD

Well. You needn't tell me where he is. Not in so many words. D'ye understand?

THORD

O, Ingiald.

INGIALD

Let's come to some arrangement. You don't want your neighbours to call you a traitor. I understand that. You don't want me to burn your house down, or to stick this knife into you. I understand that, too. Well. You give up Thorolf to me quietly.

THORD

I can't, Ingiald. They'd know. They'd know. Vigdis would tell them.

INGIALD

I don't say "betray him," you silly gowk.

THORD

But what then, Ingiald?

INGIALD

Give me some hint where he is, so that I can find him. I'll

pretend to search the house, and light on him, as it were, by chance. Come now.

THORD

But——

INGIALD

Come now. D'ye see this bag? [*Produces a purse.*]

THORD

Yes.

INGIALD

D'ye hear it? Eh? Chink. Eh? Chink? Where is he?

THORD

I couldn't.

INGIALD

Come now. Hark? Three silver marks. Eh? Just whisper. Where? Come now.

THORD

Three silver marks.

INGIALD

Three silver marks. You needn't say it right out. Hear it jingle.

THORD

It's a lot of money.

INGIALD

You could do with it, eh? Come now, old man, where is he?

THORD

Let me weigh it in my hand.

[95]

INGIALD

Certainly. Here you are. Now then. Whisper here. Where is he? Tell me where he is. Where is he? Is he in the chest here?

THORD

No, not in the chest.

INGIALD

No? What is in the chest?

THORD

Things of Vigdis's.

INGIALD

Is he upstairs, then? Eh? Upstairs?

THORD

No. He's not upstairs.

INGIALD

Outside? Eh?

THORD

[*Putting the bag on the table.*] Ingiald.

INGIALD

Yes. Well. What is it?

THORD

You won't take it to heart my hiding him?

INGIALD

No. No. Of course I won't.

THORD

Swear you won't. You won't fine me? Nor take my cattle?

INGIALD

Not if you tell me where he is.

THORD

You'll search the house first, Ingiald.   In pretence?

INGIALD

Yes.   I'll pretend to search the house.   And then?

THORD

You see that door there?

INGIALD

Yes.   Yes.   What then?

THORD

You must go through that door.   No.   No.   Go through *this* door, and then round the house.

INGIALD

Yes?   Where to?   Among the ricks?

THORD

No.   Not among the ricks.

INGIALD

In the dairy?

THORD

You might look in the dairy.

INGIALD

Where else, eh?

THORD

Just to the left of the dairy.

INGIALD

The cowbyre, eh?

THORD

No. No. You might look in the cowbyre, though.

INGIALD

Where else?

THORD

Ingiald.

INGIALD

Yes.

THORD

Swear you won't tell anyone. Swear you won't say I told you.

INGIALD

Of course I won't tell anyone.

THORD

You might count the sheep. You understand?

INGIALD

To the left of the dairy, eh?

THORD

To the left of the dairy.

INGIALD

I'll see them counted. Thank'ee, Thord.

THORD

Now, you'll pretend to look upstairs?

INGIALD

Yes. We'll let in Vigdis, now.

THORD

No, not Vigdis, no.

INGIALD

Yes, man. Hey there. Erik!

ERIK

Sir.

INGIALD

Tell the lady to come in.

ERIK

Tell the lady to come in, sir. You may go in now, mum.

[*Enter* VIGDIS]

VIGDIS

Well. Have you had a nice talk?

INGIALD

No. Not so nice as I could have wished, perhaps. Your husband's very low to-night. Excuse me a moment. Hi there. Hrapp, Hoskuld.

SOLDIERS

[*Entering.*] Sir. Sir.

INGIALD

I'm sorry, Vigdis. But I must search the house. Your husband has given me permission. I must look through all the rooms.

VIGDIS

Search my house, indeed.

INGIALD

I won't disarrange it more than can be helped.

VIGDIS

Search my house, indeed. For what will you search my house?

INGIALD

For your cousin, Thorolf.

VIGDIS

My—cousin—Thorolf. And why should you want my cousin Thorolf, I should like to know?

INGIALD

Come, Vigdis, I'm sorry. Now don't let's have a scene.

VIGDIS

A scene, indeed. And why should you have a scene? I'm not going to have my house pulled to pieces.

INGIALD

They won't do any harm, Vigdis.

VIGDIS

Harm or no harm, I won't have anyone spying around in my house. I never heard of such impudence. This is *my* house. It isn't Thorolf's house. What d'ye want Thorolf for?

INGIALD

You know perfectly well, Vigdis, what I want Thorolf for.

VIGDIS

[*To* THORD.] And I'm to be insulted in my own house! I wonder you sit there and let your wife be insulted. As for you, Ingiald, for all your lordship, you never had more manners than one brought up in a pigstye. It is what I might expect from you. But as for you, Thord, I'm ashamed of you. Defend your wife, man. Don't let these louts throw the whole house overboard.

INGIALD

[*To his men.*] Upstairs with you. Search every room in the house.

VIGDIS

How dare you insult a woman so? You great captains want humbling. If I were a man now, you wouldn't dare.

ERIK

[*To* INGIALD.] Beg pardon, captain.

INGIALD

What is it?

ERIK

That box, captain. [*Points to chest.*]

INGIALD

Well. What about it?

ERIK

I was thinking he might be in that box.

INGIALD

O, nonsense. Upstairs with you.

[*They all run upstairs*]

[*To* THORD.] You come, too, Thord. If anything's missing you'll blame my men.

THORD

[*Aside.*] Let Vigdis go, Ingiald. Take Vigdis.

INGIALD

[*Glancing at her.*] No. She suspects nothing. You come.

THORD

No. I don't think she suspects. No, she suspects nothing.

VIGDIS

Where are you going, Thord?

THORD

Upstairs with Ingiald.

VIGDIS

Am I married to a man or to a bleating old sheep with the staggers? Do you call yourself a human being, Thord? [*Aside.*] What's Ingiald going to do?

INGIALD

Come, Thord. Come on, now.

THORD

[*To* VIGDIS.] Get supper ready. Don't stand there.

[*Exit with* INGIALD]

VIGDIS

Get supper ready. Get supper ready. What's he going to do? Why didn't Thord give me a hint? He'll search the sheep-fold. Of course he'll search the sheep-fold. He'll be going to the fold in another minute. Why did I leave him in the sheep-fold? Why did I let him stay at all? What can I do? What can I do? He'll be down in a minute. What's this bag of money? What's this bag of money? Thord's sold him. It's blood money, I know it. What can I do? O God. What can I do?

THORD

[*Above.*] Vigdis.

VIGDIS

Yes, Thord.

THORD

All right. Nothing. I only wanted to know if you were there.

VIGDIS

What can I do? I know. I know. It's a bare chance. It's a bare chance.

[*She runs softly and swiftly from the room.*]
[*In two seconds she returns with* THOROLF]
[*Noise above, and shouts*]

VIGDIS

Quiet. Quiet. Not a whisper.

THOROLF

What shall I do?

VIGDIS

Not a whisper.

THORD

[*Above.*] Vigdis. Are you there still?

VIGDIS

I'm still here, Thord. What's the matter with you? Into the chest, Thorolf. Get into the chest. [*She opens chest.*]

THOROLF

[*Kissing her.*] Good-bye, in case, Vigdis.

VIGDIS

O you silly boy. Get in. I must lock you in. Don't sneeze, for God's sake. Press your upper lip if you want to sneeze. It's a bare chance, Thorolf. [*She locks the chest on him and takes key. Then she hurriedly and softly puts bread and beer upon the table as for supper.*]

[*Re-enter* INGIALD, THORD, *and* SOLDIERS]

VIGDIS

Well, my lord. Did you find my cousin Thorolf by any chance?

INGIALD

I've not finished looking yet.

VIGDIS

Haven't you? You might look on the dresser there. I would if I were you. Or in the oven. Yes, look in the oven, Ingiald. Show him the oven, Thord.

INGIALD

[*To some of his men.*] Step into the kitchen, and look in the oven. You. Come with me the rest of you. We must look through the farmyard.

VIGDIS

Don't disturb your elder brother, Ingiald.

INGIALD

What elder brother?

VIGDIS

The donkey.

INGIALD

Ah, you're funny, Vigdis. Well, he laughs best who laughs last, *I* say.

[*Exit with* MEN]

VIGDIS

Thord. Thord Goddi.

THORD

Yes, Vigdis.

VIGDIS

What's this bag of money, here?

THORD

Bag of money?

VIGDIS

This bag of money here. What is it?

THORD

It's what I brought from market.

VIGDIS

It's nothing of the sort.

[105]

THORD

Oh no. Nor it is.

VIGDIS

Well?

THORD

Well? I suppose Ingiald left it there when he came in.

VIGDIS

Did you see Ingiald leave it there? O, what am I thinking of? [*Aside.*]

THORD

Now for Heaven's sake stop nagging. Hark!

VIGDIS

What is it?

THORD

I thought I heard a noise in the yard. A cry.

VIGDIS

My God. A cry. [*They go to the door.*]

THORD

I hope they won't find him.

VIGDIS

Thank God I did what I could for him. O, may Heaven blind them.

THORD

I'm afraid they're sure to find him. What was that?

VIGDIS

My God. They're brave, aren't they, thirteen to one?

THORD

Didn't you hear a sort of groan then?

VIGDIS

Poor Thorolf. Poor Thorolf.

THORD

We did our best, Vigdis.

VIGDIS

Yes. May God always help you, Thord, as well as you helped Thorolf!

THORD

Yes, I shall always be glad I did my best for him.

VIGDIS

Yes, Thord. I suppose you will be. I hope you will be.

THORD

Poor fellow.

VIGDIS

Poor Thorolf.

THORD

Don't take on, Vigdis. We must all die. Ah. Ah. Come away from the door. Come. [*Cries without.*]

VIGDIS

[*Covering her eyes.*] O, my dear, my dear. O Thorolf, little brown-haired Thorolf.

[107]

THORD

There. There. It's all over now.

VIGDIS

O my Thorolf, my cousin Thorolf.

THORD

There. There. Now don't take on. Don't take on; you get on my nerves when you cry like that.

VIGDIS

O, you had brown hair, Thorolf. Bonny hair you had. O my boy, my poor cousin. [*Cries without.*]

THORD

[*Aside.*] They've got him. They've got him. [*He rubs his hands.*] We all owe Heaven a death. Poor Thorolf. Poor fellow. And him so young.

VIGDIS

It was a sight for sore eyes on a sunny morning to see him going over the hills. O Thorolf, you were the joy of a woman's eyes. You were as stately as a stag. You were as comely as a king's darling. O my boy, my poor cousin, my own dear, my heart's darling, Thorolf!

THORD

And him so young. And such a promising young fellow. To be cut short. Life is but a span. And him so young. Idle, vicious, drunken blackguard, it's a good job you are cut short. [*More noise without.*]

VIGDIS

He had soft brown hair with threads of gold in it like the bright bird's feathers.   Now it's dabbled with blood, dabbled with blood, dabbled with blood.

THORD

Dabbled with blood. O! O me!

VIGDIS

O young man, O treasure of the west, O white, comely, handsome Thorolf! Yours will be a cold bride bed under the winter grass.

THORD

O, do for Heaven's sake be quiet.

VIGDIS

A cold bed, a lonely bed, a white bed.

THORD

You'll waste none of our sheets, laying of him out. Let me tell you that.

VIGDIS

Three white lonely candles in a draught, three flames guttering, but you will lie still beneath them, Thorolf.

THORD

Vigdis. Do you want to drive me mad? Have done now.

VIGDIS

O bonny Thorolf. Swimming and rowing and going among

[109]

young men you were like a king. None could sail a boat like you. No queen ever loosed her hair about a lovelier lover than you. You were courteous, you were kind, you had strength and beauty, you were brave; now you will lie in the ground, and the sheep will crop the grass there.

THORD

Here. Vigdis. A little of that goes a long way. Thorolf's dead. Here's Ingiald coming back. Hold your noise now, for Heaven's sake.

[*Re-enter* INGIALD *with* MEN]

INGIALD

I've a bone to pick with you, Thord.

VIGDIS

Bring me my dead. Give me my dead, you butchers, you bloody men.

INGIALD

D'ye hear?

VIGDIS

Thirteen to one. Thirteen to one. You butchers. You bloody men. Bring me my dead. Bring me my dead darling. You cowards. You cowards.

INGIALD

What's wrong with *you*, Vigdis?

VIGDIS

Let me look upon the boy's dead face. You butchers. O

[110]

fair, white face. O white face with the red blood upon it. O my boy, my dear boy, Thorolf.

INGIALD

He'll be a white face when I get him and that's a fact, Vigdis. I'll promise you that much. Thord, I'll wring your ears off.

VIGDIS

Where is my dead lad? You dogs. You butchers. Take me to his corpse.

INGIALD

Your dead lad? There's no dead lad.

VIGDIS

Not dead. O, Heaven! [*Pretends to swoon.*]

THORD

What?

INGIALD

I'll tell you what, you creeping rot. You cur. You Judas. What have you done with him?

THORD

Done with him?

INGIALD

With Thorolf. Eh. Where is he? Eh? What have you done with him?

THORD

I've done nothing, Ingiald. Nothing.

[111]

Ingiald

Don't tell me you've done nothing.

Thord

I didn't do anything with him.

Ingiald

You lying knave. D'ye dare to sit there and say you haven't got him off?

Thord

I haven't got him off.

Ingiald

You lie.

Thord

How could I have got him off?

Ingiald

How? How do I know how? But I'll know how. I'll flay you alive. I'll skin you and salt you. I'll—I'll—I'll——

Thord

O, don't. Ingiald, I swear—I swear I thought you'd get him.

Ingiald

I tell you, you've got him off.

Thord

I haven't, Ingiald.

Ingiald

[*To his men.*] Look at him. Look at this liar, here. I

[112]

come here to this liar and tell him I want Thorolf. And he
cringes and whines and licks my boots. So I just speak to him
kindly, like a father. I'm always kindly and like a father.
I'm too kind. And he cringes and whines, and begs me not
to hit him. Only spare my precious hide, he says, and I'll
tell you where Thorolf is.

THE MEN

Hear that now. He betrayed him, etc.
Then he wants a little money, for saying where Thorolf is.
The money on the table there. Three marks of silver, no less.
He'd sell his own mother for a little money. Wouldn't you, eh?

THORD

I wouldn't.

INGIALD

You would, you know it. Three marks of silver you begged.
And then you told me to look in the sheep-fold.

THE MEN

Treacherous swine. His own cousin. His own cousin.

INGIALD

And then he sneaks his man off while we're rummaging in
the wrong place. And now he expects me to be out three marks
of silver.

THE MEN

Tie him to the bull's tail, master; and let's hunt him.

INGIALD

So you'd sell your cousin, would you, and then try to go back

[113]

on your bargain? [*Going to him.*] Where have you taken
Thorolf to? Eh?

THORD

He was in the sheep-fold where I told you, Ingiald. He was.
Indeed he was.

INGIALD

O! Was he? And where is he now? Gone to Olaf's, I suppose.

THORD

He may have gone to Olaf's.

THE MEN

Olaf's is a likely place. We'd better go on there at once.

INGIALD

Lord help you, Thord, if we don't get him. Understand?
I mean it. Come on there.

A MAN

You never looked in that chest yet, captain.

INGIALD

O yes, that chest. [*He tries lid.*] Where's the key, Thord?

THORD

Ask Vigdis.

INGIALD

Where's the key of this chest, Vigdis?

VIGDIS

Key of the chest, indeed. Who are you to ask for my keys? I'm not going to have you spying in my chests. You and your gang have done harm enough here. You'll get no key. Let that be enough.

INGIALD

Come now. The key.

VIGDIS

I tell you, you shall not have the key.

THE MEN

Break it open, captain.

A MAN

O, let the chest alone. Thorolf'll be safe at Olaf's if we don't hurry.

INGIALD

Give me the key.

THORD

Give up the key at once.

VIGDIS

I tell you, you shall not have the key. You've thrown the house overboard as it is. Get out now. Go.

INGIALD

Give me that key at once, Vigdis.

VIGDIS

[*Flinging key on floor.*] Take it then, and bad luck go with it. Here it is. Now open.

[115]

INGIALD

[*Giving it back.*] Thank you. That's all I wanted. Now, Thord. Give back that bag of money.

THORD

O Ingiald, you gave it to me.

INGIALD

Now you will give it back.

THORD

O Ingiald.

VIGDIS

Give it, Thord. Give it, you Judas, you. D'ye think I'll have blood money in the house? Give it up at once.

[*The* MEN *go out and linger at the door*]

INGIALD

Come on now.

VIGDIS

[*Taking money bag.*] I've only one thing to say to you, Ingiald. I say, take your money and get out of my house, now. [*She makes him back to the door.*] Take your dirty blood money. [*She smites him over the face with the money bag and drives him out. She watches them go.*] Go on to Olaf's with you, and try some other Judas. That's all I've to say to you, my lord. [*She turns and unlocks chest. Then, instead of opening, she turns to look at Thord. Thord goes to door and looks out, comes back and sits on chest. Vigdis backs away from him.*]

[116]

THORD

Well. They've gone. [*A pause.*] They've gone. [*No answer.*] Can't you answer when I speak to you?

VIGDIS

Yes. I can answer. Listen to me, Thord Goddi. You and I will part from now. You took money to betray Thorolf, your guest and my cousin. I always knew you for a mean man. Now I know you are base, and a dastard, and a dog. God forgive me, I once loved you. Pah. I let you kiss me. I held you in my arms. There. There. There. Take it. [*She flings her wedding ring at him.*] Now we'll part, my sir. I thank God I never bore you a child.

THORD

[*Laughing nervously.*] I've got a headache. I can't—Ow— [*The chest lid rises.* THORD *leaps from it.* THOROLF *appears.*] Thorolf!

THOROLF

Thorolf!

THORD

Thorolf, I didn't mean—I swear I didn't. I didn't mean. It was only a joke. I'll explain.

THOROLF

Thord. Pah. You're not worth it.

THORD

O Thorolf. You shall have—I'll give you my money. All of it——

THOROLF

Pah. Vigdis, my dear, where are they?

VIGDIS

They've gone, Thorolf. We can slip away to Broadfirth now. It's quite safe. Come. Come. We'll go together, my friend. [*They turn to go.*]

THORD

I'll change my religion.

CURTAIN

Written in 1906.

THE SWEEPS OF NINETY–EIGHT

THE SWEEPS OF NINETY–EIGHT

Scene: *An inn at Dunleary. A parlour.* Tiger Roche, *an old, well-preserved man, with his left arm in a sling.*

Roche

I have been in seven lost causes. This is the seventh; and it comes to an end like the others. There were good fellows with me. They poured out their lives like water. Good fellows they were. They are all gone now. Shears, and all of them. My God! but they were brave. And to think of those swine at the Castle ruling men like they were! [*He rings the bell.*]

[*Enter* Hostess]

Well, what did the ship-captain say?

Hostess

There'll be a boat below the door here in half an hour from now.

Roche

And he'll engage to land me in France?

Hostess

In France itself.

Roche

You said half an hour?

Hostess

Yes, sir.

Roche

So I've half an hour more in Ireland. Half an hour more in Ireland, and then—

Adieu for ever more,
My love,
Adieu for ever more.

Well, there's no sense in sorrow; I may as well have some wine.

HOSTESS

What wine would you like, sir? Claret? Burgundy?

ROCHE

Have you any Miss Taylor?

HOSTESS

Why, sir, that's a common drink. Only sailors drink Miss
Taylor.

ROCHE

I drank a cup of Miss Taylor the day I landed at Killala.
I would drink it again to the memory of the friends who pledged
me in it. [*Soliloquizing.*] It ought not to have failed. But
the honest purpose does fail, for it is fighting the knavery
of the world. It's a harsh alternative, to fail or be British.
Fail, aye, and I'm proud to fail.

Better be trampled out by asses' hooves
Than be the thing the asses' mind approves.

[HOSTESS *goes out and returns with bottle and glass*]

HOSTESS

Here it is, sir.

ROCHE

I thank you.

[HOSTESS *goes out*]

[*Pouring out a glass of wine and holding it up.*] I drink to you, my comrades. You fought a good fight, my comrades. You were spent like water. Your names shall be written in fire.

[*Re-enter* HOSTESS]

HOSTESS

There's some gentlemen coming, sir. Perhaps you'd like to step aside, sir. The cellar's dark, and there's a good place in the henhouse.

ROCHE

I'll stay where I am, thank you.

HOSTESS

It may be dangerous for you to stay, sir. One of them's that Major Sirr.

ROCHE

I shall be glad to meet him.

HOSTESS

[*Looking out.*] It may be very dangerous, sir. One of them's that Major Sandys.

ROCHE

O! Who's the third?

HOSTESS

Sir, would you not be advised, since it might be your death? He's the drunken fat man who flogged poor Mr. Wright. I must go out, sir.

[*Exit*]

ROCHE

Old Fitzpatrick! I shall have pleasant company for my last half-hour in Ireland. [*He sits down.*]

[*Enter* MAJOR SIRR, MAJOR SANDYS, *and* THOMAS JUDKIN FITZPATRICK, J. P.]

FITZ.

And so, sir, when he said that, sir, there was no use bothering a jury.

SIRR

Aha. Very good, very good. You are a wag, sir.

FITZ.

Yes, sir, the rebellious dog.

SAND.

All the same, the rebellion's not stamped out. I shall be glad when that new regiment comes in.

SIRR

What new regiment?

SAND.

O, a Kentish regiment. Fencibles and that. They'll be marching through here, by the way. Before we go, I expect.

SIRR

Well, the more the merrier. But all the same, I think we've scotched the rebellion. Let's sit down and be merry.

SAND.

All the same, I'm glad the new regiment's coming. And I'm

[124]

glad it'll pass this tavern. We are in the enemy's country, so far from Dublin.

SIRR

Come, let's be merry. Mr. Fitzpatrick, I hear you hanged the last of these rebels yesterday morning.

FITZ.

Yes, sir; the rebellious dog. Under God's providence I hanged that rebel, sir. The rebellious dog, sir, he was little better than a common atheist. If we could catch that arch-traitor, Tiger Roche, sir; why, honest men, sir, could sleep in peace again.

SAND.

Why, I thought Tiger Roche had died twenty years ago.

FITZ.

That's an instance, sir, of the lengths these rebels go to. It's their subtlety, sir; their canting, lying, hypocritical subtlety. He pretended he was dead, sir. He gave out a report that he was dead, sir. And then, sir, if you please, he lands at Killala with a troop of pike-men. Dead? A crocodile's tears, sir. Twenty years of scheming and plotting; and pretending all the time he was in his grave. [*Staring hard at* ROCHE.] Who's the old put with his arm in a bag?

SIRR

O, some old put or other. Let's be merry. [*He rings the bell.*]

[*Enter* HOSTESS]

SIRR

Mine's brandy. What's yours? What's yours, Sandys?

[125]

FITZ.

A bottle of brandy, woman. Bring a bottle of brandy. [HOSTESS *brings bottle and glasses. Then lingers.*] Well, ma'am. And why don't you go, ma'am?

HOSTESS

The brandy is half a guinea, sir.

FITZ.

You saucy jade. Hark ye, mistress. I'd have you know, ma'am, that I'm a justice of the peace, ma'am. I shouldn't wonder if you're another of these pernicious atheistical Friends of Ireland, as they call them. Pernicious, lying, murderous dogs.—Well! What are you waiting for?

HOSTESS

I'm waiting for my money, sir. I don't like to be put upon.

FITZ

What? Rebel, would you, against the King's Peace? I am the King's Peace, madam. Not another word, or I'll commit you.

[*Exit* HOSTESS]

SIRR

You are a wag, sir. You are merry.

SAND.

Excellent. Excellent.
[*They draw to the table, unbuckle their belts, put down their swords and papers, and prepare to enjoy themselves.*]

[*To* Fitz.] They say you made a great haul of rebels in Tipperary, about six weeks back.

Fitz.

Under God's providence, I did, sir. I caught seven, sir. I had them all flogged, sir, and then hanged the eldest. Strong measures, sir; but without strong measures we shouldn't sleep in peace, sir. No, sir. If we didn't exert the strong arm, sir—and you will agree with me that might is right—there'd be a subversion of all Liberty. But I thank God, sir, that we have a Constitution. Let me hear no cant about Equality and Liberty, and the Rights of Man, sir. Show me a man who talks of Truth, and I will show you a rebel.

Sirr

Hear, hear.

Sand.

Well, about the rebels. How did you catch them?

Fitz.

Catch them? I saw them in the streets, sir. The effrontery of these rebels knows no bounds, sir.

Sand.

What, with arms in their hands?

Fitz.

Arms in their hands? No, sir. In Tipperary, sir—under God's providence—they know better.

[127]

SAND.

Well—but how did you know them?

FITZ.

Know them, sir? I knew them by their waistcoats, their canting, atheistical, seditious red French waistcoats. There was "Down with Church and State" in every button. Sir, the evidence was plain, sir. Those waistcoats would have condemned a Christian martyr, sir.

ROCHE

[*Aside.*] It seems they did.

FITZ.

What's the old put there muttering?

SAND.

Ah, don't pay any heed to him. Tell us of the man who didn't take off his hat to you.

SIRR

Yes, tell us of that. You are a wag, Mr. Fitzpatrick. I'm afraid you're a merry wag, sir.

FITZ.

Sir, your very good health.

SIRR

O, sir, your servant, I'm sure.

[*They drink*]

SAND.

Well, about the man——

FITZ.

O, yes. The rebellious hound. He didn't take off his hat to me, sir. Well, sir. He that affronts me, sir, affronts King George, sir. For I, sir, under God's providence, am King George's Justice of the Peace, sir; so, sir, when a man does not salute me, he does not salute King George, sir. He is a rebel, sir. A *sans-culotte*, sir. A murdering pike in the hand of a *sans-culotte*, sir. He is a rebel on the face of it. And so, sir, to make a short tale, I gave him fifty lashes. And d'ye know, sir, he had the brazen-faced effrontery to contradict me when I called him a rebel to his teeth. Beat that if you can, sir. What d'ye think of that, sir? Beat it if you can for cold-blooded, brazen-faced, rebellious audacity. These people are possessed of the devil, sir.

SAND.

Look at my case. Only last week. I had a traitor. He was taken in the fact, as it were. That man Hevey. Why, he was a known traitor. There was no need to try him. The thing was evident. I condemned him to be hanged. Well, he had a mare, a grey mare, a famous creature. I told him to send her round to me. I told him straight out that a mare like her should never again load her loyal loins with the vile burden of a convicted traitor. And he'd the heaven-sent impudence to complain to General Craig.

FITZ.

These people are possessed of the devil, sir. But come, a bumper. A bumper.

[129]

SIRR

[*Aside.*] I think that old put's a rebel. He blushed like fire, Major, when you told your story.

[*They look at* ROCHE, *who is reading a little book*]

FITZ.

What's he reading? These reading people, they're generally deep ones.

SIRR

[*Peeping.*] It seems to be poetry.

FITZ.

[*Aside.*] Poetry? He is a rebel without doubt. [*Aloud.*] I would make it a capital offence to read poetry. Yes, sir. When a man deliberately starts to poison his mind with incendiary cant about Truth and Beauty, he is as good as damned, sir. I would hang any man who read poetry. A man who has a book of poems in one hand has always a rebel's pike in the other. You mark my words, sir. Ahem! You, sir! You with your arm in the sling.

ROCHE

You were pleased to speak to me?

FITZ.

Yes, sir, I was pleased, as you call it, to speak to you. Don't trifle with me, sir. For I am, under God's providence, a Justice of the King's Peace, King George's deputy, under God's providence, if you know what that means.

ROCHE

Sir, I know what that means. Yes, sir, I know what that means. Its meaning is written red across this island.

FITZ.

So, sir. I am glad to find you so well affected. Are you an honest man, sir?

ROCHE

Come, Mr. Fitzpatrick. A man is known by the company he keeps.

SIRR

You are a wag, sir.

FITZ.

So, sir, I see you know me?

ROCHE

Not know Mr. Fitzpatrick!

FITZ.

Why then, sir, you will let me see what book you are reading.

ROCHE

With pleasure, sir. The Odes of Horace.

SAND.

I know that Odes O'Horace to be a pamphleteering rebel. Mr. Fitzpatrick, we must secure this man.

SIRR

[*Looking at book.*] There's mighty few rebels understands Hebrew, let me tell you that, Sandys.

[131]

Roche

[*To* Sirr.] I thought I couldn't be mistaken. Can it be—tell me—Am I not in the presence of Major Sirr, the saviour of this benighted country, the apprehender of that arch-offender, that rebel chief, Sir Peter Keogh? O happy day! A glorious privilege!

Fitz.

Yes, sir, that is Major Sirr, sir. Our Saviour under God's providence, Major Sirr, sir. Come, sit down and be merry, Mr.—Mr.—what's your name?

Sand.

All very well, Fitzpatrick. But you and I are of the Commission. Hark! There's the fifes. The regiment's coming. We'd better send him in with the regiment and have him properly examined.

Sirr

Don't be an ass, Sandys.

Fitz.

Major Sandys, sir. When you are drunk, sir, you are a credit to your King and your religion, sir. But Major Sandys, sir, when your are sober, sir, you are a dry toast, sir. You stick in an honest man's throat, sir. Damme, sir, sit down and drink like a Christian.

Sand.

Well. The regiment's coming. The band are out of tune. These militia are the deuce. Well, Mr. Rebel, or Mr. Honest Man, whoever you are, the bottle lies with you.

FITZ.

Give us a toast, Mr. Honest Man.

ROCHE

Gentlemen, pass up your glasses. I will give you a toast.
Hand up your glasses. I will give you a toast.

SIRR

What is it you're drinking?

ROCHE

Tokay, Major, a kind of Imperial Tokay.

FITZ.

A man who drinks Tokay, sir, is a man of principle. Did the
rebels drink Tokay? No, sir, they drank vile atheistical whisky.

ROCHE

Come, don't abuse whisky. I've known whisky get a grocer
knighted.

FITZ.

Sir, a King, sir, is above the law, sir. Come, give us your
toast.

SAND.

Yes, give us your toast.

SIRR

Fill fair, now, honest man.

[ROCHE *lines up the three glasses and fills them full*]

FITZ.

Your toast, now.

[133]

ROCHE

Gentlemen, I give you a toast—" The Trinity of Judas."—
There, sir, is yours; there's yours, Major Sandys; there's yours,
Major Sirr.

[*He flings the glasses one by one into the faces of the trio*]

Gentlemen, I am Tiger Roche.   I hope you like your wine.

SIRR

Traitor!   Help me, you two.   There is a thousand pounds
reward.

FITZ.

My religion forbids re—retaliation.

SAND.

[*To* ROCHE.]   Well, you bully.   The regiment's coming.
Then we'll see about Mr. Tiger Roche, with his toasts and his
Hebrew.

[SIRR *tries to reach his sword*]

ROCHE

[*To* SIRR.]   I should be sorry to have your blood upon my
sword, Major Sirr.

[SIRR *relapses*]

[*To* SANDYS.]   Now, Mr. Sandys, about your regiment.   That
is not your regiment.   Your regiment is a red ruin at Rathnew.
Those fifes are the fifes of the Friends of Ireland.   In five minute's time I hope to be leading them to Dublin.

ALL

What!   O God, we are lost!

ROCHE

Sit down, you carrion.

SIRR

And I've a wife and two sons.

ROCHE

What! Human feeling in a Sirr!

FITZ.

O Mr. Roche, sir; Captain Roche, sir. Have pity; I am not fit to die.

ROCHE

Truth from a Fitzpatrick!

SAND.

O Captain Roche. You shall have the grey mare. Hevey's famous mare, that won the trotting match.

ROCHE

Generosity in a Mr. Major Sandys.

ALL

O Mr. Roche, we'll reform. O, hide us, Mr. Roche. Not the mob, Mr. Roche. We shall be torn limb from limb.

ROCHE

Well, you'd better get up that chimney.

FITZ.

My belly'll never go up there.

[135]

ROCHE

Well, it had better go there.

SAND.

It won't hold us all. You must stand out, Fitzpatrick. Stand by, Sirr. I go first. [*He gets up the chimney.*]

SIRR

O God, will I be in time? [*He gets up the chimney.*]

[*The fifes sound clearly*]

FITZ.

My belly will bring my grey hairs in sorrow to the grave. O you inhuman Sandys. Help me up. O, help me up. I'll squeeze in somehow. O Mr. Roche, help me up. Do now, kind Mr. Roche. O, I shall choke. [*He gets up the chimney.*] [*An agonized voice from the chimney:*] Do our legs show?

[*The band sounds without. ROCHE gathers up their papers in a pile. Then goes to the window.*]

ROCHE

Ho, there. Captain!

VOICE WITHOUT

What d'ye want?

ROCHE

Bring in a file of men. There are some rebels secreted here.

[*The troops ground arms and halt. Enter CAPTAIN and file*]

CAPTAIN

Well, sir, where are the rebels?

[136]

Roche

Sir, I hold the King's Commission. I have traced these rebels here. Five minutes since we were drinking at this table. They are up that chimney. Do your duty.

Soldiers

[*Running to chimney.*] Here's a leg. Here they are all right. Yank them down, sons. We'll give you Killala Bay. We'll give you Erin-go-bragh. In the neck we'll give it to you. [*They pull down three filthy, blinking scarecrows.*]

[*As they wipe the soot from their eyes* Roche *indicates them*]

Roche

This [*pointing to* Sandys] is Mr. Napper Tandy. This [*pointing to* Sirr] is Captain Tiger Roche. He looks a tiger, I must say. This [*pointing to* Fitzpatrick] is that arch-felon, Mr. Wolfe Tone. Guard them carefully, Captain. They are worth some seven thousand pounds.

All Three

[*Recognizing the King's uniform through the soot.*] Unhand us, Captain. We are the King's Justices. That man there is the rebel. That is Tiger Roche, Captain. We are the King's Justices.

A Soldier

Bleeding fine Justices the King's got, then.

A Soldier

You and your Justices. We'll give you all the justice you need. An ounce of lead is the justice you'll get.

[137]

All Three

Unhand us, will you! Captain! What are you doing. That is the rebel. That is Tiger Roche. Take off your men. We are the King's Justices.

Captain

I've heard that song before. Shut your damned seditious heads or I'll make you chew a trooper's cook.

Roche

[*Smiling.*] What in the world's a trooper's cook? Captain.

Captain

It's a piece of wood, sir. It's all the cook a trooper has. Between the teeth, it is an effective gag.

All Three

But hear us, Captain.

A Soldier

Blimy! Shut your heads. Don't you hear what the Captain tells you?

Sand.

Damn it, Captain. You shall suffer——

Fitz.

If there's justice in Ireland.

A Soldier

There's no justice in Ireland.

SIRR

But there's law, sir. And you shall have it.

CAPTAIN

Yes, there's law, and you shall have it. There's man-o'-war
law—"over the face and eyes."

SERGEANT

Like the cat give the monkey.

ROCHE

You've secured their hands, sir. They are three desperate
felons.

SERGEANT

Their hands won't give no trouble.

CAPTAIN

[*To* ROCHE.] Well, sir. What next?

ROCHE

[*Writing at table*.] O, march them into Dublin—this note will
explain—and give them in charge to General Craig.

CAPTAIN

I presume you will come, too, sir.

ROCHE

I will follow in a moment. I must place a seal on these
papers I have found here.

[139]

The Three Justices

That proves it, Captain. He's the rebel. He's Tiger Roche.
Don't let him stay behind, Captain.

Roche

Captain, remove those babblers. Silence, you felons. Give
them the trooper's cook. Stay a moment. Leave a file of men.
They can bear witness to my sealing the papers.

Captain

I've a reputation to keep up. What! Leave my men in a
tavern? No, sir, and I'm obliged to you. The hostess will be
witness enough. Forward, my croppy boys. Quick march.

Roche

But you'll have a drink before you go, Captain?

Captain

Not in working hours, thank ye. Now, my croppy boys.

The Three

You shall hang for this, Captain.

Captain

There's some I know will hang too. Quick march, I say.
[*He nods to* Roche.] I'll see you later, at the General's.

Roche

At General Craig's. But I shall probably overtake you on
the road.

CAPTAIN

"We will meet at that beautiful shore." Quick march, my sons.

[*Exeunt. The troops pass on*]

[*A pause, during which* ROCHE *watches them from the window*]

ROCHE

Well, the fire's out and the guests are gone. There's only the bill to pay. [*He empties a purse on the table.*]

[*Enter* HOSTESS]

HOSTESS

The boat is waiting below, sir.

ROCHE

It is good-bye, then.

HOSTESS

You'll be coming again, sir. There'll be other friends going the same road.

ROCHE

I shall be too old when they try again. Good-bye.

Now with his useless steel the beaten rebel goes
To that proud misery's peace no victor ever knows.

Written in 1905.

THE TRAGEDY OF NAN

Tragedy at its best is a vision of the heart of life. The heart of life can only be laid bare in the agony and exultation of dreadful acts. The vision of agony, or spiritual contest, pushed beyond the limits of the dying personality, is exalting and cleansing. It is only by such vision that a multitude can be brought to the passionate knowledge of things exulting and eternal.

Commonplace people dislike tragedy, because they dare not suffer and cannot exult. The truth and rapture of man are holy things, not lightly to be scorned. A carelessness of life and beauty marks the glutton, the idler, and the fool in their deadly path across history.

The poetic impulse of the Renaissance is now spent. The poetic drama, the fruit of that impulse, is now dead. Until a new poetic impulse gathers, playwrights trying for beauty must try to create new forms in which beauty and the high things of the soul may pass from the stage to the mind. Our playwrights have all the powers except that power of exultation which comes from a delighted brooding on excessive, terrible things. That power is seldom granted to man; twice or thrice to a race perhaps, not oftener. But it seems to me certain that every effort, however humble, towards the achieving of that power helps the genius of a race to obtain it, though the obtaining may be fifty years after the strivers are dead.

This country tragedy was written at Greenwich in February, March, and September, 1907. Part of it is based upon something which happened (as I am told) in Kent about a century ago. As I am ignorant of Kentish country people I placed the action among a people and in a place well known to me.

JOHN MASEFIELD.

4th April, 1911.

TO
W. B. YEATS

THE TRAGEDY OF NAN

PERSONS				PLAYED BY
JENNY PARGETTER.	.	.	.	. Miss Mary Jerrold
MRS. PARGETTER .	.	.	.	. Mrs. A. B. Tapping
WILLIAM PARGETTER	.	.	.	. Mr. Horace Hodges
NAN HARDWICK .	.	.	.	Miss Lillah McCarthy
DICK GURVIL	.	.	.	. Mr. A. E. Anson
ARTIE PEARCE	.	.	.	. Mr. Percy Gawthorn
GAFFER PEARCE .	.	.	.	. Mr. H. R. Hignett
TOMMY ARKER	.	.	.	. Mr. Allan Wade
ELLEN .	.	.	.	Miss Marion Nugent
SUSAN .	.	.	.	. Miss Bokenham
THE REV. MR. DREW	.	.	.	Mr. Edmund Gurney
CAPTAIN DIXON .	.	.	.	. Mr. H. Athol Forde
THE CONSTABLE .	.	.	.	Mr. Christmas Grose

This play was produced by the Pioneers at the New Royalty Theatre, on 24th May, 1908, under the direction of Mr. H. Granville Barker. At its revival as a matinee at the Haymarket Theatre, in June, 1908, the part of the Rev. Mr. Drew was played by Mr. Cecil Brooking.

ACT I

SCENE: *A kitchen in the house of a small tenant farmer at Broad Oak, on Severn.* 1810.

[MRS. PARGETTER *and* JENNY *rolling dough and cutting apples.*]
[JENNY *takes flour from cupboard.*]

JENNY

It do seem quiet 'ere, Mother, after service.

MRS. P.

P'raps now I'll 'ave some quiet.

JENNY

Only think, Mother, the ladies 'ad cups of tea in bed of a morning.

MRS. P.

P'raps now you're come 'ome, I'll 'ave my cup of tea, it's time I'd a little something after all I gone through.

JENNY

Why, Mother?

MRS. P.

What with that girl—Mooning round with 'er great eyes.

JENNY

Do 'ee mean Cousin Nan, Mother?

MRS. P.

Mind your work.   I wish them groceries'd come.

[147]

JENNY

Us'll 'ardly 'ave the things ready, Mother. Company be coming at dark.

MRS. P.

Things'll 'ave to be ready. 'Old your tongue.

JENNY

'Oo be coming, Mother, besides Dick Gurvil?

MRS. P.

Young Artie Pearce, wold Gaffer Pearce, them girls o' Robertses, and Tommy Arker.

JENNY

Us shall be quiet a pearty, shan't us?

MRS. P.

It won't be much of a pearty to me, with that Nan in the room. She tokens 'er dad too much.

JENNY

Why, Mother?

MRS. P.

Always so prim and well be'aved, thinking 'erself so much better than anyone.

JENNY

Ah!

MRS. P.

Always 'elping 'er friends as she calls them.

[148]

JENNY

'Elpin' them, Mother?

MRS. P.

Barthin' their brats for 'em. 'Oo knows what dirt they've been playing in? Or mending their linen. Flying in the face of Providence. She might bring us all the fever. [*Going over to get a chair.*] 'Ow many more times am I to tell yer I won't 'ave your things left about? Look 'ere at this chair.

JENNY

What be it, Mother?

MRS. P.

Look 'ere at your coat. 'Oo's to get you a new coat when this is wore out? I will 'ave you careful. Every day of my life I'm putting your clothes away. Idle lawkamercy girl——

JENNY

That ben't mine, Mother. That be Cousin Nan's.

MRS. P.

It's a wonder you couldn't say so at once. Oh! so its 'ers, is it. Wot's she got in 'er pockets, I wonder. [*Looks in pockets.*] Wot's 'ere. Oh! ribbons for our white neck, indeed. Wot's 'ere. Ho, indeed. [*Taking paper.*]

JENNY

Wot's that, Mother, a letter?

MRS. P.

So this is wot's up, is it? [*She glances at paper.*]

[149]

JENNY

[*Peeping.*] It looks like Dick Gurvil's 'and, Mother——

MRS. P.

You 'eed your duty. [*Puts paper in her own pocket.*] I'll give it 'er. 'Ere, out of my way. None of your rags in my way. [*Flinging coat into a corner.*]

JENNY

Oh, Mother, it's gone into the pigwash.

MRS. P.

Wot if it 'as?

JENNY

She won't be able to wear it again, Mother. Never.

MRS. P.

Let 'er go cold. Learn 'er not to leave 'er things about. Where are you going now?

JENNY

I was just going to hang it out, Mother.

MRS. P.

Don't you dare to touch it. Stand 'ere and do your work. Let that dirty gallus bird do 'er own chores.

JENNY

Whatever do 'ee mean, Mother?

MRS. P.

A gallus bird; that's all she is.

[150]

JENNY

Cousin Nan, Mother. Why do 'ee call 'er that?

MRS. P.

Oh, p'raps your Father 'aven't a-told you.

JENNY

No, Mother.

MRS. P.

Run and see if that be Dick with the groceries.

JENNY

[*Goes to window.*] No, Mother.

MRS. P.

Drat 'im. Well, this mustn't go beyond yer—it ain't to be known about. 'Er father—your cousin Nan's father—wot married your father's sister——

JENNY

Yes, Mother.

MRS. P.

Don't interrup' when your Mother's talking to yer. 'Er father, as she's so stuck on— 'E was 'ung.

JENNY

'Ung, Mother?

MRS. P.

At Glorster ja-il.

JENNY

Whatever 'ad 'e gone for to do?

MRS. P.

'E stole a sheep. That's wot 'e did.

JENNY

And so 'e were 'ung

MRS. P.

There's a thing to 'appen in a family.

JENNY

So be that why Nan come 'ere?

MRS. P.

Thanks to your father.

JENNY

I didn't think, when I left service I should 'sociate with no gallus birds.

MRS. P.

Nor you wouldn't if your father was in 'is right mind. The Lord 'ath laid a 'eavy judgmink on your father. Wot 'e wants with 'er I can't think.

JENNY

Her may remind he of Auntie.

MRS. P.

'E's no call to be reminded of any woman, 'cept 'er the Lord 'ath bound to 'im. Wot I gorn through with that Nan in the 'ouse'd a kill a Zebedee. They do say they be 'ard to kill.

JENNY

'Ere be Father coming.

[152]

MRS. P.

'E 'as 'is lunch of a mornin' now. Take 'is cider off the 'ob.

JENNY

Where's 'is bread and cheese? [*She takes mug off hob, looks about carelessly, and drops and smashes mug on hearth.*]

MRS. P.

There now.

JENNY

Oh, Mother, I've broke it.

MRS. P.

What a clumsy 'and you 'ave.

JENNY

It's Father's fav'rit mug. O Mother, whatever will 'e say.

MRS. P.

'Ere. Get upstairs. Get into the next room.

JENNY

Whatever will 'e say! 'E will be mad. (*Cries.*)

MRS. P.

I'll talk 'im round. There! It's all a accident. Quick! before 'e comes now.

JENNY

'E will be that mad! A dear, a dear! (*Goes out.*)

[153]

Mrs. P.

[*Taking out letter.*] So this is wot it's come to: [*Declaiming.*] Dick Gurvil to 'is fond beloved:

> "As I was a-walking a lady I did meet
> I knew it for my true love by the roses on 'er cheek
> The roses on 'er cheek so sweetly did grow
> My 'eart out of my bosom, like a engine did go."

I'll watch yer Master Dick.

[*Enter* Mr. Pargetter, *walking with a stick. He is an old, shortish thick-set man, still hale.*]

Mr. P.

[*Advancing towards* Mrs. P. *and gravely saluting.*] Well, Mother.

Mrs. P.

Did you see the fiddler?

Mr. P.

I saw the fiddler.

Mrs. P.

Is 'e coming to-night?

Mr. P.

'E is coming. Us be going to 'ave great wonders to-night. 'Ot mutton parsty pies.

Mrs. P.

You won't eat of no 'ot mutton parsty pies. You know 'ow that sheep died as well as I do. 'E was *oovy*. [*Pause.*] A apple parsty's no great wonders.

Mr. P.

A fiddler *and* a apple parsty's wonders.

[154]

Mrs. P.

It'll fare to be a girt wonder if th' apple parsty be set. The amount of 'elp I get in the 'ousework——

Mr. P.

At it again.

Mrs. P.

Yes, I am at it again, as you call it.

Mr. P.

What is it, now?

Mrs. P.

'Ow much longer 'ave I got to put up with that Nan in the 'ouse?

Mr. P.

My niece Nan'll stay in this 'ouse till—till I go to church-yard. Or—till she marries. [*A pause.*] Now you know my mind. The girl's a good girl, if you'd let up in your naggin' 'er 'ed off.

Mrs. P.

Naggin', Will?

Mr. P.

'Ow's any girl to be good with you naggin' 'er 'ed off all day long.

Mrs. P.

When did I ever nag, as you call it?

Mr. P.

When? 'Ave you ever give 'er a kind word since she come 'ere.

[155]

MRS. P.

I 'ave my 'eavenly warrant for all I done, Will. Them as the Lord afflicts we must come out from and be ye separate.

MR. P.

I wonder the Lord can let you prosper, talking like that.

MRS. P.

'E knows 'is own, Will. You mark my words.

MR. P.

I will mark 'em. And you mark mine. You'll treat my niece Nan as you'd treat your daughter Jenny.

MRS. P.

Our daughter Jenny is the child of respectable parents. That—that charity girl is the daughter of——

MR. P.

My sister. That's 'oo she's the daughter of.

MRS. P.

And a thief 'oo was 'ung. I've always been respectable; and I've always kep' my girl respectable. I will not 'ave to do with the common and the unclean.

MR. P.

You'll 'ave Nan 'ere, and you'll stop your nagging jealous tongue.

MRS. P.

Jealous?

Mr. P.

Yes, jealous. You make 'er life a burden acos she tokens my sister. You was sweet on 'er dad yourself. That's why you make 'er life a burden.

Mrs. P.

Ho, indeed! Ha, ha, ha! Wot notions.

Mr. P.

That's the truth though. I know yer. I seen somethink of yer in these twenty years.

Mrs. P.

'Ark you to me, Will Pargetter. Could you look on and see your daughter wronged?

Mr. P.

What's that got to do with it?

Mrs. P.

I'll tell you. When first we 'ad that charity girl 'ere——

Mr. P.

You call 'er Nan. Wot are you waivin' that bit of paper at me for?

Mrs. P.

We 'ad 'opes as our Jenny'd marry Dick Gurvil soon as she come back from service.

Mr. P.

That depended on Dick, not on Jenny.

MRS. P.

Oh, but Dick was no difficulty. They kep' company before Jenny went to service. Dick was sweet on 'er all right.

MR. P.

Dick was sweet on twenty girls.

MRS. P.

No. Since that—that idle mooner come 'ere—Dick's been sweet on *'er*. Look 'ere. Look at this. [*Shows letter.*]

MR. P.

I don't want no letter. Put it where yer got it. That's the best thing I ever 'eard of Dick. Dick wants a wife with sense.

MRS. P.

You'll let 'er marry 'im, after 'is carrying on along o' Jenny. And break your own daughter's 'art.

MR. P.

Jenny's got no 'art.

MRS. P.

Jenny'd resolve 'er 'eavenly crown for Dick Gurvil. 'Ow dare you blacken your own child?

MR. P.

Blacken 'er. She's a cold 'eartless little baggage, Jenny is. Our Nan's worth a 'undred of 'er.

[158]

Mrs. P.

And you expect me to see that great-eyed, ugly, scrawf marrying my daughter's man.

Mr. P.

He's not your daughter's man. Dick's everybody's daughter's man. If 'e steps up and marries our Nan—it'll be the making of 'im. Give me my lunch.

Mrs. P.

Ah! I was forgetting. You put me out of patience. I'm afraid I spoke 'asty, Will. I've a 'asty tongue [*with suavity*].

Mr. P.

There, there! Where's my vittles?

[*She puts down bread and cheese*]
[Pargetter *gets up to fetch mug from the hob*]

Mr. P.

Thank ye, Mother. [*He sees the mug broken.*] Law, Mother. You 'aven't a broke my Toby.

Mrs. P.

There, there now, Will, it was a accidenk.

Mr. P.

Not my Toby, broken?

Mrs. P.

It was a accidenk. [*She picks up the pieces.*]

[159]

Mr. P.

'Ooever 'ave a broke my Toby. Why weren't I told to onst?

Mrs. P.

She were goin' to tell yer, she said.

Mr. P.

Not—not Nan? It wasn't Nan broke it?

Mrs. P.

'Er said 'er'd tell you to onst. It was a accidenk.

Mr. P.

But no accidenk could a broke my Toby.

Mrs. P.

There, there. Us'll buy another's good as 'er.

Mr. P.

But I've a 'ad my zider outen ov 'er this fifty year, like my gran'fer 'ave a done. I'd a value for that Toby.

Mrs. P.

'Er'll tell 'ee 'ow it was. It was a accidenk. She was in a 'urry, you see. Getting things ready for the pearty. It was quite a accidenk.

Mr. P.

'Ow could it be quite a accidenk?

[160]

MRS. P.

'Er 'ands were wet, you see; she's particular about 'er 'ands——

MR. P.

Clumsy 'anded——

MRS. P.

They was all soapy from washing. It was quite a accidenk.

MR. P.

And so she let it slip.

MRS. P.

She didn't see where she was going. The sun was in 'er eyes or somethink. She's goin' to tell yer 'ow it was.

MR. P.

My wold Toby jug as Granfer 'ad. 'Er could a broak my 'eart sooner. 'Er could. 'Er could. [*He pushes away his bread and cheese.*] I can't eat my vittles after that. That I can't. Careless girt gowk!

[*Enter* NAN—OLD PARGETTER *stares at her hard all through this scene.*]

NAN

You be back early, Uncle.

MRS. P.

Well?

NAN

Yes, Aunt.

MRS. P.

"Yes, aunt." 'Ave you looked at yourself long enough in the glass?

[161]

NAN

What glass?

MRS. P.

The glass upstairs.

NAN

The beds are made.   I suppose that's what you mean.

MRS. P.

That's not the way to talk before your uncle.

NAN

May I help you cut them apples, Aunt?

MRS. P.

No, you mayn't 'elp me cut these apples.   You get your own work.

NAN

I've done all my work, Aunt.

MRS. P.

None of your impudence.   [*Very sharply.*]

NAN

I have.

MRS. P.

If you 'ave, it's not done properly I know.   I've a good mind to make you do it over.   A very good mind.

NAN

Is that the dough for the pasty?

Mrs. P.

None 'o yer business.

[Nan *picks up a rolling pin*]

Put down that pin when you're told.

Nan

I wish you'd let me 'elp, Aunt? Comp'ny be coming at dark.

Mrs. P.

What's it to do with you? I know w'en comp'ny's coming
without your dinnin' it into me.

[Nan *goes softly to the dresser*]

Wot are you creepin' about on tiptoe for? One'd think you
were a thief, like your father.

Nan

[*Meekly.*] I didn't want to disturve you, Aunt.

Mrs. P.

Disturve me! You couldn't disturve me more if you tried.

Nan

I'm sorry, Aunt.

Mrs. P.

You know that perfectly well.

Nan

I'm sorry, Aunt.

Mrs. P.

'Ere, you give me the fidgets.

NAN

'Ave you one of your sick headaches, Aunt?

MRS. P.

You give me the sick 'edache. One would think you might 'ave 'ad a little gratitood.

NAN

When I *was* grateful you called me a 'ipocrit.

MRS. P.

Oh! *When* was you grateful, as you call it?

NAN

When I first come 'ere. I did my best, I did. I thought you'd like me if I work' 'ard, and 'elped you.

MRS. P.

Did yer think!

NAN

I used to make you tea afore you got up of a morning: I wash up the dinner things, so as you could 'ave your nap of a after-noon. I never let you do the week's washing, not once, since I come 'ere.

MRS. P.

One 'ud expect a little something. After all that's been done for you.

NAN

Done for me! What have you ever done for me?

MRS. P.

Given you a 'ome.

[164]

NAN

A home?

MRS. P.

There's not many would 'ave took in a girl 'er dad being 'ung. But I says to your Uncle——

NAN

I know what you said to Uncle. That the Rector 'ad asked you to take me in. That's what you said to Uncle. You was afeared the Rector'd let it be known if you refused. You was afeared folk'd get to know you for what you are. That's why you took me in. [*More softly.*] D'ye think I don't know, Aunt. I feel I do. [*Pause.*] And down in the shop they tell me what a friend you've been to me. "Mrs. Pargetter *'ave* been kind tiv ee," they say. And Mrs. Drew at the Rectory. She's another. "'Ow grateful you must feel towards your aunt." That's what she says. And you smile. You take it all in smiling. You lick your lips over all their praise. Or you play the martyr. You play the martyr. D'ye think I haven't heard you? "A lot of return I get," that's what you say. They praise you for being good to me. *Good! You!* And you make my life here a hell. You lick your lips to make life hell to me. And you tell lies about me. You mean woman. You so holy, you tell lies.

MR. P.

[*Angrily.*] Now none of that now. That's enough. You leave the room.

MRS. P.

No, she'll not leave the room. I'll learn 'er to be'ave first. [To NAN.] I'd 'ave you remember as your daily bread as you're so fond of is give you by me and your Uncle.

[165]

NAN

Given me?

MRS. P.

Per'aps you'll deny as you 'ave your food—God knows you eat enough.

NAN

And every morsel bitter. Bitter. You make it burn in my throat.

MRS. P.

And a roof over you 'ed, which is more than your merits.

NAN

So 'as a man in a prison a roof.

MRS. P.

Yes. You're right. 'E 'as till 'e's 'ung. And you 'ave your clothes. The very clothes on your back. Talking of clothes, that reminds me. Take that dirty coat of yours out of the pig-wash where you put it. I suppose you want to poison the pigs next.

NAN

[*Turning to pig wash trow.*] Oh! 'Oo've bin and done that? [*At the point of tears.*] I suppose you think it funny to spoil a poor girl's clothes. And now it's spoiled. [*She takes ribbon from pocket.*] And this is spoiled. What I'd saved up for. Now I shan't have any. You put that in the trow. You know you did.

MRS. P.

You say I put your dirty things in the trow and I'll put you in. Talk like that to me, will yer? One of these days I'll give you the cart whip, like what you deserve.

NAN

[*Turning to hide tears*]. You read your Bible, and you go to church, and you do a thing like that. You put a poor girl's coat in the trow and as good as deny it afterwards.

MR. P.

Now come, come, come. 'Ow d'yer expect to be ready for to-night? Let's 'ave no more catanddoggin' here.

MRS. P.

I'm not talking to you. 'Old yer peace. [*Furiously at interruption.*] I'm talking to *you*. [*To* NAN.] You're a black, proud, ungrateful cat. Wot your 'eart'll look like on the Day of Judgmink beats me.

NAN

Oh! [*Contemptuously—she opens out the sopping coat.*]

MRS. P.

I'll give yer "oh." 'Ere. Don't go dripping the pigwash all about the place. You drop it. Give it to me 'ere—'ere. [*She snatches at the coat and tries to wrench it from* NAN'S *hands.*]

NAN

Don't you dare to touch it. Let go of it.

MRS. P.

Will yer. Leggo now.

[167]

NAN

I won't. No you don't. You'll tear it in another minute. I'll kill you if you tear it.

MRS. P.

Wot'll you?

NAN

I'll kill you. I'll kill you.

MRS. P.

[*Putting both hands to the coat and wrenching it free; then slashing it into* NAN's *face.*] I'll show you 'oo's mistress 'ere, my lady. Now—see. [*She tears the collar off and stamps on it.*] There. You'll do what you're told 'ere, my lady.

[NAN *holds table and glares at her aunt then picks up the cutting knife.*]

NAN

[*Slowly.*] My dad gave me that coat. [*A pause.*] My dad.

MRS. P.

Mind, Will, she's got the knife in 'er 'and.

MR. P.

[*Going to her.*] Give me thicky knife. [*He takes it from her.*] No temper 'ere. I've got one score against you already. Wot's come to you to-day?

MRS. P.

The devil's come to 'er. She's pretty near tore my arm off.

NAN

[*Slowly.*] You be careful.

[168]

MRS. P.

But I'll teach yer.

NAN.

You be careful.

MR. P.

Nan, you go to your room.

[NAN *sullenly picks up the torn coat and then bursts into tears*]

NAN

My dad give me this coat. It's a dear coat. [*She smooths out the torn and crumpled stuff.*] And now it's all torn. [*The* PARGETTERS *watch her with a sort of hard scorn.*] I'll never be able to wear en again. Oh, my dad, I wish I was dead. I wish I was dead.

MR. P.

No sinful talk like that, now. I won't 'ave it.

NAN

Uncle! I 'ave tried, I 'ave, Uncle.

MR P.

Don't turn to me, girl. You'd ought to turn to God—giving way to the devil—No—and you've not been straight. If you'd told me at once I'd 'ave let it pass. Though I felt it. [*A pause, then testily.*] Come now, be straight. That's above all things.

[*A pause,* NAN *sobs*]

Eh?

[NAN *sobs*]

MR. P.

[*Rising.*] 'Aven't you something to tell me?

[169]

Nan

No! No!

Mr. P.

[*Grimly.*] I thought you 'ad. [*Turning.*]

Nan

Oh, Uncle! Do 'ee.

Mr. P.

[*Going*]. I didn't think it of you.

Nan

Uncle.

Mr. P.

I didn't think it.

[*Exit*]

Mrs. P.

[*Going up to her.*] I'll make your belly bitter, like in the Bible.

Nan

You! Oh! [*Turns from her.*] Oh, Dad, I wish I were with 'ee, I do.

Mrs. P.

[*Bitterly.*] You'll spoil yer looks for to-night, I shouldn't wonder. You won't 'ave yer young men neighing after yer. Dirty 'ogs.

[Nan *picks up apples and begins to cut them, still crying*]

Mrs. P.

I'll watch you with your young men! I'm not going to 'ave no mothers coming round complaining.

NAN

[*Slowly.*] I 'ope you may never feel wot I feel.

[*Enter* JENNY]

JENNY

Mawther!

MRS. P.

'Ush!

JENNY

There be Dick's trap with the groceries.

MRS. P.

Time too. 'Ere [to NAN] go and get them!

NAN

Me?

MRS. P.

Yes, you. 'Oo else. Do something for your living for once in a way.

[*Exit* NAN]

JENNY

Mother, wot 'ave Dad say?

MRS. P.

'Ush yer tongue. I've made *that* right.

JENNY

O mother. I thort 'e'd 'ave my 'ed off for it.

[171]

MRS. P.

Never you 'eed of that. I've somethink else to say to you.
That girl, Nan——

JENNY

Wot, Mother?

MRS. P.

[*Speaking very rapidly.*] You better watch out she don't tread
a thy corns, as well as thy mother's she've a done.

JENNY

Wot do 'ee mean, Mother?

MRS. P.

Dick Gurvil's 'oo I mean.

JENNY

Oh!

MRS. P.

Yes, Dick Gurvil! She've set 'er cap at Dick.

JENNY

Oh!

MRS. P.

[*Mimicking.*] Oh! Oh! *Yes*, and Dick be sweet on 'er.

JENNY

I don't care, Mother.

MRS. P.

Yes, you do care. 'Ave done o' your folly.

JENNY

Dick can please 'isself so far as I'm concerned, I'm sure.

MRS. P.

No 'e can't please 'isself, as you call it. 'Oo else'd yer get if you lose 'im? You take a man when you can get 'im. There ain't too many, let me tell yer.

JENNY

I do-an't care, I'm sure. I don't want no men.

MRS. P.

Don't you want. You listen to me. You got ter want. Whether you like or not. I ain't goin' to 'ave you the talk of the town.

JENNY

Lor, Mother! I didn't think of that.

MRS. P.

No, I know you didn't think.

JENNY

Lor, mother.

MRS. P.

'Oo 'ad 'er man took by a gallus-bird.

JENNY

Would they say that, Mother?

MRS. P.

'Oo's she to take Dick Gurvil? If you'd any pride——

[173]

JENNY

Be you sure she be a-trying for Dick?

MRS. P.

Well, you best find out.

JENNY

I'll watch it, I will.

MRS. P.

[*As* NAN *enters.*] Ah! you'd a better! Now I got to see to the 'ouse work. I'll expect you to 'ave everythink ready against I come back. [*To* NAN.] You may think as you're someone. I'll learn you different. None o' your tricks, 'ere. No! Nor none of your mother's carryings on (*a pause*) with men. That's wot I mean. . . . Gallus bird.

[*She goes out,* NAN *draws a chair to the table*—JENNY *is already seated*—*and begins to cut apples. She is crying. She gathers the torn coat together tenderly.*]

JENNY

Never mind Mother, Nan. She don't mean nothin'!

NAN

I don't——

JENNY

She be only put out by 'avin' comp'ny to-night.

NAN

It's not! It's not! Oh, she'd ought to leave my father.

[174]

JENNY

There, there now—let I get 'ee some warm warter off the 'ob. Your eyes'll be as red as red.

NAN

I don't care, I don't care.

JENNY

Why, come now. Us be going to be girt friends, us be, ben't us? Mother be a 'ard woman to please. But 'er don't mean it.

NAN

Her do speak so bitter. They be all against me! The 'ole world be against me.

JENNY

[*With bowl of water and a handkerchief.*] Do 'ee jest mop thy eyes. Or let I.

NAN

It be kind of you to trouble. What a girt silly I be to cry so!

JENNY

Your eyes'll be as red. Come, come! There be 'andsome young men a-comin'. I wouldn't wonder as they be all sweet on you! I wouldn't wonder as you'd 'ave a sweet'eart some Easter.

NAN

A sweet'eart! A charity girl!

JENNY

Don't take it to 'eart. Us be goin' to be friends, ben't us, dear?

NAN

It be kind of you to speak kind.

JENNY

And us'll go out of a Sunday. Why, us'll be girt friends. It go to my 'eart to think of thy trouble.

NAN

Will 'ee be a friend, cousin Jenny?

JENNY

There, there. Wot pretty eyes you 'ave. Your 'air's thicker than mine. 'Ow you do a set it off. Us'll 'ave no secrets, will us?

NAN

'Ee will be my friend, won't 'ee, Jenny? Do-an't 'ee be agen me—I couldn't bear it if you turned against me. I've sometimes been near killing myself since I came here. Your Mother's been that bitter to me.

JENNY

Don't 'ee say such things.

NAN

Jenny, I'll tell 'ee why I didn't kill myself.

JENNY

Lord, Nan, doa-n't 'ee.

NAN

I want 'ee to bear with me, Jenny. I'll tell 'ee why I didn't

[176]

kill myself. I thought . . . there . . . it's only nonsense. Did you ever think about men, Jenny? About loving a man? About marriage?

JENNY

I've 'oped to 'ave a 'ome of my own. And not to be a burden 'ere and that.

NAN

Ah! But about 'elping a man?

JENNY

A man 'as strength. 'E ought to 'elp a woman.

NAN

I could 'elp a man, Jenny.

JENNY

Wot ideyers you do 'ave!

NAN

When a girl's 'eart is breaking, Jenny, she 'as ideyers.

JENNY

Ah!

NAN

Jenny!

JENNY

Yes, Nan?

NAN

I've never talked to a woman like this afore. I felt I'd die if I couldn't talk to someone.

[177]

JENNY

I know, exackly!

NAN

When I see you so kind, and you so pretty, Jenny, I felt I must speak.

JENNY

Do you think me pretty, Nan?

NAN

Yes, Jenny.

JENNY

In service they thought me pretty. All but cook.

NAN

You are pretty, Jenny.

JENNY

Cook was a unpleasant old thing. She did 'er 'air in papers. No ladies do their 'air in papers! Ow! she was 'orrid of a morning. O! the waste I see go on in that 'ouse. They 'ad pastry every day. And the ladies had milk and biscuits at eleven of a morning.

NAN

You must tell me all your secrets, Jenny.

JENNY

That I will. And will 'ee tell I all yourn?

NAN

If you like, Jenny.

[178]

JENNY

And will 'ee tell I when you 'ave a sweet'eart?

NAN

Ah! A sweet'eart. You must tell me about yours, Jenny.

JENNY

Ah! I ain't got one yet.

NAN

'Aven't you, Jenny?

JENNY

Noa. Not one special like.

NAN

You'll 'ave one soon, Jenny. O Jenny, I hope you'll be very 'appy.

JENNY

Love be queer, ben't it? The things it makes people do. Could 'ee fancy a man, Nan?

NAN

Perhaps.

JENNY

Ugly girt scrawfs, I think they be.

NAN

Not all of them.

JENNY

Perhaps you 'ave a fancy, Nan? 'Ave you, dear. 'Ave you? 'Oo be it, Nan? Tell me, dearie. I wouldn't tell a single soul. Tell me, Nan. You said as you'd 'ave no secrets from me.

NAN

Ah!

JENNY

Is it anyone I know?

[NAN *goes to her and puts an arm round her and kisses her*]

NAN

Yes, dear.

JENNY

Be it Artie Pearce?

NAN

No, Jenny.

JENNY

'Oo be it. It be a shame not to tell me!

NAN

Jenny dear?

JENNY

Yes, Nan. Tell me now. Whisper.

NAN

It be Dick Gurvil, Jenny.

JENNY

Dick Gurvil?

NAN

I love him. I love him.

JENNY

Do you love him very much?

[180]

NAN

It feel like my 'eart was in flower, Jenny.

JENNY

Ah! It must. [*A pause*] I 'ope you'll be very 'appy. You
and Mr. Gurvil.

NAN

God bless you, Jenny.

JENNY

What eyes you have got, cousin Nan. To think of you fancy-
ing Dick! It *be* nice to 'ave you for a friend, cousin Nan.

NAN

Kiss me, dear. You've never kissed me.

JENNY

There! Go and bathe thy eyes, Nan. They'll be red if 'ee
don't. 'Ee mustn't 'ave them red for Dick to-night. Bathe
'em in cold.

NAN

I could cry, I could. [*She goes slowly out.*]

JENNY

[*At the other door.*] Mother. [*A pause.*] [*Softly.*] Mother.

MRS. P.

[*Off.*] Yes!

JENNY

Come 'ere a moment.

MRS. P.

[*Wiping her hands.*] What d'yer want now?

JENNY

About Nan.

MRS. P.

Wot? Wot about 'er?

JENNY

[*Giggling.*] She be soft on Dick, Mother. Her've a-told me.

MRS. P.

Ho!

JENNY

[*Giggling.*] Us'll 'ave to watch it, Mother.

MRS. P.

I'll watch it.

CURTAIN

[182]

ACT II

SCENE: *The kitchen.* NAN *tidying up. She places tray, glasses and bottle in inner room.*

NAN

[*Sings.*] . . . .

> Blow, blow, thou winds of winter blow,
> And cover me with sparklen snow,
> And tear the branches from the tree,
> And strew the dead leaves over me.

DICK

[*Coming in.*] Miss Nan.

NAN

Why, Mr. Gurvil! What a start you give me. You be early.

DICK

Ah? When'll the others be 'ere?

NAN

Not yet. It's not half past yet.

DICK

When'll the others—Mrs. Pargetter—be down?

NAN

They won't be down this ten minutes. They be dressing.

DICK

And 'aven't the fiddler come?

NAN

No.

DICK

Per'aps I'd a better go out again.

NAN

No. Come in and sit down, Mr. Dick. They'll be 'ere di-reckly. I'll be done. Tell me the news in the great world. What be 'appening?

DICK

They do say there be a criminal a-broak loose. Out of Glor-ster jail.

NAN

Indeed!

DICK

And come 'idin' 'ere somewhere, they think.

NAN

What makes them think that?

DICK

I dunno. But there be a Bow Street Runner. And there be a gentleman come. They were askin' where Parson live. They must be 'avin' a hue and cry. Hope they'll catch 'im and 'ang 'im. I'd like to sick the dogs at 'em.

NAN

They be 'uman beings, like us be, Mr. Dick.

DICK

[*Undoing his neck-cloth.*] No, they ben't like us. That be where you women go wrong. Along of your 'earts, that is. I'd like to see all criminals 'anged. Then us honest ones might fare to prosper. [*He takes off neck-cloth.*]

NAN

What'll you take, Mr. Dick, after your walk?

DICK

What be going?

NAN

'Ave some zider and a cake. They be in the next room, ready.

DICK

If it ben't troubling you, I ull.

[NAN *fetches mug and plate*]

DICK

[*Taking a cake.*] I'd ought to be a-waiting on you, not you a-waiting on me. Only I 'avent any angel-cakes 'ere. None but angel-cakes 'd be fit eating for you, Miss Nan.

NAN

Oh, now, I wonder how many girls you've made that speech to.

DICK

None, I never.

NAN

Well, I hope you like your cake?

DICK

It be beautiful. A spice-cake, when it be split and buttered, and just set to the fire, so as the butter runs. I don't mean to toast it; but just set to the fire, and then just a sprinkle of sugar to give it a taste. No so as to make it sweet, you know. It go down like roses. Like kissing a zweet 'eart at 'arvest time. When the girt moon be zhining.

NAN

If they be all that to you, Mr. Dick, you must 'ave another. Try and think the clock be the moon a-zhining.

[*She gets more cakes*]

DICK

It be lovely 'aving cakes and you bringing them to me. [*Bites*]. But there ben't no sugar, not on this one. Miss Nan, will 'ee jest put thy pretty 'and on this cake, and then it'll be sugared lovely.

NAN

I'm not going to do anything so silly. 'Ere. Take this one. This one be sugared.

DICK

[*Eating.*] It 'ud be just 'eaven if you'd 'ave 'alf of it. So's I might feel—some'ow—as——

NAN

No. I won't 'ave any. 'Ave another drop of zider.

[186]

DICK

[*Tasting.*] Your zider be too peert, Miss Nan. I like zider to be peert, like I likes my black puddens done, up to a point. But zider's peert's this—I tell you what it want. It want to 'ave a apple roast therein, and a sod toast therein, and then it want to 'ave a nutmeg grated ever so light, not rough, yer know. And then it be made mellow, like, like tart of a Sunday.

NAN

Why, Mr. Dick, you'd ought to have been a cook, I think.

DICK

My father say to me—"Mind thy innards," he say. I 'ad to do for my father, arter mother died. Very pertiklar about his innards dad were. I learned about innards from 'im.

NAN

It be wonderful to 'ave a father to do for. To think as he knowed 'ee when you were a little un. To think as perhaps 'e give up lots o' things, so's you might fare to be great in the world.

DICK

My dad never give up. 'E said 'e try it once, just to try like. It never'd 'ave suit my dad.

NAN

It be always 'ard for a man to give up, even for a child, they say. But a woman 'as to give up. You don't know. You never think per'aps what a woman gives up. She gives up 'er beauty and 'er peace. She gives up 'er share of joy in the world.

All to bear a little one; as per'aps'll not give 'er bread when 'er be wold.

DICK

I wonder women ever want to 'ave children. They be so beautiful avore they 'ave children. They 'ave their red cheeks, so soft. And sweet lips so red's red. And their eyes bright, like stars a-zhining. And oh, such white soft 'ands. Touch one of 'em, and you 'ave like shoots all down. Beau-ti-vul. Love-lee.

NAN

It be a proud thing to 'ave a beauty to raise love in a man.

DICK

And after. I seen the same girls, with their 'ands all rough of washing-day, and their fingers all scarred of stitching. And their cheeks all flaggin', and sunk. And dull as toads' bellies, the colour of 'em. And their eyes be 'eavy, like a foundered wold ewe's when 'er time be on 'er. And lips all bit. And there they do go with the backache on 'em. Pitiful, I call it. Draggin' their wold raggy skirts. And the baby crying. And little Dick with 'is nose all bloody, fallen in the grate. And little Sairey fell in the yard, and 'ad 'er 'air mucked. Ah! Ugh! It go to my 'eart.

NAN

Ah, but that ben't the all of love, Mr. Dick. It be 'ard to see beauty gone, and joy gone, and a light 'eart broke. But it be wonderful for to 'ave little ones. To 'ave brought life into the world. To 'ave 'ad them little live things knocking on your 'eart, all them months. And then to feed them. 'Elpless like that.

DICK

They be pretty, little ones be, when they be kept clean and that. I likes 'earing them sing 'imns. I likes watching the little boys zwimming in the river. They be so white and swift, washing themselves. And the splashin' do shine zo. Diamonds. 'Oo be coming 'ere to-night—'sides us?

NAN

Old Gaffer Pearce be a-comin' to fiddle.

DICK

He'd ought to be in mad'ouse, Gaffer did. Dotty owd gape. He ben't wholly stalwart in uns brains, folk do observe. But——

NAN

He been a beautiful fiddler.

DICK

He been a wonder, that old man 'ave.

NAN

'E play wonderful still, when 'e gets thinking of old times, and of 'is girl as 'e calls 'er. Why, she've been dead fifty years and more.

DICK

She was beautiful. They call 'er the Star of the West. My dad 'ave tell of 'er. She 'ad a face like cream.

NAN

He made beautiful poems to 'er; and music, 'e did. I 'eard

'im sing 'is poems once. He was fiddlin' quiet-like, all the time 'e were a-singing; and the tears standing in 'is eyes. 'E's never been quite right since the Lord 'ad mercy on 'er.

DICK

'Oo else's comin' 'sides Gaffer?

NAN

Tommy and Artie. What a 'andsome boy Artie be grown.

DICK

Ah? I 'ear 'em say that. I couldn't ever see it.

NAN

He be just like his mother. Black and comely.

DICK

I likes a good black. I likes a good brown, a good bay brown. I likes a good black too. There be bright blacks and there be dull blacks. Now what be the black as I likes? You 'air is jest the very colour. Beautiful I call it.

NAN

[*Getting up.*] If you ben't going to 'ave more zider I'll take your mug, Mr. Dick. Mr. Dick.

DICK

Yes.

NAN

We've 'ad a sheep die on us last week. Don't you 'ave none of our 'ot mutton pies to-night.

[190]

DICK

Ah? I 'ope you'll give me twice of trotters, instead like, I can do with a trotter, I can. I s'pose us be going to 'ave great times 'ere to-night, Miss Nan.

NAN

Yes, indeed. Us'll dance the moon down to-night.

DICK

I s'pose you be a girt lady to dance?

NAN

I've not dance now, for more'n a year, Mr. Dick.

DICK

I s'pose you 'ad dancings when you were to 'ome.

NAN

Us used to dance on our doorsteps at 'ome. There was an old man used to fiddle to us. Every night there was a moon, we danced. The girls would dance in their pattens. They used to go clack, clack, their feet did. You'd a thought it was drums, Mr. Dick.

DICK

I wish I'd bin there to 'ave dance with you.

NAN

And then we used to sing "Joan to the Maypole" and "Randal" and all the old songs. And there'd be beetles a buzzin'. And sometimes one of the shepherds come with 'is flute. It was nice at 'ome, then.

Dick

What times us be 'avin' since you come 'ere. It be always sad to leave 'ome. But I s'pose you'll be going back afore long. Your dad and your mother'll be a-wanting you. Sure to be.

Nan

They be dead, Mr. Dick.

Dick

Now, be they indeed! Mrs. Pargetter do talk's though you 'ad both your folk.

Nan

Mrs. Pargetter! She has 'er reasons, Mr. Dick, for letting folk think that.

Dick

What reasons can 'er 'ave for that, Miss Nan?

Nan

Some day, per'aps I'll tell you 'er reasons. Now let I take your coat and hat.

[*She takes coat, hat, etc., and puts them in inner room. Then Re-enters.*]

Dick

'Ow brave you be a-looking, Miss Nan.

Nan

Soap and water tells, they do say.

Dick

You be all roses, Miss Nan. And you be all lilies.

NAN

Why, Mr. Dick! You be quite the courtier.

DICK

Ah! [*Producing a rose.*] Miss Nan?

NAN

Yes?

DICK

I brought a rose——

NAN

For Jenny, Mr. Dick?

DICK

No, for 'ee. Will 'ee wear it, Miss Nan?

NAN

Yes, if you'll give it to me.

DICK

'Ere it be. Will 'ee say thank you for it?

NAN

Thank you, Mr. Dick. What a beautiful rose!

DICK

'Er be a Campden Wonder. 'Er be red. Like love. Love be red. Like roses.

NAN

Oh!

[193]

DICK

I see that rose growing, Miss Nan—an' I—I thought 'er'd look beautiful if—if—if you were wearing of 'er, like.

NAN

Well, I hope it does.

DICK

You put 'er to the blush, Miss Nan—Miss Nan——

NAN

Yes?

DICK

Will you do I a favor?

NAN

What is it?

DICK

Will 'ee wear that rose in your hair?

NAN

In my hair, Mr. Dick! Why?

DICK

I 'ad a dream once of you with roses in your hair.

NAN

[*Putting rose in her hair.*] In the old times women always put roses in their hair. When they danced, they wore roses in their hair. The rose-leaves fell all about 'en, my mother told me.

DICK

It looks like it were growing out of your 'ed.

NAN

I must light the lamp.

DICK

No, don't 'ee. Don't 'ee.

NAN

[*Striking a match.*] They must have looked beautiful, those women must, in the old time. There was songs made of them. Beauty be a girt gift, Mr. Dick.

DICK

It be wonderful in a woman.

NAN

It makes a woman like God, Mr. Dick.

DICK

You be beautiful, Nan; you be beautiful.

NAN

Ah, Mr. Dick.

DICK

You be beautiful. You be like a fairy. The rose. You be beautiful like in my dream.

NAN

Ah! Let go my hands. Let go my hands.

DICK

You be beautiful. Your eyes. And your face so pale. And your hair with the rose. O Nan, you be lovely. You be lovely!

[195]

NAN

O don't! Don't!

DICK

My love, my beloved.

NAN

Ah!

DICK

I love you, O Nan, I love you.

NAN

Let me go; let me go, please.

DICK

Do 'ee care for me? Do 'ee love me, Nan?

NAN

You don't know! You don't know! You don't know about me.

DICK

I love you.

NAN

Ah! You mustn't. You mustn't love me.

DICK

There be no high queen 'as a beauty like yours, Nan.

NAN

O! let me go.

DICK

My love! My 'andsome!

[196]

NAN

O! Dick.

DICK

Nan, O Nan, do 'ee love me?

NAN

Ah!

DICK

Dear sweet. Will 'ee marry me? Do 'ee love me?

NAN

I love you, Dick.

DICK

My love! My pretty!

NAN

My dear love.

DICK

My beautiful. I'll make a song for you, my beautiful.

NAN

Your loving me, that's song enough.

DICK

Nan, dear, let I take the pins out of your hair. Let me 'ave your 'air all loose. Your lovely hair. O Nan, you be a beautiful woman.

NAN

Ah, God! I wish I were beautiful.

DICK

Dear love, you be.

[197]

NAN

More beautiful.   Then I'd 'ave more to give you.

DICK

Kiss me.   Kiss me!

NAN

There be my 'air, Dick.   It ben't much, after all.

DICK

[*Kissing the hair.*]   Oh, beautiful.   Beau-ti-vul.   My own Nan.

NAN

I am yours, my beloved.

DICK

When shall us be married?   When shall us come together?

NAN

Ah, my love!   Now is enough.   Now is enough.

DICK

When shall us marry?

NAN

Kiss me.

DICK

Shall it be Michaelmas?

NAN

Kiss me.   Kiss me.

DICK

My winsome.   My beauty.

[198]

NAN

Now loose me, darling. [*They break.*] I have had my moment. I have been happy.

DICK

Nan! Nan!

NAN

I cannot marry you. O Dick, 'ee must go away. Go away. [*He goes toward her.*] Don't 'ee. Us can never marry. You'd 'ate me if you knew. I can't tell you. Not to-night, dear. They'll be coming down directly. If I married you, Dick? Oh, I can't. I can't—if I married you—if we lived 'ere—I might bring shame upon you. They'd call names after me. They'd know. They'd know.

DICK

My pretty! My Nan. Tell thy Dick.

NAN

Ah, no, no. Don't touch me. You don't know yet. I'm—not a fit—I'm not a fit woman for you to marry, Dick. My father. My poor dad—[*she breaks down*] O Dick! O Dick! You don't know what sorrows I gone through. I think my 'eart'll break.

DICK

There, there, Nan. Tell thy Dick. My poor dearie. You be my dear love now, Nan.

NAN

If you love me, Dick—O, my love! Us together! Us needn't fear what they say. Us could go away, Dick. To America. Us'd be 'appy there. O Dick, take me out of this. All we 'ave is our lives, Dick. With love, us'd never want. Us'd 'ave that, my love. Take me, Dick.

DICK

I'll take you, darling. To-night. To-night I'll tell them.

NAN

In spite of—even if—what I 'ave to say?

DICK

No matter what it is, dear. To-night, now. To-night. When the fiddler comes.

NAN

Ah! my beloved!

DICK

I'll claim you. Before them all, I'll claim you.

NAN

Your wife, my blessed.

DICK

Kiss me, once more, dear.

NAN

Before they come.

[*Outside the door there is a shuffling and giggling*]

A VOICE

They be in. I hear 'em.

A VOICE

They ben't.

A VOICE

Don't, Artie. [*Together, rapidly.*]

A VOICE

Sh!

A VOICE

All together.

A VOICE

One after the other.

DICK

Here they are.

NAN

My beloved! My own.

VOICES

"Joan, to the maypole away let us on
The time is short and will be gone—"

[*They stop and giggle*]

ANOTHER

They ben't.

[*One hums the tune*]

DICK

To-night. Before them all. When the fiddle begins. My
wife.

NAN

My husband.

VOICES

"Where your beauties may be seen." Bang! Bang! Bang!
[*They knock the door. The* LOVERS *break.* MRS. PARGETTER
and JENNY *run downstairs as* NAN *flings the door open. Enter
old* GAFFER PEARCE, ARTIE *of that ilk,* TOMMY ARKER, *and*
TWO GIRLS.]

[201]

Mrs. P.

'Ere you be. 'Ow nice it is to see you.

[*She kisses the girls and looks hard at* Nan]

Jenny

[*To* Dick.] Ah, Mr. Gurvil. 'Ave you brought I the rose as you promised?

Dick

You don't want no roses.

Jenny

You ain't very polite, Mr. Dick.

Dick

You got roses in your cheeks, you 'ave.

Mrs. P.

'Ow be you, gaffer?

[*General salutation*]

Artie

Granfer doan't 'ear you, unless you 'it 'im. [*Shouts in his ear.*] 'Ow be you, granfer?

Gaffer.

[*Looking at* Nan.] Twice I seen her, twice. Her've gone by on the road. With a rose in 'er 'air. And 'er eyes shone. Twice. In April.

Artie

'Ere, gaffer! Sit down 'ere. 'E can fiddle still, th'owd granfer do; but 'e doan't talk, not to strangers.

[202]

A GIRL

Us seed some strangers in the village, Mrs. Pargetter.

MRS. P.

Ah?

TOM

They were askin' where your 'ouse was. Them and parson.

ARTIE

'Ave you been a-robbin', Mrs. Pargetter?

MRS. P.

A-robbin'! No. I 'ave enough of thieves without me going stealin', I 'ope.

ARTIE

Well. One of 'em be a runner, 'e be.

DICK

Yes, for I seed 'en too.

MRS. P.

O! So you didn't come with th' others, then, Dick?

DICK

Noa. But I seen 'en.

ALL

I wonder whatever they do want!

MRS. P.

Well. If they're coming 'ere, us shall soon know. I should a-thought the pleece could a-caught their own thieves.

[*Old* PARGETTER *comes downstairs, buttoning his waistcoat*]

Mr. P.

Aha! Aha!

All

'Ow be you, Mr. Pargetter?

Mr. P.

[*Saluting.*] Why, 'ow beautiful all you girls be looking! 'Ullo, Dick! You be quite the bridegroom. Why, gaffer, what a old Pocahontas you be, to be sure! 'Ave you brought your fiddle?

Gaffer

[*Still staring at* Nan.] 'Oo be her? On the roads, shining, I've seen 'er. Scattering blossoms, blossoms.

Jenny

[*After glancing at* Gaffer.] So you come 'ere early, Dick. Why Nan, do look. You 'aven't a-done your 'air. Look, mother, at Nan's 'air!

Mrs. P.

What in the name of Fate d'you 'ave that rose in your 'air for? And why d'yer come down with your 'air like that?

Nan

I had to open the door. I had to light the candle.

Gaffer

Give I a cup of red wine and a cup of white wine, and honey [*coming towards her*] and a apple and a—I be goin' to fiddle joy to the feet of the bride.

[204]

ARTIE

You be going to do wonders, you be. Sit down, you old
stupe. Ain't no bride 'ere.

MR. P.

[*To the* GIRLS.] There be brides for us all. With all you
lovely young things. Nothing like 'aving a sweet'eart. Now!
You ladies, you'll want to take off your things.

ARTIE

'Ow about us?

MR. P.

One sect at a time. Like the sheep goin' through a 'edge.
Per'aps you ladies'll go up-stairs with Nan and Jenny 'ere.

NAN

Come, Ellen.

JENNY

'Ere! Give I your brolly.

[*The* GIRLS *go upstairs*]

MR. P.

Now, you gentlemen. Come on in 'ere with me. [*He leads
them to the inner room.*]

MRS. P.

[*As* DICK *follows.*] Oh, Dick.

DICK

Ess, Mrs. Pargetter.

[205]

MRS. P.

I see you 'ave your things off. Just 'elp me a moment, there's a good lad.

DICK

Ess, Mrs. Pargetter. What do 'e want done?

MRS. P.

Us must 'ave all clear for dancing. I'll nip them candles over 'ere to the dresser. There. Now 'elp me lift the table over. There! You was 'ere early, wasn't yer, Dick?

DICK

Nothin' to speak of. 'Ow about them chairs?

MRS. P.

They'll do nicely. I suppose Nan let you in?

DICK

Ess. Miss Nan done.

MRS. P.

You two been 'aving a fine game, I know.

DICK

Ah?

MRS. P.

Don't tell me you 'aven't. Did she kiss yer?

DICK

[Sullenly.] Never you mind.

Mrs. P.

Oh, I don't mind. But I got eyes, I 'ave.

Dick

Oh! What good 'ave they done yer?

Mrs. P.

O, when I see a girl with 'er face all flushed, and 'er 'air all 'anging down, and a rose stuck over 'er ear, and a young man by 'er as flustered as what you are—Well—I can——

Dick

What can you?

Mrs. P.

Well, I know they don't come like that of their own.

Dick

[*Sullenly.*] Do you?

Mrs. P.

I ain't blaming yer, mind.

Dick

Aren't yer?

Mrs. P.

I know what it is to be young, myself.   But all the same——

Dick

What?

Mrs. P.

Oh, nothing.

[207]

DICK

What were you going to say?

MRS. P.

Nothing.

DICK

You were going to say something.

MRS. P.

No, I weren't. Only it mid seem strange. You see, your dad's so partikler.

DICK

Oh! 'im.

MRS. P.

'As 'e took you in 'is partner yet? Your dad?

DICK

No.

MRS. P.

No, I know 'e 'aven't. I could tell yer something. A little surprise—about your dad.

DICK

What's that?

MRS. P.

Somethin' 'e said to me. I don't know as I've a right to tell yer.

DICK

About my being took in as partner to 'im?

Mrs. P.

It was meant as a secret. But there—since—us can 'ave no secrets, can us?

Dick

Why, no—I'm——

Mrs. P.

Well—your dad says to me, "Mrs. Pargetter" 'e says, "I'm gettin' to be a old man, I want to see my boy settled. Now then," 'e says. "The day my boy marries I 'ave 'im bound my partner. And £20 to 'elp 'im furnish."

Dick

Good iron! A old chanti-cleer. Balm in Gilead, as the saying is.

Mrs. P.

"Yes," I says, "And more no mother could ask." [*Change of voice.*] That girl'd forsake 'er 'eavenly crown for you, Dick. She's drooped like a lily of the vale since she's been away. If you'd seen that girl as I seen 'er, you'd 'ave yourself arst this Sunday. Or you'll 'ave 'er goin' into a decline. 'Ave you arst 'er yet?

Dick

Yes. I arst 'er just now. Just this minute ago.

Mrs. P.

When she was at the door 'ere?

Dick

When I come in.

Mrs. P.

Wot did she say, I wonder? No tellin', I suppose?

Dick

I thought as you'd seen. I mean, from what you said.

Mrs. P.

No. I never seed.

Dick

From 'er 'avin' 'er 'air down. The rose and that.

Mrs. P.

'Air down? She 'adn't 'er 'air down. I done it myself.

Dick

Yes, she 'ad 'er 'air down. You said—just now——

Mrs. P.

Jenny 'ad?

Dick

No, Nan.

Mrs. P.

Nan: wot's she got to do with it?

Dick

I've just arst 'er to marry me, Mrs. Pargetter. And her 'ave
said yes. [*A pause.*] It'll be nice bein' a partner and that, won't
it. I'll be able to 'ave the trap of a evenin'. And I'll 'ave money
for——

Mrs. P.

[*Grimly.*] *You* be 'is partner! You'll be your dad's partner if you marry Jenny—that's your dad's arrangement. That's wot 'e's planned.

Dick

My dad 'ave planned——

Mrs. P.

"'E shall marry as I choose," 'e says, "my son shall. If 'e don't know which side 'is bread is buttered, there's the door. 'E can beg."

Dick

'E can beg!

Mrs. P.

"Not a penny will 'e ever 'ave from *me*," 'e says. Now.

Dick

So!

[Mrs. Pargetter *watches him*]

Mrs. P.

D'you think we'd let you throw Jenny over, after getting 'er talked about?

Dick

It be different 'avin' a kiss or two of a girl and wantin' to marry 'er.

[*Re-enter* Pargetter *slowly, looking hard at* Dick *who is very white. He walks to the dresser, picks up a corkscrew, and walks slowly out, looking hard at* Dick *but saying nothing.*]

Mrs. P.

Now then.

DICK

[*Moistening his lips.*]   Per'aps my father'll 'ear me explain.

MRS. P.

Wot'll you tell 'im?

DICK

Tell 'im as Jenny ain't no more to me 'n what a pig's milt is. Tell 'im as I love Nan.   And as I be goin' to marry 'er.

MRS. P.

[*Slowly and grimly.*]   You'll tell 'im for instans, you'll tell your father, for instans, as you're goin' to marry a girl whose dad was 'ung at Glorster, like the thief 'e was.   Just afore last Christmas.

DICK

Nan's dad wos?

MRS. P.

[*Nods her head.*]   And 'er mother 'ad men come to see 'er. [*A pause.*]   'Ow'll yer tell that to yer dad?

DICK

My Lord Almighty!   Daughter of one of them!

MRS. P.

Two of them.

DICK

My 'oly Saviour!

MRS. P.

Your 'art out of your bosom like a engine it does go.

DICK

I'll marry 'er yet to spite yer.

[212]

MRS. P.

Wot'll yer marry 'er on? You ain't got a penny. She ain't got a penny. [*A pause.*] I wonder she never told yer about 'er dad's being 'ung. They 'ad yeomanry in front of the gaol. Quite an affair. Didn't she never tell yer?

DICK

No. 'Er was going to. My! Oh my——

MRS. P.

Per'aps she waited till she 'ooked yer. 'Ark at 'em in there!

[*Laughter inside and one crows like a cock*]

She is artful. I never see a deeper girl than wot she is.

DICK

Oh, 'old yer tongue, you old devil! I've 'ad my gruel.

MRS. P.

Come, come. Be a man.

DICK

Mrs. Pargetter. I mean, I'm—Mrs. Pargetter——

MRS. P.

Yes? Wot?

DICK

I dunno—I dunno wot to think.

MRS. P.

Your dad'll know wot to think.

[213]

DICK

I dunno! If I 'ad I a little of my own!

MRS. P.

Oh, if yer like to starve, starve. Walk. Pad yer 'oof.

DICK

Ah! A tramper! My 'eavenly King!

MRS. P.

Lots on 'em pass 'ere. Dirt on 'em. Feet comin' through
their boots. You see 'em nick crusts out of the gutter. Berries
of a 'edge, some on 'em. Froze stiff, some on 'em, under a rick.
Lots on 'em.

DICK

Ah! Don't! I can't! [*A pause.*]

MRS. P.

Well, Dick? Wot's it to be? Is it Jenny?

DICK

O damn it, yes, it's Jenny, Jenny. Like 'avin' a cold poultice!
Very well, it's Jenny then. Now I 'ope yer satisfied.

MRS. P.

[*Kissing him.*] There. *I* knew yer wouldn't act dishonour-
able. I knowed you better.

[*The door opens, the men come in, singing and laughing.* ARTIE
PEARCE *crows like a cock. The* GIRLS *come down, hearing the
noise.*] Wot a time you people 'ave been.

[214]

Mr. P.

Wot 'a you been doin' all the time?

Artie

[*Singing.*]　　Making love in the evenin'
　　　　　　　Making love in the evenin'

A drop of zider sets one up like [*wiping his mouth*].

Mrs. P.

[*To* Pargetter.] You'll 'ear later. All in good time. 'Ere Jenny, 'elp me with these chairs! I've watched it all right. Dick and you I mean. It's settled.

Jenny

[*With a chair.*] Give I that one, Mother. O Mother, wot fun us shall 'ave.

Mr. P.

Now us be goin' to 'ave a dance.

A Girl

Be you a-goin' to dance, Mr. Pargetter?

Mr. P.

Course I be. Come, gaffer. Out with that fiddle 'o yourn.

A Girl

I do love a fiddle.

Jenny

A barrel hargin be good, too.

[215]

Mr. P.

Now, gaffer. Now, no long faces, anybody. Us be goin' to 'ave great times, ben't us?

Nan

Wait till I set thy chair right, gaffer.

Gaffer

[*Querulously.*] On the roads, I seen you. Surely. And it was all—all a-blowing?

Nan

Sit 'ere, now. And 'ave this cushion.

Artie

Don't let granfer fall into the fire. 'E will, if you don't watch it.

Gaffer

[*Bowing in the old style.*] Beauty makes women be proud. There be few beauties 'as the 'umbleness to 'elp a old man. Ah, there be no pleasure for the old; but to 'muse the young. I be a old man. A old, old man!

Nan

The old be wise, gaffer. The old 'ave peace, after their walking the world.

Mrs. P.

Stuff! [*A giggle.*]

Gaffer

There be no peace to 'im as sees you, goin' by in beauty, puttin' fire to 'em.

Girls

Us be waitin'. Us be all ready!

Mr. P.

Take your——

Gaffer

[*To* Nan.] What tune will the bride 'ave? A ring of bells
and the maids flinging flowers at 'er. Like me and my girl 'ad.
[*Pause.*] I 'ad a flower of 'er to go to church with. [*Pause.*]
They put my flower under the mould after. [*Pause.*] I 'eard
the mould go knock! [*He tunes his fiddle as he speaks.*] No
one remembers my white flower. [*Pause.*] That's sixty year
ago.

Nan

You'll meet her again, gaffer. Per'aps she's by you now.

Gaffer

[*With a lifting voice—half rising.*] So you've a come, my
'andsome——

Mrs. P.

'Ere. [*She taps* Gaffer's *hand.*] Play! 'Ere! Fiddle. [*To*
Nan.] Don't you see you're upsettin' 'im. Move away. One'd
think you'd no feelings.

Mr. P.

Take your partners.

Mr. P.

Now, 'ave you all got your partners?

All.

No. Don't be so silly, Artie. Now, do be quiet. 'Ow are
us to dance! [*Etc., etc.*] You come over 'ere by me.

[Nan *stands a little apart, looking at* Dick, *waiting on him*]

Mrs. P.

Now, now, we're all 'ere. 'Ush a moment. Afore we begin there's a little bit o' noos just 'appened, as I'd like to say about.

Artie

'Ear! 'Ear!

Mr. P.

[*To* Artie.] You be quiet! [*He grins at* Artie *approvingly.*]

Mrs. P.

As I'm sure 'll come as a great surprise. Really, it quite took my breath away! It did, really. Now, I mustn't stop you young people dancing. But I must just tell you this little bit of noos. He, he! Why——

Artie

We ain't lookin'.

A Girl

Be quiet, Artie.

Mrs. P.

Jenny and Dick 'ere 'ave made a match of it. I 'ope the present company'll wish the 'appy couple joy! Dick! Jenny! Give me your 'ands. There. [*She clasps them.*] I 'ope you'll be very 'appy together. Dick, [*kissing him*] you're my son now, ain't yer?

Artie

Spare 'is blushes, Mother.

All

Why, who'd ever a-thought it! I do 'ope you'll be 'appy. 'Ow sudden! Quite took my breath away! Jenny, come 'ere,

[218]

and let I kiss 'ee. I s'pose us can't kiss you, Mr. Dick? No, Mr. Dick'll be quite the married man. 'E looks it already.

NAN

Dick, Dick, oh, Dick! What, oh, Dick, you weren't playing, Dick?

DICK

Don't Dick me. Get out!

MRS. P.

Wot are yer bothering Dick for?

NAN

I thought 'e'd something—something to say to me.

DICK

You thought I was a oly scrawf, didn't yer?

NAN

I thought I was a 'appy woman, Dick. [*She looks at him and goes slowly over to a chair. As she goes.*]

MR. P.

Now, Nan. What are you waitin' for? Take your place 'ere and dance, now.

MRS. P.

Per'aps Nan is like 'er father.

JENNY

[*Sliding her feet about.*] 'Ow's that, Mother?

[219]

MRS. P.

Per'aps she can only dance on air.

NAN

[*Going to her.*] Yes, yes, I am like my father. You coward to say that.

MR. P.

Wot are you thinking of, with company present?

MRS. P.

You leave her to me. I'll deal with her. [*To the company.*] She thought if she 'ad 'er 'air down an' 'er neck un'ooked as *she* might 'ave a go in at Dick, 'ere.

TOMMY

'Ope us didn't come too soon, Dick.

JENNY

She believes in giving all for love, Cousin Nan do.

MRS. P.

She'll give no more in this house. Why, 'er dad was 'ung for a thief only last Christmas.

MR. P.

Now, Mother, that's—No, she deserves it. She ain't been straight.

ALL

Ah.

NAN

Yes. I'd like you all to know that. My dad was 'ung at Glorster. I'd oughtn't to a shook your 'ands without I'd told you. I tried 'ard to tell you, Dick. Dick. Dick. I give you all I had. You 'ad me. Like I never was. Not to any. O Dick, I 'ope you'll be very, very 'appy.

DICK

'Ere. Go and say your piece to Gaffer there. 'E 'asn't many pleasures, I've done with yer. 'Ere, Jenny, you be goin' to dance with I.

JENNY

[*Giggling.*] I think I could 'elp, Dick Gurvil.

DICK

'Elp me then. Come on.

JENNY

Law. It make my heart all of a flower. That's wot Cousin Nan says. I s'pose it must be very clever if 'er says it.

NAN

I wish—I wish the grass was over my 'ed.

DICK

'Ere. Us wish to dance.

[*Nan goes aside*]

GAFFER

A bride's tears be zoon a-dried. But love be a zweet vlower. A girt red vlower. Her do last for ever. For ever. [*He plays "Joan to the Maypole."*] Like me and my girl, for ever!

[*They dance*]

CURTAIN

ACT III

[SCENE: *The same*. NAN *at table at back*. *A noise within*. GAFFER *in his chair*.]

NAN

Life be that bitter. O dad, life be that bitter.

GAFFER

You be young to 'ave life bitter on you.

NAN

It isn't time makes us old.

GAFFER

Some on us is glad to go away. Quite early.

NAN

I wish I could go away. I wish I could go away.

GAFFER

Us'll all be took away, afore long.

NAN

I'd like to be took away now.

GAFFER

I've a-wanted to be took away ever since my vlower were took. Many a long year. And I grawed to be a old, old man. I were out of work sometimes. And I be old now. Very old.

[222]

NAN

Per'aps you'll join 'er soon, gaffer.

GAFFER

Noa. Not for a girt while. I 'ave 'er little grave. I 'ave 'er little grave to see to. With vlowers and that. If I 'ad girt bags of gold like Squire, I could 'ave a 'edstone put. I'd 'ave 'er little grave all carved. I'd 'ave posies cut. And 'er face down on the stone. All in white I'd 'ave my vlower cut. White stone. There be no kings 'd 'ave whiter. But I can't never avord a 'edstone. So I ben't goin' to die. Noa. I ben't goin to die.

NAN

When love be dead, gaffer, what be there else?

GAFFER

There be the grave. It be all the poor 'as, just the grave. And I got my vlower's grave. Eight maids in white there was. No older than my vlower they was. And there were all white vlowers on 'er. Eight maids in white, maidy. And the bell tolling. Oh, my white blossom to go under the grass.

NAN

She was very young to be took, Gaffer.

GAFFER

They was eight maids in white when they carried 'er. Then they was women. Beautiful they were. Then they grew old. One by one. And then their 'ouses were to let, with the windows broke. And grass and grass. They be all gone. When I be gone there'll be none to tell the beauty of my vlower.

[223]

There'll be none as knows where 'er body lies. I 'ave 'er little grave all done with shells. And the vlowers that do come up, they be little words from 'er. Little zhining words. Fifty-nine year them little words come.

NAN

I got a grave, too, gaffer. And I 'ave fifty-nine years to come.

GAFFER

My bright 'ansome. 'Oo 'ave you in yer grave?

NAN

I 'ave my 'eart in the grave, gaffer. But there'll be no vlowers come up out of 'er. I shall be 'ere fifty-nine year per'aps. Like you been. Fifty-nine year. Twelve times fifty-nine is—and four times that. Three hundred and sixty-five days in a year. Up, and work, and lie down again. But dead, dead, dead. All the time dead. No. No. Not that. Gaffer. How did thy vlower die?

GAFFER

There come a gold rider in the evening, maidy.

NAN

You was by 'er, Gaffer?

GAFFER

She looked out of the window, my white vlower done. She said, "The tide. The tide. The tide coming up the river." And a horn blew. The gold rider blew a 'orn. And she rose up, my white vlower done. And she burst out a-laughing, a-laughing And 'er fell back, my white vlower done. Gold 'air on the

pillow. And blood. Oh, blood. Blood of my girl. Blood of
my vlower.

NAN

In your arms, gaffer?

GAFFER

On my 'eart. My white vlower lay on my 'eart. The tide.
The tide. The tide coming up the river.

NAN

She was 'appy to die so, gaffer. Along of 'er true love. You
'ad the sweet of love along of your vlower. But them as 'as
the sharp of love. Them as never 'as no sweet. O I wish the
tide was comin' up over my 'ed, I do.

GAFFER

It be full moon to-night, maidy.

NAN

Full moon. It come up misty. And red.

GAFFER

It was red on the pillow. Then.

NAN

The harvest-moon.

GAFFER

There'll be a high tide to-night.

NAN

A high tide.

GAFFER

For some on us.

NAN

Why for some on us, gaffer?

GAFFER

The tide be comin' for some on us.

NAN

For you, gaffer?

GAFFER

Ther've come no message yet for me. But the tide be a'comin' for some on us. It 'ave someone every time. It 'ad my vlower one time. O it be a gallows thing, the tide. First there be the mud and that. Sand banks. Mud banks. And the 'erons fishing. Sand in the river, afore the tide comes. Mud. The cows come out o' pasture to drink. They come on the sand. Red cows. But they be afraid of the tide.

NAN

They 'aven't no grief, the beasts asn't. Cropping in the meadows when the sun do zhine.

GAFFER

They be afraid of the tide. For first there come a-wammerin' and a-wammerin.' Miles away that wammerin' be. In the sea. The shipmen do cross theirselves. And it come up. It come nearer. Wammerin', Wammerin'! 'Ush it says. 'Ush it says. 'Ush it says. And there come a girt wash of it over the rock. White. White. Like a bird. Like a swan a-gettin' up out of the pool.

NAN

Bright it goes. High. High up. Flashing.

GAFFER

And it wammers and it bubbles. And then it spreads. It
goes out like soldiers. It go out into a line. It curls. It curls.
It go toppling and toppling. And on it come. And on it come.

NAN

Fast. Fast.
A black line. And the foam all creamin' on it.

GAFFER

It be a snake. A snake. A girt water snake with its 'ed up.
Swimming. On it come.

NAN

A bright crown upon it. And hungry.

GAFFER

With a rush. With a roar. And its claws clutchin' at you.
Out they go at the sides, the claws do.

NAN

The claws of the tide.

GAFFER

Singing. Singing. And the sea a-roaring after. O, it takes
them. They stand out in the river. And it goes over them.
Over them. Over them. One roarin' rush.

NAN

Deep. Deep. Water in their eyes. Over their hair. And
to-night it be the harvest tide.

[227]

GAFFER

[*As though waking from a dream.*] The salmon-fishers 'll lose their nets to-night.

The tide'll sweep them away. O, I've known it. It takes the nets up miles. Miles. They find 'em high up. Beyond Glorster. Beyond 'Artpury. Girt golden flag-flowers over 'em. And apple-trees a-growin' over 'em. Apples of red and apples of gold. They fall into the water. The water be still there, where the apples fall. The nets 'ave apples in them.

NAN

And fish, gaffer?

GAFFER

Strange fish. Strange fish out of the sea.

NAN

Yes. Strange fish indeed, gaffer. A strange fish in the nets to-morrow. A dumb thing. Knocking agen the bridges. Something white. Something white in the water. They'd pull me out. Men would. They'd touch my body. [*Shuddering.*] I couldn't. I couldn't.

[*Loud laughter from within, and a clatter of knives. The door opens. Enter* JENNY *from inner room, carrying a dirty plate, with dirty knife and fork. As* JENNY *comes in,* MRS. PARGETTER *is heard off.*]

MRS. P.

Is *she* in there?

JENNY

Yes.

MRS. P.

Tell 'er to come in.

JENNY

[*To* NAN.] You're to go in, mother says.

MR. P.

[*Heard off.*] 'Ere, shut that door behind yer. It blows my 'ed off. [JENNY *turns and shuts the door.*]

NAN

What 'ave you got there, Jenny?

JENNY

[*Uneasily.*] You're to go in, mother says.

NAN

[*Rising.*] Never mind what mother says. Answer my question, my friend, my girt friend, my little creeping friend. What 'ave you got there?

JENNY

[*Shrinking.*] A mutton parsty pie for gaffer, as mother sent. It'll be a little treat for 'im.

NAN

[*Looking.*] Whose plate have you brought it on, my little friend?

JENNY

[*Stammering.*] Mother's plate.

NAN

It is a dirty plate. And the knives and forks are dirty.

[229]

JENNY

[*Confidently.*] Gaffer won't know any different. It's good enough for an old man like 'im. 'Ere, gaffer. 'Ere's some supper for yer.

NAN

[*Going up to her.*] No, my friend, my girt friend, my little Judas friend, my little pale snake friend. It's not good enough. Did *you* 'ave one of them pies?

JENNY

[*Blustering.*] You can—I ain't goin' to——

NAN

Did you? The sheep died. The sheep died last week. Did *you* eat one of them pies?

JENNY

No, I know what the sheep die of. Gaffer won't mind. 'Ere, gaffer.

NAN

[*Fiercely.*] Sit down, my little friend. Sit down and eat that pie yourself. Eat it. Eat it or I'll kill you. Eat it. You with no charity to old or young. You shall eat the charity of the uncharitable. Eat it. You little snake. Eat it.

JENNY

I'll—I'll send mother to you.

NAN

[*Preventing her.*] No. Oh, no. [*Forcing her into a chair.*] Eat. Eat. [JENNY *in great terror begins to eat.*]

JENNY

I be goin' to be sick.

NAN

Eat. [JENNY *eats. Then shrinks back.*]

JENNY

[*After a mouthful.*] Wot are you lookin' at me for?

NAN

I'm looking at my friend. My friend.

JENNY

[*After a mouthful.*] I can't eat with you watchin' me.

NAN

Yes, Jenny. It is your bride cake. Your bride cake. Your bride cake for your marriage, Jenny.

JENNY

[*Screaming.*] *Don't* look at me like that.

NAN

[*Coming up to her and glaring down into her face.*] Yes. Jenny. I must look at you like this. I must look into your soul, Jenny. Into your soul. [*Slowly and quietly.*]

JENNY

Ah-h.

NAN

You 'ave pale eyes, Jenny. Pale eyes. I can look into your soul. D'you know what I see, Jenny? [*A pause.*] I see your

[231]

soul. It is cold, Jenny. It's a little mean cold, lying thing. You're a lucky one, Jenny. You cannot love nor hate. A dog loves more and hates more. A worm do. D'you know what comes to such souls, Jenny?

JENNY

[*Gasping.*] Mother! Mother!

NAN

I'll tell you, Jenny. I'll tell your future to you. I see your life very plain in your pale eyes. I see a girt town, with lamps. And I see you in a public 'ouse, Jenny, with red on your white cheeks. And your pale eyes are swollen with drink. And you've a raggy skirt. And you cough. And you tremble. That is the pay in this world, Jenny, for a little cold mean lying thing. And I see a dirty room with a dirty bed, and you lying dead on it. Your painted cheeks on the pillow. Till the town dead-cart come. Out with you. Out with you. Out with you. [JENNY *totters, gasping, to the door.*]

JENNY

Ah. Ah-h! [*She leans up against the door, holding it by the latch, in terror; she is only half conscious.*]

GAFFER

[*Rousing and shading his eyes looking up.*] Be you ready for your journey, maidy?

NAN

My journey.

GAFFER

You must eat and drink, my 'andsome. 'E be coming.

[232]

NAN

Who be coming?

GAFFER

The gold rider, maidy. 'E be comin' on the road.

NAN

The gold rider. We will eat and drink, gaffer. It be a long road to go. [*She opens oven and brings out the apple-pasty; then takes a carving knife, and plate. Then the brandy bottle. She cuts the pasty and gives food to* GAFFER.]

GAFFER

[*Rising unsteadily and holding up his hands.*] Bless this food to thy service. Bless the Giver of all good things. Amen. [*He eats.*]

NAN

Amen. [*The outer door is knocked. Footsteps outside.*] Drink, gaffer. [*She gives him a sup of brandy.*]

GAFFER

[*Drinking to her.*] A fair journey. Vlowers on the road afore you. O gold 'oofs. Gold 'oofs. Be swift. Swift. [*A knocking at outer door.*]

A VOICE

Is anyone inside there? Open.

NAN

Drink, gaffer. [*Violent knocking outside. The inner door is shaken by those within.* JENNY *holds the latch and keeps them from entering.*]

[233]

JENNY

O! O! Don't let 'er in on me. Don't let 'er in on me. [*Falling against the wall.*] Oh, oh.

[*Enter the* PARGETTERS *and* DICK. *The others cluster at the doorway.*]

DICK

[*Seeing* JENNY *and glad to have* NAN *for once in the wrong. Angrily.*] Wot 'ave you been doin' to 'er? Eh?

MRS. P.

[*Advancing on* NAN.] Why can't you open the door? Standing staring there.

MR. P.

Wot 'ave she done to you, Jenny?

MRS. P.

[*Turning.*] Never you 'eed wot she's done to 'er. You go and open the door. 'Ere, Jenny. Go on inside. Go on now. Before they see yer.

DICK

She's—she's—Best 'ave 'er locked up, mother.

MRS. P.

Open the door, there.

[JENNY *totters out*]

MR. P.

Wot's brought 'er into that state?

Nan

She has seen herself, uncle. There's few can bear that sight. A worm in the dust fears it.

Mrs. P.

You don't mean to say as you've cut the parsty.

Mr. P.

'Ush. They'll 'ear yer.

Mrs. P.

[*In a blood-curdling voice.*] And look at your uncle's bottle. If I don't give it yer for this. [*A knock.*]

A Voice Without

Come on. Come on. I've got no time to waste.

Mrs. P.

[*Going to the door with her best society smile.*] I didn't 'ear yer knock. Wot with comp'ny. I 'ope I 'aven't kep you waitin', I'm sure. [*Peering at visitors.*] Good evenin', sir. Will, fetch chairs for the gentlemen. Why, it's Mr. Drew. Come in, sir. Won't you please ter come in, sir.

Drew

Thank you.

[*Enter* Parson Drew, Captain Dixon *and a* Constable *carrying a handbag.*]

Mr. P.

[*Fetching chairs*]. Good evenin', sir.

[235]

Drew

Good evenin', Pargetter.

Mr. P.

[*To* Dixon.] Good evenin', sir.

Dixon

[*Coldly to* Constable.] Put that bag on the table.

Drew

Well, Dick. Is that you, Ellen? You grow so fast. Nan. Yes. Yes. Good evening, everybody.

Mr. P.

[*In a stage whisper to* Mrs. Pargetter.] 'Ave the table cleared.

Dixon

[*Irritably.*] Never mind the table.

Mrs. P.

You must excuse things bein' a bit untidy, sir. Wot with 'avin company, we're all topsy turvy, as you mid say. [*Suavely to* Nan.] Jest take that parsty off the table, Nan, there's a good girl.

Nan

I've done with make-believes, Aunt. One makes believe too long.

Mrs. P.

[*To* Drew.] She loves a bit of play-actin', sir. She do it wonderful, considerin'.

[236]

DIXON

Oh, Drew. Drew. [*Irritably.*]

MRS. P.

She's been givin' us a bit out of Shakespeare as they call it.

DREW

Yes. Yes. Yes. Now hush, please, a moment everybody. [*Everybody is silent.*] [*Raising a hand.*] I'm afraid we come at a very inconvenient time. But—[*Seeing those in the door.*] Oh, just come in there, will you? Yes. Yes. It's a very pleasant duty. It's not often that I have such a pleasure as I have to-night. [*Taking chair.*] Yes. Thank you. Sit down, Mr. Dixon.

DIXON

[*Coldly.*] *Captain* Dixon.

DREW

Yes, yes, to be sure. Captain Dixon, to be sure. I beg your pardon, Captain Dixon. I'm sure you'll all be very glad when you hear what it is that makes us interrupt your evening's pleasure.

DIXON

[*Tartly.*] Excuse me. Mr. Drew. But hadn't we better come to business?

DREW

Yes, yes, but——

DIXON

[*Mildly.*] I shall miss the coach back to town.

[237]

DREW

O, no, no, no, no. O, no, no, no. Oh, you've ten minutes yet. More. You've got lots of time. You'll hear the horn long before the coach is due.

MRS. P.

Yes, sir. You'll 'ear the horn a long ways off. If it's the coach you want.

GAFFER

The horn. The horn. Gold hoofs beating on the road. [*He advances to the table.*] They beat like the ticking of a 'eart. Soon. Very soon. The golden trump.

MRS. P.

[*Angrily.*] Could ever anything! [*Quietly.*] You old stupe. Take 'im out, Will. Don't let 'im begin in 'ere. [*To* DIXON.] Don't mind 'im, sir. 'E's silly.

[GAFFER *goes to the door and looks out into the moonlight*]

GAFFER

[*At the door.*] Maybe I'll meet 'im on the road.

[*He goes out*]

DREW

One of our—You know, eh. [*Taps his forehead.*]

DIXON

[*Sourly.*] I thought it was another bit out of Shakespeare as they call it.

[238]

Mr. P.

Yes, sir. 'E talks very strange sometimes.

Drew

Yes, yes, poor fellow.

Dixon

I suppose this is the right house?

Drew

Yes, of course. Yes, certainly, certainly.

Dixon

[*Taking bag and unlocking it.*] I thought it might be the—the —Yes. Ye-es. Very well, then. [*Suddenly.*] Which of you is Nan Hardwick?

Nan

I am that one.

Dixon

Ye-es. You. Very well then. Is that correct, Mr. Drew?

Drew

Certainly. Certainly.

Dixon

Daughter of Mary Hardwick, and of—of Edward Hardwick who was—eh?

Nan

Who was hanged at Gloucester.

Dixon

Of Swanscombe, in the Hundred of—Yes. Very well then. [*Turning to others.*] You certify that this is that Nan Hardwick?

The Others

Yes, sir. That be 'er.

Dixon

Very well, then. That's not the horn, Drew?

Drew

O, no, no.

Dixon

[*Taking bag and papers out of handbag.*] Have you a pen and ink in the house?

Mr. P.

[*Taking them from the dresser.*] This is a pen and ink, sir.

Dixon

Ye-es. [*Writes.*] This pen's—Drew, have you got a pen? [*To* Mrs. Par.] Give me a penwiper. [*He wipes, and then mends pen with a penknife.*] Ye-es. Ye-es. [*Sharply.*] Nan Hardwick, your father was—er—put to death for stealing a sheep near Aston Magna. No. Don't answer. That is the fact. Ye-es. Very well then. The sheep was the property of Mr. Nicols. Now it has been proved that your father, Edward Hardwick, had nothing to do with that sheep.

Nan

And you come here, do you, to tell me that? You have a thousand men beneath you, a thousand strong men like the man there. And you have judges in scarlet, and lawyers in wigs. And a little child out of the road could have told you that my dad was innocent. A little child of the road. By once looking in his eyes.

DIXON

I can't go into all that. You must keep to the point. [DREW *whispers*.] What? Yes. Yes. I daresay.

DREW

[*To* NAN.] Let Captain Dixon finish what he's got to say.

MRS. P.

Where's yer manners gorn? You wait till afterwards.

DIXON

To continue. The sheep was stolen by Mr. Nicol's shepherd, who was the chief witness against your father.

NAN

The sheep was stolen by Richard Shapland.

DIXON

[*Staring at her.*] Who has since confessed.

ALL

Ah. Confessed. Think of that. There now.

DIXON

A sad miscarriage of justice. Very well then. While we support the laws, we must be content to suffer from their occasional misapplication. [*Glances at his watch.*]

DREW

Lots of time. Lots of time.

DIXON

Ye-es.   But in this instance, the Home Office has decided to offer you some compensation.

NAN

Some blood-money.   Thirty pieces of silver.

DIXON

No.   It's more.   It's fifty pounds.   [*He empties bag.*]   Will you count it over please, before signing the receipt?

NAN

No.   No.   The blood and tears are sticky on it.

DREW

She's upset.   I'll count it.

MR. P.

[*Pouring brandy for* NAN.]   'Ere, Nan.   'Ave just a drop.

[*She refuses*]

OTHERS

Fifty pou-und.   Fifty pou-und.   Did you ever.

DICK

[*Muttering.*]   A 'orse and trap.   And furnish a 'ouse.

DREW

Fifty.   Would you like to count it over, Pargetter?

MR. P.

No, thanky, sir, I'm sure.

[242]

DIXON

[*To Nan.*] Are you satisfied? [*Sharply.*] Nan Hardwick.

NAN

What d'you want more?

DIXON

Are you satisfied that the sum is correct?

NAN

Oh. The money. You know it is. Why go to all this trouble? Give me your pen. There. There's my name to your paper. Received. By me. Fifty pounds in gold.

DIXON

And the date. Ye-es. I'll just add the date. [*To the* CONSTABLE.] Witness it, Horton. [*The man signs. He looks at his watch again.*] I shall miss that coach.

DREW

Won't you think better of it, and stay the night? Stay, man, stay and see the tide. It's a wonderful sight.

DIXON

No, thanks. No, thanks. [*He gathers up his handbag.*] Here you are, Horton. [*Gives him bag.*] I hope the money may be a comfort to you. [*To* NAN.] Where can I catch this coach?

MRS. P.

Just down the lane, sir. It is but a step. Keep on right down, sir. You can't miss it, sir.

[243]

MR. P.

You'll 'ear the 'arn go, sir.

DIXON AND HORTON

Good night. [*Going.*]

ALL

Good night, sir. Good night, Officer.

DICK

[*To* PARGETTER.] Wouldn't 'e take a drop of somethin'?

MR. P.

Noa. It's not for the likes of us to offer.

DICK

You can't ever tell.

DREW

I'm sure that what we have just heard has given us all a great deal of pleasure. I won't dwell on the satisfaction to yourself, Nan, for fear of giving you pain. But I am sure that your good aunt, who has been so kind to you——

MRS. P.

No more than my sacred dooty, Mr. Drew.

DREW

[*Gallantly.*] I will spare your blushes, Mrs. Pargetter. And all your young friends who are here to-night. I'm sure that they all feel with me——

[*Re-enter* DIXON]

[244]

DIXON

Excuse me, Drew. Do show me the way to where the coach passes. These beastly lanes are——

DREW

Yes. Yes. Certainly. Certainly. [*To the Company.*] I must wish you all good night. So sorry to have interrupted your evening's amusement.

MRS. P.

A pleasure I'm sure, sir.

DREW

[*To* NAN.] By the way, Nan. Perhaps I should say Miss Hardwick, now you're an heiress. Mrs. Drew would like to see you at the Rectory to-morrow—She thinks you might like to live with us as our housekeeper.

DIXON

Come on. Come on.

DREW

Coming, Captain Dixon. But we'll go into that to-morrow Shall we?

NAN

Thank you, sir. I hope you'll thank Mrs. Drew, too, sir. But I shall not come to the Rectory to-morrow. Unless—Unless the fishers bring their take to you. For you to choose your tithe.

DREW

[*Puzzled.*] Well. Ah. Ah yes. Well, think it over. Sleep on it.

NAN

I shall sleep soundly on it.

DREW

Good night, everybody. Now. Captain Dixon.

[*Exit*]

[*Returning.*] Mrs. Pargetter!

MRS. P.

Yes, sir. [*He draws her aside and whispers, pointing to* NAN.]

DREW

[*In stage whisper.*] To bed at once.

[NAN *smiles bitterly*]

MRS. P.

Yes, sir. Pore thing, it's been too much for 'er. I don't wonder.

[*Exit* DREW]

MRS. P.

'E's gone at last. [*To the others.*] Go on in back to supper. Us'll be with yer in a minute. Shut the door. There's sech a draught.

[*They go*]

DICK

I'll fetch in Miss Nan a bit of supper.

[246]

Mrs. P.

It's a pity you don't 'eed the mote in yer own eye without 'eedin' the camel in yer neighbour's. Go in and see to Jenny.

Mr. P.

Well, Nan, it be a long lane as 'as no turning, as they say. I knew thy pore dad when us was boys. When us goe'd a nesting after ardiestraws. Dear, dear. 'E won the prize for kiddy potatoes, and for kiddy beans. I be glad, that I be, to 'ear— wot we've 'eard to-night.

Nan

So you are glad, are you? Glad.

Mrs. P.

If you 'adn't a black 'eart, you'd be glad yourself, I should a-thought. Some people a-got no feelin's.

Mr. P.

Fifty pound be a lot of money, too.

Nan .

The worth of a man's life 'ad need to be a lot of money.

Mr. P.

There's two things you could do with all that money. You could put er into the Bank and that. Or you could—I'd be very glad to borrow it of you, to 'elp me on the farm. And pay you the interest, like.

Nan

And if I'd refuse. What then?

Mrs. P.

Refuse? Refuse? I don't doubt you give yerself airs. It's wot we'd expect of yer——

Mr. P.

[*Interrupting.*] I'm only asking.—To keep it in the family.

Mrs. P.

[*To* Par.] Asking? Givin' in to 'er wills and 'er won'ts. Wot's asking got to do with it? 'Ere. You're under age. We're yer guardians. *We'll* take care of that money for yer.

Nan

Yes. You'll want some money, for Jenny's portion.

Mr. P.

[*Controlling his temper.*] I 'aven't said nothink yet——

Mrs. P.

No. You 'aven't got the sperrit of a 'og with the twitters.

Mr. P.

[*Angrily.*] I don't want none of *yer* jaw.

Mrs. P.

Don't you nag at me, for I won't 'ave it. See?

Nan

The money is mine. Not yours. I have a use for it.

Mr. P.

[*To* Nan.] Then I've done with yer. You talk rude to the

quality. You give all sorts of talk to—Talk as 'd sick a savage. Do wot y' like with yer money. But you'll make good my Toby jug, at least. Now then.

NAN

Your Toby jug?

MR. P.

You know wot I mean.

NAN

Aha. The little friend. My little friend. [*A cry within.*] That's 'er soul's voice that cry is. So *that* is wot——

MRS. P.

And you 'ad the cold blooded cheek to 'ave your go at the parsty, wot's more.

MR. P.

And—there—I'll leave you to your conscience. [*Going.*]

MRS. P.

Stop a moment, Will. Us'll settle 'er with 'er, onst for all.

NAN

[*Going to the money bag and cutting its tape.*] Yes. We'll settle. Look at it. Look at it. [*She pours the gold into a heap.*] Gold. Gold. Little yellow rounds of metal. Fifty little yellow rounds of metal. This. This is for a man's life. Oh, you little yellow rounds that buy things. Look at 'em. Hear 'em. [*Pause.*] Don't you speak to me. [*Intensely.*] There was a strong man, a kind man. He was forty-nine years old. He was the best thatcher in the three counties. He was the sweetest singer. I've known teams goin' to the field stop to 'ear my dad sing. And the red coats come. And a liar swore. And that

[249]

strong man was killed. Sudden. That voice of his'n was choked out with a cord. And there was liars, and thieves, and drunken women, and dirty gentlemen. They all stood in the cold to see that man choked. They stop up all night, playing cards, so as they should 'ear 'is singin' stopped. For it goes round the voice the cord do. And they draw a nightcap down so as 'e shan't see 'is girl a-crying. [*Pause.*] And for that, I get little yellow round things. [*Pause.*] And there was a girl, a young girl, a girl with a sick 'eart. D'you know what came to 'er? You know what came to 'er. She came among them as might have made much of 'er. For she'd 'ave give a lot for a kind word. 'Er 'eart was that broke 'er'd 'ave broke out a-crying at a kind word.

Mrs. P.

When you've done with your fal-lals, I'll 'ave my say.

Nan

Don't you speak. Don't you threaten. You'll listen to me. You 'ad me in your power. And wot was good in me you sneered at. And wot was sweet in me, you soured. And wot was bright in me you dulled. I was a fly in the spider's web. And the web came round me and round me, till it was a shroud, till there was no more joy in the world. Till my 'eart was bitter as that ink, and all choked. And for that I get little yellow round things. [*Pause and change of voice.*] And all of it—No need for any of it. My dad's life, and your taunts, and my broke 'eart. All a mistake. A mistake. Somethin' to be put right by fifty pound while a gentleman waits for a coach. 'E thought nothing of it. 'E thought only of getting the coach. 'E didn't even pretend. [*A cry within.*] It were a game to 'im. 'E laughed at it. [*A cry within.*] Yes. She has seen herself. No wonder she cries. She sees the parish dead-cart coming.

[DICK *puts his head in at the door*]

DICK

Mother. Come to Jenny. Quick.

MRS. P.

To 'ell with Jenny. I've somethin' to attend to 'ere.

DICK

She's in a fit or somethink. Us can 'ardly 'old 'er down.

MRS. P.

[*To* NAN.] More of yer work. You wait till I come back.

A GIRL

[*At the door.*] Quick, Mrs. Pargetter.

[MRS. PARGETTER *snatches the brandy bottle and goes out*]

MR. P.

I don't know 'ow all this'll end, Nan.

[*He goes out*]

[*Re-enter* DICK]

DICK

I brought you a little bit o' supper, Miss Nan.

NAN

What then?

DICK

I thought—Won't you sit down and 'ave it, Miss Nan? There. Let me put this chair comferable.

NAN

Why do you bring this to me?

DICK

I thought—some'ow—I thought you'd like a bit of cossitin'.

NAN

I want nothin'. Nothin'.

DICK

Miss Nan. I want just to say. Some'ow, it be 'ard to explain. But I ask—I ask your forgiveness. 'Umbly I ask it. Oh, Miss Nan. My beauti-vul. My beautivul as I wronged.

NAN

As you wronged. Yes?

DICK

I was—I dunno—I was led away, Miss Nan.

NAN

Yes, Dick. You were led away. How were you led away? Why?

DICK

I was that. When I 'eard as your dad was. I mean when I 'eard of your dad. I doan' know. It seemed—I felt some'ow. I be that dry I can't 'ardly speak. Miss Nan——

NAN

You felt some'ow? Yes?

DICK

As your 'air was, was a cord round my throat. Choking. I was sick. I couldn't—no—I. couldn't.

NAN

And was that the only reason why?

DICK

Yes, Miss Nan.

NAN

And why did you choose Jenny? My kiss was still warm upon your lips. [*Going to him.*] Your blood was singing in your veins with me, when you turned—Why did you turn to 'er?

[*A pause*]

She was not a—a gallus-bird. Eh?

[*A pause.* DICK *licks his lips and swallows*]

[*Re-Enter* GAFFER *slowly, with a few roses plucked in the garden. He goes to* NAN.]

GAFFER

The moon be at full, O wonder. The cows in the meadows kneel down.

The rabbits be kneelin'. The vlowers in the 'edge do kneel—
Roses for your 'air, my beauty. O my bright 'ansome of the world.

[*He gives the roses reverently*]

Roses in your 'air. And the bride's 'air loose.

[NAN *places a rose in her hair and loosens it about her*]

[253]

NAN

[*Taking some money.*] For a 'eadstone, Gaffer. [*Sharply.*]
Well, Dick.

DICK

I was.—O, I can't. To show that I 'ad done with yer. I
was angry.

NAN

Because I didn't tell you of my dad?

DICK

Yes.

NAN

There be three times, Dick, when no woman can speak.
Beautiful times. When 'er 'ears 'er lover, and when 'er gives
'erself, and when 'er little one is born. You—You'd have been
the first to stop me if I'd spoken then.

DICK

I thought as you'd—not been straight—I thought——

NAN

And now you turn again from Jenny. Why have you left
Jenny, Dick?

GAFFER

[*Jangling and counting money.*]
" Nine. 'Ow the bells do chime,
" Ten. There's a path for men."

DICK

Because I don't care for 'er. Because now——

GAFFER

" 'Leven. From the earth to 'eaven."

DICK

Be quiet, Gaffer.

NAN

Because?

DICK

O, Miss Nan. It be you as I love. My dad 'ave stop me afore. But now your name be cleared——

NAN

Is that the only reason?

GAFFER

[*Talking through.*] Twelve. Twelve. Us rang out a peal at twelve. Angels. Gold angels. The devil walks the dark at twelve. Ghosts. Ghosts. Behind the white 'edstones. Smite 'em, gold rider. Smite 'em with thy bright sharp spear.

NAN

Is that the only reason? You love me, then?

DICK

Yes. That's the only reason. I love you, Nan.

NAN

And what will my aunt say?

DICK

Damn 'er. It's 'er that came between us.

[255]

Nan

I know what you can say to 'er.

Dick

What?

Nan

Go to her now. Take her that bag of money. Tell her she may have that. But that you will marry me, not Jenny.

[Dick, *rather staggered, takes up the bag and walks slowly to door*]

Dick

Wouldn't it be better, Miss Nan, if us—if us just told 'er, without—without bein'——

Nan

I knew it. I knew it.

[*A horn is heard faintly off*]

Gaffer

There be a music on the sea, a soft music. The ships be troubled at the music.

Nan

Come here, Dick. They said my dad kill a sheep. A foundered old ewe as'd feel nothin'; 'ardly the knife on 'er throat. And my dad was 'ung; only acos they said 'e kill a beast like that. They choked 'im dead, in front of 'alf a city. But you come. And you 'ave yer love of a girl. You says lovely things to 'er. Things as'd move any girl—and only because you be greedy. Greedy of a mouth agen your mouth; of a girl's lips babblin' love at you. And a sour old woman's word'll make you 'it that girl across the lips you kissed. In ten minutes. You'll take 'er lovin' 'eart and 'er girl's pride, and all 'er joy in the world, and stamp it in the dust. And you'll dance on 'er white body; and all you'll feel is the blood makin' a mess on your boots.

[*The horn blows nearer*]

GAFFER

The horn. The horn. O night owl laughing in the wood.

NAN

And you go to another girl. And you give 'er a joy in the world. And then you see your old love not wot the old woman said. No. But as sweet to the taste, as dear to your greedy mouth. And with gold—yellow round things—to buy vanity. 'Ouses, 'orses, position. Then you come back whining. Whining! For 'er to take you back. So as you mid 'ave that gold.

DICK

O, you can talk. You've a right. But I love you, Nan. I do love yer.

NAN

I see very plain to-night, Dick. I see right, right into you. Right down. You talk o' thieves. You talk o' them as kills—them as leads women wrong. Sinners you calls them. But it be you is the sinner. You kill people's 'earts. You stamp them in the dust, like worms as you tread on in the fields. And under it all will be the women crying, the broken women, the women cast aside. Tramped on. Spat on. As you spat on me. No, no, oh no. Oh young man in your beauty—Young man in your strong hunger. I will spare those women.

DICK

[*Scared, and speaking loudly, so as to attract them in the inner room.*] I never! Mother! Mother!

GAFFER

O Love you be a King. A King.

NAN

I will spare those women. Come here to me.

DICK

Ah! Ah! Mother! [*He backs towards the door.*]

GAFFER

On the road. They come. Gold hoofs. Gold hoofs.

NAN

Spare them. Spare them. Spare them the hell. The hell of the heart-broken. Die—you—die. [*She stabs him with the pastry knife. He falls.*]

DICK

[*Raising himself stupidly.*] The drums be a-roaring. A-roaring. [*He dies.*]

GAFFER

[*Clapping his hands.*] Oh Beauty, beauty. Oh beauty of my white vlower.

[*A murmuring and rushing noise is heard as the tide sweeps up from the sea.*]

Gaffer

[*Shouts.*]   It be coming.   Out of the wells of the sea.   The eagles of the sea hear it.   They sharp their beaks.

[*Enter hurriedly the others*]

Mrs. P.

[*Running to* Dick.]   Dick.   Dick.   Oh!   [*Screams.*]   Look at it all smoking.

Mr. P.

'Ere.   The brandy.   Quick.   'E's gone.

Nan

[*As the noise increases.*]   The tide.

Gaffer

The tide.

Nan

[*Laughing.*]   The tide coming up the river.

Mrs. P.

Take the money, Will.   Don't 'eed the brandy.

A Girl

The pleece, Artie.   Get the pleece.

Nan

[*Going to the door as the noise increases*.]   A strange fish in the nets to-morrow.

[*She goes*]

GAFFER

Singing. Singing. Roaring it come. Roaring it come. Over the breast. Over the lips. Over the eyes.

[*The horn blows*]

MRS. P.

[*Putting the money hastily in the locker.*] That's something. Wot are we to tell them?

[*The coach-horn blows loudly and clearly*]

GAFFER

The horn! The horn!

CURTAIN

THE TRAGEDY OF POMPEY
THE GREAT

TO

MY WIFE

ARGUMENT

In the years 50 and 49 B. C., Cneius Pompeius Magnus, the head of the patrician party, contested with C. Julius Cæsar, the popular leader, for supreme power in the State. Their jealousy led to the troubles of the Civil War, in which, after many battles, Cneius Pompeius Magnus was miserably killed.

ACT I. The determination of Pompeius to fight with his rival, then marching upon Rome.

ACT II. The triumph of Pompey's generalship at Dyrrachium. His overthrow by the generals of his staff. His defeat at Pharsalia.

ACT III. The death of that great ruler on the seashore of Pelusium in Egypt.

PERSONS

ANTISTIA.

PHILIP.

A Lute-Girl.

CORNELIA.

JULIA

Q. CAECILIUS METELLUS PIUS SCIPIO.

CNEIUS POMPEIUS MAGNUS (called Pompey the Great).

CNEIUS POMPEIUS THEOPHANES.

MARCUS PORCIUS CATO.

A Gaulish Lancer.

LUCIUS DOMITIUS AHENOBARBUS.

COTTA, a Centurion.

MARCUS ACILIUS GLABRIO.

LUCIUS LUCCEIUS.

LUCIUS AFRANIUS.

PUBLIUS LENTULUS SPINTHER.

A Ship-Captain.

A Ship-Boy.

A Mate.

A Boatswain.

ACHILLAS EGYPTIAN.

LUCIUS SEPTIMIUS.

Centurions, Sentries, Soldiers, Trumpeters, Sailors.

	SCENE.	TIME.
ACT I.	Rome.	January A. U. C. 705 (B. C. 50).
ACT II.	Dyrrachium.	July A. U. C. 706.
	Pharsalia.	August A. U. C. 709 (June B. C. 48).
ACT III.	Pelusium.	September A. U. C. 706 (Aug. B. C. 48).

THE TRAGEDY OF POMPEY THE GREAT

ACT I

A room in Pompey's *house near Rome. Walls hung with dra-
peries of a dark blue. Doors curtained. Balcony, open,
showing distant lights. A gong and mallet. Wine, glasses,
etc. Papers in a casket. Lamps.*

Horns without as troops pass. Antistia *alone, lighting lamps
with a taper.*

ANTISTIA

[*Looking towards the window.*] More soldiers. Blow your
horns. Spread your colours, ensign. Your colours'll be dust
the sooner. Your breath will be in the wind, a little noise in
the night. That's what you come to, soldiers. Dust, and a
noise in the trees. Dust, and the window rattling. No more
flags and horns then. [*Lighting the last lamp.*] I wish I knew
the rights of it. [*Settling books on table.*] I wish Philip would
come.

A VOICE

[*Without, in the balcony.*] Pompey.

ANTISTIA

What was that?

THE VOICE

Pompey.

ANTISTIA

[*Frightened.*] Who calls Pompey?

[267]

THE VOICE

Not so loud. Not so loud, Pompey.

ANTISTIA

What is it? What d' you want with Pompey?

THE VOICE

Philip must tell Pompey at once.

ANTISTIA

What must he tell him?

THE VOICE

To stamp his foot at once.

ANTISTIA

To stamp his foot at once?

THE VOICE

[*Amid laughter.*] Stamp your foot, Pompey. Aha! Ha! Pompey.

ANTISTIA

[*Going to the window.*] What's this? Who are you?

THE VOICE

[*Going.*] Aha! Pompey. Stamp your feet, Pompey.

ANTISTIA

[*Going to a door R. scared.*] Philip, Philip.

PHILIP

[*Putting down tray.*] What's the matter? What's happened?

ANTISTIA

There was a voice. A voice. Something at the window.
Jeering Pompey.

PHILIP

[*Opening window.*] Come out of that. There's no one there
now. Was it a man?

ANTISTIA

There was no one. It had a man's voice. It spoke. It
laughed.

PHILIP

It's gone. It's gone, my dear. Don't. Don't. It's gone.

ANTISTIA

They say that the dead come back. To cry in the night
[*pause*] whenever bad times are coming. Dead men's souls.
They want blood. Licking. Licking blood in the night. Whenever Rome's in danger.

PHILIP

Hush. Hush. Don't talk such things. It gives them life.
What was it saying?

THE VOICE

Stamp your foot, Pompey. Stamp your foot, Pompey.

ANTISTIA

Ah!

PHILIP

[*Exorcising at window, with things from tray.*] Wine for blood.
[*Pours wine.*] Bread for flesh. [*Breaks bread.*] Salt for life.
[*Flings salt.*] A cloak of blue on Rome. A net of gold over this
house. To the desert. To the night without stars. To the
wastes of the sea. To the two-forked flame. [*Returning heav-*

[269]

ily.] God save my dear master, Pompey. I fear there's trouble coming.

ANTISTIA

[*Hysterically.*] Ah! Ah!

PHILIP

[*Pouring water.*] Drink this. Drink this. I'll fetch another glass.

ANTISTIA

[*Hysterically.*] Not off that tray. Not off that tray.

PHILIP

There. There. God save us! Why, Antistia, they've no power.

ANTISTIA

I see the marching of armies. Dust. Dust. That is what the trumpets mean. War. Civil War. Pompey and Cæsar. Like eagles struggling.

PHILIP

No. No. Don't say that. You bring things to pass.

ANTISTIA

What else could it mean? What did it mean?

PHILIP

[*Distractedly.*] I don't rightly know what it said.

ANTISTIA

About stamping? About Pompey stamping?

PHILIP

Pompey said it. In the Senate yesterday. Reports came in.

[270]

There was a panic. The Senators were at their wits' ends. News came that Cæsar was marching on Rome. They asked Pompey if he had an army. If he could defend them.

ANTISTIA

Is Cæsar coming?

PHILIP

It was one of these wild rumours.

ANTISTIA

What did Pompey say?

PHILIP

He said if he stamped his foot, soldiers would spring up all over Italy. Armies of soldiers. To drive Cæsar back into Gaul.

ANTISTIA

And now he must stamp his foot. Cæsar's on the road with his army.

PHILIP

It's time for the house to shake when the door-posts quarrel. [*Pausing at distant tumult.*]

ANTISTIA

They're proud ones, to set the world on fire so as one of them may warm his hands.

PHILIP

Pompey's only defending the State. He thinks he's a great one, Cæsar does, now that he's conquered Gaul. What are the Gauls? The Gauls are naked heathen, with copper swords like the savages. Why, Cæsar would never have been anybody if Pompey hadn't backed him.

ANTISTIA

That's reason enough for him to fight Pompey now.

PHILIP

Pompey made him what he is. Pompey got him his place in Gaul. He was no one before that. [*Pause.*] And now he hopes to put Pompey down. So he can rule Rome instead. Put my master Pompey down.

ANTISTIA

I suppose Cæsar couldn't beat Pompey, Philip?

PHILIP

Antistia. [*Solemnly.*] Don't you talk like that, Antistia. I believe wherever Pompey goes, there goes a god in front of him. Like fire. It's that makes him what he is. Oh, my dear beloved master. I'm that drove mad, I can't hardly talk of it. That he should have a civil war with Cæsar. And him only newly married.

ANTISTIA

It was a civil war that first made Pompey famous, Philip.

PHILIP

He was with Sulla, against Marius. In the civil wars then. And ever since then he's gone on. Just as though a god went before him, brushing a road for him. You would see nothing but dangers all round. And Pompey would ride up. And [*he blows in his hand*] puff. They'd fade. They'd go. [*Pause.*] I've seen all Rome out on the roofs to see my master, Pompey. Triumph? There were horns blowing, you couldn't hear. And forty kings marching barefoot in the streets. I've seen him grow to be the greatest man in the world.

ANTISTIA

Eh? The greatest man in the world. And all through being
with Sulla in the civil war. Supposing he were not great, Philip.
Only a big clay statue. A statue propped up by sticks. A clay
thing, gilded. Rats gnawing at it. The wind shaking it. The
sun cracking it. [*Pause.*] And dead men, Philip. Dead men
underneath it in the dust, fumbling at it to bring it down.

PHILIP

Antistia.

ANTISTIA

Time brings all about, they say. You spoke of Sulla, Philip.
I was a little girl then, when Marius and Sulla fought. My
father was a centurion under Marius. I never told you that.
What do you know of me, Philip, except that I'm to marry you?
I was in the street outside our house, and some men came
across the road. They patted my head and asked if my father
was upstairs. I said yes, Philip. And they went in and brought
him out. Out to the door in the sun. Some boys gathered to
watch. I ran up to him, Philip, to show him my doll. And one
of the men said, " We'll give you Marius." He was behind my
father. He swung his arm right back like this, to give his sword
a sweep. He knocked my dada down with a great hack on the
neck, and they all stabbed him as he fell. One of the men said,
" There's your dada, little girl; run and tell mother." And
then one of the boys knelt down and stole his sandals, and another snatched my doll away. Time brings all about, Philip.
All the lives spilt then by Pompey and Sulla. They are coming
out of the night. Out of Spain. Out of Rome. Out of Asia.
Souls have power, Philip, even in the darkness, when the time
comes.

[273]

PHILIP

[*Awed.*] What time?

ANTISTIA

Pompey's time. There. There. It's beginning. [*Noise of a tumult. The horns of Soldiers.*]

PHILIP

[*At window.*] Some of Rome seems to be burning. Pray God the Senate's safe. [*Pause.*] We shall have to put off our marriage, Antistia.

ANTISTIA

Why, thus it is. We put off and put off till youth's gone, and strength's gone, and beauty's gone. Till two dry sticks mumble by the fire together, wondering what there was in life, when the sap ran.

PHILIP

I must be with my master, Antistia.

ANTISTIA

Your master. When you kiss the dry old hag, Philip, you'll remember these arms that lay wide on the bed, waiting, empty. Years. You'll remember this beauty. All this beauty. That would have borne you sons; but for your master. [*A noise of a lute off.*] Your mistress too, perhaps. Here she comes. Here comes the young wife, that will have little joy of her man. She with her lute girl, twanging a march for her. Here she comes. Open the door.

PHILIP

Our mistress.

[*Enter*, CORNELIA *and* JULIA. *The* Servants *place chairs for the ladies*]

[274]

CORN.

That will do, Antistia. Philip, you may go. [*Exeunt* PHILIP *and* ANTISTIA.]

JULIA

But tell me. What's going to happen? Is Cæsar really going to fight your husband, or is it only a feint to get your husband out of Rome?

CORN.

I don't know what to think, Julia. He's a danger. He's got such power with the mob. He's got this army in Gaul. Of course, that's a very great menace.

JULIA

But what are his plans? What does he want?

CORN.

He wants to rule Rome. He plans to be elected Consul. He is lying in Gaul there, thinking, I think, to frighten every one into electing him.

JULIA

I wish you could make your husband put down all this rioting. [*Noise without.*]

CORN.

[*Going to the window.*] I wish my father would come in, Julia, I'm anxious. What has the Senate decided? [*She walks up and down.*]

JULIA

That Cæsar must dismiss his army. I don't think it's anything to make you anxious. How is your father? What does he think?

CORN.

He thinks that my husband ought to put Cæsar down with a strong hand.

A VOICE WITHOUT

Present arms.

CORN.

Who's that? Come in. [*The door is shaken and opened violently.*]

[*Enter her father,* METELLUS SCIPIO]

Father.

JULIA

We were just talking about you.

MET.

Where's your husband? Is he here? Has he been here?

CORN.

No, father. What is it?

MET.

Still at the House? He must have had my note. Has he sent round to you?

CORN.

No. What has happened?

MET.

I must talk to you, Cornelia.

JULIA

[*Rising.*] Good-bye, dear.

[276]

MET.

No, Cornelia. She mustn't go. You'll have to sleep here, my dear girl. The streets aren't safe to-night. Sit down. Please sit down. We're all in the same boat. [*Pause.*] Cornelia. What's your husband going to do?

CORN.

Father. But I don't know. He tells me nothing. Nothing at least that is not common knowledge.

MET.

I've had letters. Cæsar's advancing into Italy. With all his army.

CORN.

To fight us? To attack Rome?

MET.

Yes. It's what I always feared. But I never thought the man would be such a blackguard.

CORN.

Does my husband know of this?

MET.

Yes. I sent word to him at the Senate to meet me here. I had to ride out to the camp. Cornelia. I don't understand your husband. My dear girl, he's been playing with the situation. I don't think you understand even now. It means that the whole of Rome is being handed over to a political brigand. All the governing classes, the religion of our fathers, all that has made Rome great. This cut-throat is marching to destroy it. Something happened at the camp.

[277]

CORN.

What, father?

MET.

The men. The soldiers. Roman soldiers. Men who had eaten the bread and salt. They refused duty. Romans. Bribed to that. By this upstart, Cæsar.

CORN.

They will stand and see Rome sacked by this outlaw.

MET.

I must see your husband. He's played with us. He must save us.

CORN.

There. There. He's coming. There's the sentry.

A VOICE WITHOUT

Attention. Eyes right.

MET.

Thank God.

A VOICE WITHOUT

Present arms.

CRIES

Hail! Pompey. Imperator. [*A trumpet blows a flourish.*]

A VOICE WITHOUT

Company. By the right. Quick. March.

[PHILIP *enters, opening doors wide, saluting, showing the fasces lining the door. Enter* POMPEY. *He carries a despatch box.* METELLUS *salutes.*]

[*Exit* PHILIP. *Doors shut*]

[278]

POMPEY

Ah, Julia. Ah, Cornelia. [*He goes to her, and looks into her eyes.*] Ah, beloved. [*Slowly.*] There will be always peace for me, in that calm soul. [*Turning wearily.*] I think that Sertorius was right, Julia.

JULIA

Why?

POMPEY

In our long Spanish wars, he planned to steal away to the Fortunate Islands. He could be quiet a little there. [*He goes to table dejectedly.*]

MET.

You got my note?

POMPEY

Yes. Yes. [*He sits like one stunned.*]

MET.

Man. What are you going to do? Cæsar's marching on Rome with forty thousand men.

CORN.

But you can check him. You must.

MET.

Do you understand? The whole—Does the Senate know?

POMPEY

[*Opening his despatch box.*] Sit down, dear. [*To* CORNELIA.] Sit down. The Senate knows. There were seven hundred of us in the Senate. Seven hundred of the best men in Rome, sitting there, at sunset, waiting. I had to stand up, among them.

I had to tell them that one who—that a man whom I—a man very dear to me—was marching. With an army. Against this Rome. To destroy all that that great house, in generations of honour, has built up here, of virtue, of justice, of freedom, to the wonder of the world.

MET.

Yes. Go on. Go on.

CORN.

What are they going to do?

POMPEY

Many there were in the pay of—that man.

MET.

How did they take it?

POMPEY

They were silent. But a murmur ran through the house. They moved in their chairs. Even those most glad were awed. [*Pause.*] Then Tullus, a man who owes his bread to me. He is in Cæsar's pay now. Rose up smiling. To ask me what troops I had for the defence of Rome.

MET.

Yes. And you, the guardian of Rome, what troops have you?

POMPEY

I said that with the two legions sent back from Gaul, and with those reserves called up from the country, I might have thirty thousand men.

MET.

What is all this talk of you might have? Those two legions are in Cæsar's pay. They're in mutiny at the camp. They're drawn up there. Ranged under the eagles. Their colonels are Cæsar's, body and soul. They refuse to move. As for your reserves, they're with the people. They're all for Cæsar. They came crowding out of their tents crying, Peace! Peace! They won't fight. You've mocked us. You've tricked us. You've betrayed Rome.

POMPEY

So they said in the Senate.

MET.

Why did you not prepare for this? You've had months in which to prepare?

POMPEY

I have prepared for it, Metellus. But I did not expect it. I thought that a noble act would be remembered, for more than twenty years. I thought that this Rome would be more to a man than a lust for power. And old friendship, I thought something.

MET.

I've no patience with you. [*He sits with twitching hands.*]— [*Starting up.*] Well. We know what you haven't done. At least tell us what you have done.

POMPEY

Yes. I'll tell you, Metellus. [*Pause.*] When this began between us, I thought of my own time under Sulla. I'd carried the eagles into Africa. I was a young man, then. I did rash things. But I was lucky. I conquered Africa. Sulla sent word to me then, to disband my army, and return. [*To* JULIA *and* CORNELIA.] [*Pause.*] I resented Sulla's order. My soldiers resented it. They asked me to be their King in Africa. I

[281]

obeyed Sulla. I thought—if I did—it might be easier—for
the next young conqueror—to obey, too. Not to cause civil
war.

CORN.

He thought—we both thought, father, that Cæsar would
remember that. We had planned how all our party, all the
Senate even, should go out into the fields to welcome Cæsar. As
Sulla welcomed my husband then. If he came home alone.
Disbanding his army. That would have been a triumph for
Cæsar greater than any Consulship. But Cæsar only thinks of
present power. He would see the glory of Rome pass rather
than not see that.

POMPEY

I did not think that Cæsar would be blind to the glory of
Rome. [*Going to the window.*]

MET.

I'll quote some other words to you. Something which you
said once in Sicily. "What is all this talk of law," you said,
"to us that have swords by our sides?" What? You remember
those words? Will you sit still, and see Rome sacked? See the
rabble make beastly all that seven centuries has made here?
See their filthy hands laid—laid on these delicate ladies? See
our temples spoiled that their rat-faced brats may grow up to
eat free bread, and loaf and spit outside the beer-shops. Pah!
What did the Senate say?

POMPEY

They gave me absolute power here.

MET.

What? Then send out your press. Bill every able-bodied
man. Bill the women if the men won't come.

POMPEY

No, Metellus. Not that.

MET.

What then, man? [CORNELIA *interposes. Speaking to her husband.*]

CORN.

It is a question now, dear heart, of standing for the right. The right side is always the weaker side. War is terrible. It's such a loathsome kind of spiritual death. But it is better to have war, than to see law set aside. The will of Rome must not be slighted. I don't mean the popular cry. That is all for Cæsar now, dear. It was all for you once. It will be again. I mean all the burning thought of so many generations of our fathers. That must not be set aside for the lust of one man. It is the duty of a Roman, dear heart, to go out under the eagles to defend that burning thought, the Will of Rome. Even if he goes alone. And you will not go alone. The souls of our fathers will march with you. And if you die, dear one, defending what they died to make, you will die as I would have my lover die.

POMPEY

Ah! Cornelia. You make death hard. But it would be sweet to die so for you. To die. To join that Senate of the old Romans; the wise ones. To bring them news of Rome there. In the shadows.

CORN.

Saying that you come crowned. Having played the Roman. "Having obeyed their laws."

MET.

[*Quickly.*] Go on, girl. Oh, move him, Cornelia. Goad

him to action. I cannot. For Rome's sake. Move him. Get him out of this child's mood.

POMPEY

Yes. Yes. Yes. [*Slowly.*] I shall fight Cæsar. [*Sharply.*]

MET.

Ah! [*Excitedly.*] But at once. Give him no time to win recruits by success. Give them no time here. The rabble don't hesitate. They don't understand a man who hesitates. Give me all the cavalry. Look. I'll mount six cohorts of slingers. I can worry him with those.

POMPEY

Where's the map? [*He quickly takes map from wall.*] It's the effect here, not the beating of Cæsar. We must stiffen the towns against him. Show them that they'll have to back their choice with their blood. That'll check his advance.

MET.

Cæsar's quick, mind. He marches light, and he comes a devil of a pace. [*Musingly.*]

POMPEY

You say he's got forty thousand men? Let's see your despatch. Who sent it? [*Taking paper.*] Can you trust this man?

MET.

Yes. A clever young fellow.

POMPEY

Young? Where's he served?

MET.

He was on Crassus' staff in Parthia. In the smash.

POMPEY

I don't trust ghosts.

MET.

Ghosts?

POMPEY

What escapes when an army's destroyed like Crassus'?
[*Reading.*] Forty thousand men. Shrewd. This is a shrewd
lad, Metellus. He's read a lot of school-books, this man. Come.
Forty thousand?

MET.

Yes.

POMPEY

No. It's not possible, Metellus. This is politics. Not war.
He's forcing our hand. His army's miles away. He's rushing
the frontier with a few picked men. The pick of his light foot,
and these light Gaulish lancers. It's a bold dash to put all
Rome in a panic.

MET.

[*Biting his nails.*] That's not what you'd have done.

POMPEY

That's how I know I'm right. [*Standing.*] Take the cavalry.
Get into touch with him. Harass him. Hang on to him. Worry
him all the time. I'll come on with all I can get.

MET.

Take the gladiators.

POMPEY

No. This is a Roman question. No paid slaves shall decide Rome's fate.

MET.

We shall be a desperate lot without them.

CORN.

The Navy. Land men from the ships.

MET.

They can't march. This campaign is a race.

POMPEY

No. No. Look. [*Excitedly.*] I'll send gallopers to the fleet at Brindisi. I'll tell them to lash north, forced rowing. They'd catch him at Pisaurum. They could cut in on his left flank. So much for the attack. The city here's the problem.

MET.

Damn the city here. The city's for the winner. Always.

POMPEY

[*Musing.*] Cæsar's got an army in occupation here already. Now to secure Rome.

MET.

[*Quickly.*] The patricians. Let the patricians form a Committee of Public Safety. They'll settle Cæsar's mobs.

CORN.

No. No. There'd be massacre all over Rome. All frightened men are merciless.

Met.

Be quiet, girl. Yes, man.

Pompey

No. That's the wild thing the desperate man always does to make his cause more desperate. It would madden the mob against us. Our task is to win the mob.

Corn.

Leave Cato in command here.

Met.

What?

Corn.

Let Cato raise a force purely to defend Rome. Not a party force at all.

Pompey

Yes, Cato. He stands outside parties. He has power over both.

Met.

No, I say. Power? That man with power. Bah! He reminds every one of grandpapa. That's why he's popular.

Pompey

It's popularity that's wanted.

Met.

It's power that's wanted. A few crucified mutineers. Not Cato telling us of good King Numa.

Pompey

[*Picking up the hammer of his gong.*] We'll send for Cato.

[287]

MET.

No. No.

POMPEY

Yes.

MET.

Wait a minute.

POMPEY

Well?

MET.

We want a soldier here.

POMPEY

We want a man whom everybody can trust.

MET.

Cato's not firm enough.

POMPEY

I want Rome calm, not intimidated.

MET.

I'm not going to serve if that man's left behind in Rome.

POMPEY

Oh, don't say that. What are your reasons against Cato?
In this instance.

MET.

How will Cato deal with the mutineers in camp?

POMPEY

Ah! There. [*Pause.*] Yes. We can't be hard on those poor
fellows. Try and see it as they see it. They've had the choice
of refusing duty or beginning a civil war.

MET.

A soldier's first duty is obedience.

POMPEY

Is it? I'd rather have him a man first, myself. Only very good soldiers mutiny. Did you never notice that?

MET.

No. Nor you. They must be made examples of.

POMPEY

[*Smiling.*] Come. Some wine, Metellus.

MET.

[*Crossly.*] This isn't a time for wine. [*He stalks up and down the room.*] Suppose we're beaten. I tell you if we're beaten you'll want more than old Father Cato here. You'll want a man to stamp out Cæsar's faction. I'd stop their smiling. By the time Cæsar stormed Rome he'd find few of his friends left. I'd make Rome so sick with blood. By. She'd think no more of Cæsar.

POMPEY

My God! The streets ran blood. In Sulla's time. That once. The carts drove over them.

MET.

That was child's play to what this will be.

POMPEY

Yes. Suppose we're beaten. Rome stormed. No, no, never! [*He flings the map aside.*] No. I'll give up Italy rather. I will not fight in Italy. Cæsar's rabble shall have no excuse for sacking Rome.

[289]

MET.

What? [*A pause.*] Where will you fight him then? In Spain, where your army is?

CORN.

Not in Spain.

MET.

Why not in Spain?

POMPEY

No. You know the proverb. Spain's a country where a big army starves and a little army gets beaten. I know, I've fought there. And it's far from Rome, and too near Gaul. No, Macedonia. We'll go over with the fleet to Macedonia. There are five good legions from Crassus' smash in Macedonia. We'll prepare an army there.

MET.

Yes. But your friends in Rome. Our party here? The Senate? The Consuls?

POMPEY

They must come with us at once to Brindisi, where the fleet lies. We'll take ship there. [*Writing.*] I'm writing to Domitius at Corfinium, to join me instantly with his twenty cohorts. [*Musing.*] I wonder. If he stays, he will be invested. And he will stay, he's as obstinate as a mule. If he marches south at once we shall have twenty thousand. If not, we must leave him to his fate. I must abandon Italy.

MET.

[*Slowly.*] There's something in it. Yes. I wonder.

POMPEY

It's not so risky. Fighting now is backing losing cards.

MET.

We shall lose friends.

POMPEY

We shall gain time.

MET.

Let's see the map. [*He takes another map.*] I like it. Yes. It's a good move.

POMPEY

Cæsar will attack my army in Spain, first.

MET.

Afraid of its invading his dear Gaul, you mean?

POMPEY

He'll have no choice in the matter. He's got no ships to follow us. I've got the Navy. While he's building ships, I'll build an Army. If he fights my generals in Spain, it will be a year before he can follow me. We shall have a great army by that time.

MET.

Yes. An army, eh? Macedonian phalanx, eh? We'll send out a fiery sign through Macedonia. All the swordsmen of the hills will come. Out of Dacia, out of Thrace. Jove, what an army! With Egypt at your back, too.

POMPEY

Yes. Egypt's full of my old soldiers. We can always fall back on King Ptolemy. [*He becomes sad.*] Ah, well. Ah, well.

CORN.

What is it?

[291]

POMPEY

[*Quickly.*] Nothing. [*He rises.*] I was thinking of all this kingliness wandering in little wild Greek towns.

CORN.

The kingly mind always lives in a kingly city.

POMPEY

[*Eagerly.*] Ah! Who said that?

CORN.

You said it.

POMPEY

Ah. Where's the fire that scatters those sparks? Why doesn't it burn in us always?

MET.

[*Excitedly.*] It's burning now. Look here. Listen. Look here. Your idea of Macedonia. Splendid! Cæsar won't follow. [*Slapping the table.*] He'll be afraid. Part the world between you. Let Cæsar keep the West. You be King in the East. Build up another Rome in Athens. With you in the East, we could do what Alexander did. We could——

POMPEY

No more ambitions, Metellus. You see where ambition leads.

MET.

[*Flushed.*] You wait till you see those Dacians. Big, black, clean-limbed fellows, Julia, with swords and steel shields. They charge like cavalry. [*He fills wine.*]

[292]

POMPEY

So, Macedonia.

MET.

Yes, Macedonia.

CORN.

When?

POMPEY

Now, dear.

CORN.

To-night?

POMPEY

It doesn't give you much time. It will be hard for you to leave all your pretty things behind.

CORN.

I was thinking about your night's rest. Life is book and picture to me. All that is Rome to us comes with us.

MET.

Well then [*rolling up the map with a click*], boot and saddle.

POMPEY

Take what men you have, Metellus. And press post horses. You'll want my orders though. [*He strikes the gong.*]

[*Enter* PHILIP]

PHILIP

Sir.

POMPEY

Ask Theophanes to speak to me a moment.

[*Exit* PHILIP]

[293]

Met.

That Greek writer-fellow. I don't know how you stand
that man.

[*Enter* Theophanes, *who bows and is saluted*]

Pompey

Sit down. [*He takes papers from despatch box.*] We're going
to Macedonia. We take ship at Brindisi. These orders to our
party. Have them filled in and sent round.

Theo.

Yes. But you won't want them.

Pompey

You mean that—What do you mean?

Theo.

I mean, you won't want them. Cæsar's at Cremona. He's
not marching on Rome. He's encamped in his own province.
It was a false alarm.

All

What?

Pompey

How do you know that?

Theo.

Labienus has just come in. Cæsar's right-hand man. I've
been talking to him. Cæsar's sending messengers with new
proposals to you. He's not marching on Rome.

Met.

So we go on again.

POMPEY

What are the new proposals? Does he know?

THEO.

[*Shrugging his shoulders.*] His men are beginning to shrink,
I suppose, now that it comes to the touch.   I don't blame 'em.

JULIA

Do you think it's an excuse to gain time?

CORN.

Ah, no, Julia.   Let us give Cæsar credit for a little nobleness.

MET.

Pah! He was in Catiline's conspiracy. It was proved beyond a doubt. Well, Pompey. What are you going to do?

POMPEY

It is very wonderful. I must see Cato.   [*Going.*]

MET.

The lath and plaster Spartan. Why?

THEO.

He's here.

[CATO, *in black robes, enters. He stands with arms folded, looking at them all*]

MET.

Well, sir?

POMPEY

Yes, Cato?

CORN.

You've heard? Won't you sit down?

CATO.

So this is the family party. Well, Pompey. Now I see the drags that hinder your honesty. [*To* JULIA.] You. The critic. You with neither art nor brain. Thinking you show both by condemning them in others.

JULIA

Do you show art and brain by condemning me?

CATO

Look into your heart, woman.

CATO

[*To* METELLUS.] You, sir. The General. A tailor and a love affair made you a General. Not war. War doesn't make your kind. But you long for war. You would shriek your country into war, any day, sir. So that humble brave men might make pickings for you. Invitations. Gold. What you call love affairs. Fame. [*To* THEOPHANES, *while* METELLUS *looks him up and down.*] I don't know you, sir.

THEO.

A contributor to Time's waste-paper basket.

CATO

Ah! [*To* POMPEY.] And you, the mischief-maker, the genius. Well, which of us was right, Pompey?

POMPEY

You were right. But I have acted more friendly than Cæsar.

[296]

CATO.

You have made the mischief. Can you unmake it?

POMPEY

Can you unmake it?

CATO

I? I am going into Sicily. You forget. I am Governor there.

CORN

But now. In this moment of truce. Surely it can be remedied?

CATO

Yes. At a price.

POMPEY

How?

CATO

You must go alone, on foot, to Cæsar.

POMPEY

Never.

CATO

And tell him that you come to save Rome from civil war. That a man's pride is a little thing to that. And that so you have put by your greatness.

CORN.

Ah! Ah! [*She watches* POMPEY'*s face. All turn to* POMPEY.]

POMPEY

No. I have been a King here. I have been like God here. Kings have come to me on their knees. Cæsar. Cæsar's. I made Cæsar by a stroke of my pen. No. Ah, no.

[297]

CATO

Cæsar would be shamed to tears, Pompey. Would not that victory content you?

POMPEY

I cannot. No, I cannot.

CATO

Not to save Rome, Pompey?

POMPEY

No. I should be a mock. No. No.

CORN

You would be a fire, Pompey, for all time. All the lamps of the world would be kindled at that nobleness.

POMPEY

You wish it, too, dear heart?

CORN

[*Softly.*] I wish it.

POMPEY

[*Looking round.*] To a young man. Whom I have made. Oh, Cato, Cato! Is kindness to a friend only a bitter form of suicide? [*He fumbles at the clasp of his purple.*] Very well, I will go, Marcus. [*He slings his purple aside.*]

CATO.

I thought you were Pompey the Little. I wronged you.

MET.

[*To* THEOPHANES.] So. [*They exchange glances.*]

[298]

Pompey

Old man. Old man.

[*A noise without. Cries. A sentry calls "Halt." Struggling. Shouts of "Stand back." "Let me in." The spears rattle. The door is shaken.*

Theo.

[*Opening door.*] What's this? [*Pause.*] Let him in, Sentry.

[*Enter filthy* Horseman, *dust to the eyes, tottering. The door is left open, showing* Soldiers]

Met.

One of Cæsar's lancers.

Theo.

A deserter, eh?

The Man

[*Gasping.*] Which of you is the lord?

Pompey

[*Pouring wine for him.*] I am he. Drink this. Take your time. What is it?

The Man

[*Spilling his drink like a man half dead of thirst.*] Cæsar! Cæsar! I escaped last night. Cæsar!

Corn.

What?

The Man

He's crossed the Rubicon. With all his army. Marching on Rome. Be here in two days. [*A pause.*]

POMPEY

[*Resuming his purple.*] That settles it. There can be no treaty now.

CORN.

So war has begun.

POMPEY

[*Sadly.*] There it is. Only it is more terrible now. More terrible than it was. [*Turning to go.*] It must be war now to the end.

MET.

[*Picking up the orders from the table and slapping them to command attention.*] And now. To Brindisi. [*He walks briskly towards the door, but halts opposite* CATO, *at whom he glares.* POMPEY *and* CORNELIA *halt to watch him.*] Well, sir. My Conscript Father. Will you crawl before Cæsar now, sir? It is long since a Roman bade his King to lick the dust before a traitor. You and your kind may sue to such. Rome puts other thoughts into our hearts.

CATO

There are two Romes, Metellus. One built of brick by hodsmen. But the Rome I serve glimmers in the uplifted heart. It is a court for the calm gods. That Rome. Let me not shame that city. Advance the eagles.

A VOICE WITHOUT

Present arms.

[*A trumpet blows a blast*]

CURTAIN

ACT II

Scene I

[Staff-officer's tent at Durazzo. Walls of plain canvas. Canvas door running on rings at back R. Smaller canvas door at back L. Table and camp-chairs. Everything bare and severe.]
Domitius, Lentulus, Theophanes, *at the table.]*

Domi.

So it goes on. And Spain is lost. Look at this position here. Cæsar has shut us in here like so many sheep in a pen. Has Pompey no pride? Or has he grown besotted?

Theo.

Flaccus is raiding Cæsar's lines this morning. He will attack them in three places. And break them.

Domi.

[Fiercely.] Flaccus is a boy. A whole year wasted, and half the empire lost.

[Enter Pompey hurriedly. They salute]

Pompey

Good morning. I have called you all together to tell you of the loss of my Spanish army, lately commanded by Afranius. We had expected victory, from Afranius' letters. But we are soldiers. We know what Fortune is in war. We are not merchants, to cast him for failing.

Domi.

We have given up Italy, and thrown away Spain. Africa is

[301]

invaded and Sicily taken. We have given up and drawn back
everywhere. And why? That we might come here to be cooped
up by an army half our size. I want to know why? We all
want to know why.

POMPEY

I remember Sulla saying that he could make an army love
him by talking to the privates occasionally. But that no amount
of talking would make his generals love his ideas. Be content.
And bide my time.

LENT.

Magnus. I am not given to criticism; but this biding time
is ruin. We are losing allies; we are losing Rome. Rome looked
to you to crush this upstart. Instead of that you have let a
rebellion grow into a civil war. You have watched your ad-
herents stamped out piecemeal. You have done nothing.

POMPEY

Wait.

DOMI.

We have waited for a year.

POMPEY

I ask you to wait a little longer.

LENT.

Magnus, while we wait, the rabble is stamping out aristocracy
throughout the world. [*He rises.*]

POMPEY

Sit down, Lentulus. I tell you to wait. The war is in my
hand.

Domi.

War is in the hands of the man who strikes. [*He thrusts aside the lesser door.*] There. Among the crags there. By the pine-clump. In that great red heap like an iron mine. That is Cæsar's camp. I've been out there night after night, worming over rocks and down gullies, keeping my course by the stars, so that, when a chance came, I could take an army into that camp blindfold. I've a map here. [*Throws down a paper.*] Those red dots are the sentries. Each dot was made at the risk of my heart's blood. I've grovelled in the earth before all those sentries, praying for the moon to go in, while they talked of their love-affairs. I've seen the sergeant coming his rounds with a lantern, and shut my eyes lest they should gleam, and betray me. I could take that camp with two legions in the blackest night of the year. This war is breaking the world in two. And you send Flaccus with a corporal's guard to pull down a hundred yards of paling. Justify that, before you tell me to wait.

Pompey

Flaccus is fighting the decisive battle of the war.

Lent.

This is trifling. [*He rises and moves away.*]

Domi.

The decisive. I will tell you what a decisive battle is. I took part in one for you at Massilia three months ago. At the end of that siege, there was no city. There were no people. Only some deathsheads dying of plague, and a few madmen on the walls. And outside, there were towers flinging fires at us, and slings flinging rocks at us, and miles of army coming up to the sack. That was a decisive battle.

POMPEY

Domitius, when a man thinks fixedly of anything, desiring it with his whole nature, he creates a strong pitiless devil. Domitius, you are given up to a devil. A devil of lust for battle. You are fiercer than a devil, for when there is no enemy you fight your friends, and when there are no friends you fight yourself. And when you have torn yourself bloody you fight ideas, not because you understand them, and hate them, but because when you are not fighting you are nothing. I fear you, Domitius. A man's friends are those who understand his ideas, and advance them. You are Cæsar's friend, Domitius.

DOMI.

[*Intensely.*] You killed my brother, when you were a young man. For that, I swore to tear your heart out. You dined with me once, twenty years ago. You will not remember. I put my hand upon your shoulder. I had a knife in my other hand. I could have stabbed you to the heart. And there you would have died, Magnus, before my old Marian friends. But I saw that you were a better man than my brother. Something you said. I saw that you were what Rome wanted. [*Pause.*]

[*Fiercely.*] You know better than to call me Cæsar's friend. I've made Cæsar rock in his seat.

POMPEY

You are Cæsar's friend. Your heart beats pulse for pulse with Cæsar's heart. You malign me because my hands are not red from butchery like his. And at this moment, while you malign me, Flaccus is ending the war. Take no more thought of the war. The war is over.

[*The* Generals *draw to one side and talk apart for a moment*]

[304]

POMPEY

Rome is the problem now. You would do well to think of Rome. This is the seventh democratic rising since my boyhood. Seven desperate attempts to change in fifty years. Does that teach you nothing?

LENT.

Theophanes.

DOMI.

Yes.

THEO.

Magnus.

POMPEY

I offered a broken and distracted Italy. He took it. A turbulent, useless Spain. He took it. I have flung down half a useless world, and he has gorged it and come on into the trap. I am camped in plenty, with six fleets ruling the seas. Cæsar is trenched in mud, living on roots. Besieging me, you call it? He has dug thirty miles of works. He has not enough men to guard ten miles. His men are exhausted and starving. He stays in those works during my pleasure; no longer. He cannot force me to battle. He cannot raid my lines. He cannot go back to Rome.

And I, with one slight thrust, am tumbling him into ruin.

[*Enter an* Orderly *with a despatch. He gives it to* POMPEY]

LENT.

From Flaccus?

DOMI.

You are of the Fifth?

ORDERLY

From Titus Pulcio, my lord.

POMPEY

Very well.

ORDERLY

Have you any orders, my lord?

POMPEY

No orders. Acknowledge.

[*Exit* Orderly, *saluting*]

THEO.

Is it important?

POMPEY

Read it.

THEO.

[*Reading.*] From Titus Pulcio, legate, fifth legion, to Head-quarters: "The attack under Valerius Flaccus has been repulsed with heavy loss. The survivors have fallen back upon the old works, south of the river, where desperate fighting is now going on. I am marching with what I have. The enemy is in force. Stragglers report position hopeless."

DOMI.

These thrusting youths want a lesson. Now, Magnus. Justify your plan, now.

POMPEY

Wait.

LENT.

Wait? While our right flank is being rolled up? [*Coldly.*]

POMPEY

It would take Cæsar two days to bring up enough troops to crush our right.

[306]

DOMI.

Surely you will smash this attacking force.

POMPEY

I am fighting with the thought of Rome before me. I will not march back to Rome over corpses, in the Sulla fashion.

DOMI.

At least you will march back over those whom we took last night. I killed those.

POMPEY

You killed those men?

DOMI.

They were rebels, I tell you. Traitors.

POMPEY

I will judge traitors.

DOMI.

They were my own deserters. Dogs. I will serve all traitors so. And I tell you this.

POMPEY

Not a word. You disgrace our cause, Domitius. [*Pause, and change of voice.*] I may win this war. Or this [*showing his gold eagle-clasp*] may pay a camp-trull yonder. But whether I win or go down, my men shall bear themselves nobly. Those on my side must act like knights of the bodyguard of God. See to it.

[*Enter* Chief Centurion COTTA, *battered*]

COTTA

I report the death of commander Flaccus, my lord.

POMPEY

Killed?

COTTA

Yes, my lord.

DOMI.

That is what happens in skirmishing. Nothing is done, and the good man gets killed.

COTTA

We were beaten back, my lord; the surprise failed.

POMPEY

Yes? Well?

COTTA

We rushed their wall, tore up their palisades, and set fire to two of the turrets. Then they surrounded us. I should think they had two legions on to us. We had to cut our way home.

POMPEY

And your commander?

COTTA

He was killed in the thick, my lord. After our storm, we were driven back on to the palisades. The pales were all on fire, all along the line, burning hard. I looked one minute, and saw him backed right up against the flames, with a dozen Thracians. They had a whole troop of lancers stabbing at them. I got within a few paces of him, trying to bring him off, but the fire balls burst so thick one couldn't see. My men were being cut to pieces, the cavalry was cutting in on our rear, and there came a rush of spearmen which swept me off the rampart. I saw his body falling back into the fire, all lit up. But we could never get near the place again. They cut us to pieces down on the flat. They killed eight hundred of us.

LENT.

A severe repulse.

DOMI.

Wasted. Wasted lives. Utterly useless, wicked waste.

POMPEY

And then? What happened then?

COTTA

They drove us back into the old works by the river. Over the outer wall into the ditch. [*Pause.*] We were penned up in the ditch like beasts in a slaughter-house. They swarmed up above us on the wall, pelting us. We were below them, grinding in the mud, huddled like sheep. Men will always huddle when they have no room to use their shields. It was so fierce, that I thought our men would break. But we could not break. We were shut in. We were so pushed together that the dead could not fall. And being pressed man to man gave us a kind of courage. I got up on a heap where the wall had fallen. I wanted to see. I could see all a wave of red plumes where Cæsar's Gauls were pressing up, calling to their horses. Arr. Arr. There was a roar everywhere like ice breaking up in the spring. Behind their main attack they were making a way through the wall for their horse. Every now and then their

picks flashed and the earth came scattering down. It was
worst at the gate. The noise of the axes on the gate was like a
ship-yard. They brought up a tree to batter it, and every time
they ran at it, you could see the wood give, in great splint-
ers. I thought we were lost; but it was our fight, my lord.

For I heard fifes, playing "The Day of Zama," and men singing. It was a cohort of the fifth, marching to support our left
flank. They came on slowly, in line, with their heads up, and
the fifes playing. The centurions led them, singing, marching
well ahead. It was a fine thing to see those men coming on.
Their ranks were so locked that the oak-trees on their shields
made a green breastwork across their front. It was our fight
after that. We caught them in the outer ditch. The ditch is
choked with them. Cæsar lost a full thousand there in the
ditch. They were broken. We shook them to the heart. They
will not face us again, my lord, for a long time. Nor any
enemy. Cæsar will have trouble with them.

POMPEY

Very well, Cotta.

COTTA

They are sending in the body with a trumpet, my lord.

POMPEY

Yes! Send me the returns of killed and wounded and the
centurions' reports. Your legion will stand no watch to-night.
See that your men rest. Order wine from the sutlers for them.
I will speak to them to-night.

COTTA

Thank you, my lord. [*He goes out, saluting.*]

[310]

DOMI.

One moment, Cotta. [*He goes out, after him.*]

THEO.

Cæsar is sending a trumpet. Can he be suing for peace?

LENT.

Why should he sue for peace after a skirmish?

POMPEY

It was the pricking of a bubble. He is suing for peace. And if I grant peace, I shall have these to fight. And if I refuse peace, this ruin will go on.

THEO.

Do we receive this trumpet?

[*Enter* DOMITIUS]

DOMI.

Magnus. Cæsar is in disorder. His men are leaving the trenches. He is withdrawing. His south walls are abandoned already.

POMPEY

Yes. He has learned his lesson.

He must pay them now for the life they have spent for him. He cannot pay them. The most that he can do is to save them from the result of his insanity.

THEO.

He can retreat.

POMPEY

How can he retreat? He cannot retreat. Where can he go?

My navies hold the sea. To the north there are savage tribes. The south is blocked by my garrisons. I am here in the west with my army. And to the east lies Metellus, with another army.

He has one chance of saving them. He can sue for peace.

Domi.

You are not going to receive this herald?

Pompey

Yes. Rome must have peace.
If Cæsar will make submission——

Domi. ⎰ A surrender will be useless.
Theo. ⎱ Cæsar must be destroyed.
Lent. ⎱ How will you settle Rome, with Cæsar alive?

Pompey

This war has gone on all my life. Sulla's method failed. Catiline's method failed. They shall not be tried again. Rome shall be settled this time finally.

Domi.

If you hesitate to strike now, you are a traitor, Magnus.

Pompey

I have made my plan.
[*Sternly.*] I will abide by it. To your place. Murmur no more.
No little gust of passion shall set me wavering.

[*A* Voice *without and a trumpet*]

Voice

Present arms. Port arms. Pass friend. Present arms.

[312]

POMPEY

Life is nothing. It is the way of life which is so much. Enter there.

COTTA

[*Entering*] The body, my lord. With the trumpet.

Enter Bearers *with the body of* VALERIUS FLACCUS. COTTA *and the others salute the corpse. Then, with a solemnity of trumpets blowing points of ceremony,* MARCUS ACILIUS *enters, led by two* Centurions. *He is blindfolded.* COTTA, *the* Bearers *and the* Centurions *go out, when the handkerchief is removed.*

ACIL.

I bring back your soldier, Cneius Pompey.

POMPEY

You bring a message?

ACIL.

I come from Cæsar.

POMPEY

Well?

ACIL.

He asks you to end this war. The gods have given you an equal measure of victory. You have both lost and won half the Roman world. Now that the world is shared between you, you can consent to a peace. To-morrow, if fortune favour one of you, the fortunate one will think himself too great to parley. [*Pause.*] Cæsar asks that a peace may be concluded. If you will undertake to do the same, he will make public oath to disband his army within three days. That is his proposal.

[313]

POMPEY

More than a year ago, the Senate ordered Cæsar to disband
his troops. That decree still stands disregarded. I cannot treat
with a rebel. Cæsar must obey that decree and submit to the
Senate's mercy.

ACIL.

The quarrel is between you and Cæsar, Magnus.

POMPEY

Not at all. I represent the Senate.

ACIL.

Your party of the Senate, which my party does not recog-
nise.

POMPEY

These are the facts, Acilius. Cæsar has attacked Republican rule. He has failed. I make it a condition of treaty that
he acknowledge Republican authority.

ACIL.

Cæsar has never denied that authority. He is in arms against
a perversion of that authority by unscrupulous men. That
he seeks to end the Republic is denied by my presence here,
asking for peace. Cæsar is no suitor to you. That great mind
is its own sufficient authority. Farewell, Magnus. [*Going.*]

[*At door.*] You will grant peace if Cæsar kneels in the dust.
Very well. Rome is more to him than honour. He will kneel
in the dust. In the most public place in Rome. He will submit himself, body and cause, to the judgment of the Roman
people there assembled.

Will that suffice?

POMPEY

No.

The mob has no voice in this matter. The mob must be taught to obey its rulers. Cæsar must submit to the Senate.

ACIL.

Then the blood will be on your hands, Magnus. [*Going.*]

POMPEY

It will suffice if Cæsar surrender to myself in the presence of both armies. But a public act of submission must be made. Otherwise it will be thought that Cæsar drove us from Italy, and forced us to accept his terms. That I cannot allow.

ACIL.

I am to tell Cæsar that you refuse. [*Quietly.*] From fear of what the world may think?

POMPEY

You count that a little thing, the thought of the world? For what else are we fighting; but to control the thought of the world? What else matters, Acilius?

You think that I am fighting to be a master? Not so. I am fighting because I know what Cæsar wants. I have watched his career step by step. Cæsar means to be king. He has bribed the rabble to crown him.

You see only the brilliant man, winning—what he has the power to win. I look beyond that man. I see Rome under a secret, bloody domination and a prey to future Cæsars. That shall not be.

I am an old man, now, Acilius. I have been fighting this

[315]

battle all my life. I hope now to end it. You have heard my terms. [*He strikes a gong.*]

[*A pause. Enter a* Centurion]

Do you accept them or refuse them? Take your time.

[*Pause*]

ACIL.

I refuse them.

POMPEY

[*To* Centurion.] You will take the Gemella legion, drive in Cæsar's outposts and burn the works.

[*Exit* Centurion]

ACIL.

There is no voice for peace, then. I have failed. Now that my task is done, may I speak with you privately?

POMPEY

Yes. On a private matter. Is your business private?

ACIL.

Yes. It is private.

POMPEY

[*To* Generals.] Leave us.

[*Exit* Generals]

[*To* ACILIUS.] Be brief.

ACIL.

My mother married you. Years ago. She was dragged by force from my father so that you might be propped by a vote the more. She died of a broken heart, in your bed.

[316]

You have taken worse props, now. These nobles. They are using you to stamp out democracy. So that they may plunder in peace for another fifty years.

And when you have done their task. When the war is over.

POMPEY

[*Taking up gong.*] I cannot listen to this.

ACIL.

You plan to make just those democratic reforms for which Cæsar is fighting. You mean to cripple the aristocracy. And they will stop you. Domitius hates you. Metellus fears you. Lentulus is jealous of you. They are planning to get rid of you. Even now. [*Pause.*]

Get rid of them, Magnus. Take Cæsar as your friend. End the war. Drive them out.

POMPEY

And after?

ACIL.

You could make Rome what you please.

[POMPEY *strikes the gong*]

[*Re-enter* Generals]

POMPEY

And after? [*Pause.*] Your party shall submit to mine. [*He writes a few words.*] You may take this to Cæsar. [*Gives writing.*]

Give this man safe conduct.

ACIL.

I am going, Magnus. I shall not see you again.

[317]

[THEOPHANES *goes out*]

POMPEY

[*Who has turned away.*] Well?

ACIL.

Pride is a mean thing in the presence of death. To-day you are great, and the kings bring tribute to you. To-morrow you may be this. Only this. Praised by the worm.

[*Showing corpse*]

POMPEY

You talk of the presence of death. Man, I am in the presence of life, and death's a pleasure to it.

[COTTA *and* Centurions *enter with* THEOPHANES. *They salute*]

Who cares what I may be? I may be carrion. But while I am man, and carry a faith in me, I will guard that faith. See this man through the lines.

[*With a solemn blowing of a point of ceremony*, COTTA *and the* Centurions *go out, leading* ACILIUS, *blindfolded. Murmurs. Acclamations.*

The Generals *eye* POMPEY. *He walks to the body and looks at it.*]

POMPEY

Poor boy. You have gone a long way from this inn.
When you were born, women kissed you, and watched you as you slept, and prayed for you, as women do. When you learned to speak, they praised you; they laughed and were so tender with you, even when they were in pain. And to-night you will wander alone, where no woman's love can come to you,

and no voice speak to you, and no grief of ours touch you to an answer.

The dead must be very lonely.

DOMI.

[*Coming forward and looking at the body.*] That? Why be sad at that? He was marked for it. [*Quietly.*] Magnus. I have something to say. I give you full credit for what you have done. You were right. But not so right as I would have been. Destruction's what war's for. Still. It has happened. Now there is Rome. How are you going back to Rome without the moral support of a victory?

LENT.

In Rome, it is said openly that you have been shuffled about at Cæsar's will.

THEO.

And that we have been beaten in every battle.

POMPEY

What is that noise, there?

[*Cries of* "*Victory.*" *Clapping. Trumpets. A cry of* "*Present Arms.*" *The spears rattle.*]

[*Enter* LUCIUS LUCCEIUS, *in the civil dress*]

LENT.

Lucceius.

THEO.

Lucius Lucceius.

[LUCCEIUS *stand looking at them silently. He salutes the body, and advances slowly.*]

[319]

Lucc.

[*Slowly.*] I salute you, Cneius Pompey. I come from Rome.

Pompey

What news do you bring from Rome?

Lucc.

News of your triumph, Magnus.

Cæsar's army, under Curio, invaded Africa.

Curio is killed. His army is destroyed. Africa is saved to us.
[*He takes a laurel wreath.*]

The Roman people send me with this wreath, Magnus. [*He
offers it, with reverent dignity.*]

Pompey

[*Taking the wreath and laying it on* Flaccus' *head.*] Once,
long ago, I played with you. By the fish-pools at Capua, watching the gold-fish.

You asked me for my purple, that glittering day long ago.
[*He lays his purple over* Flaccus.] All things for which men
ask are granted. A word may be a star or a spear for all time.
This is the day of my triumph, it seems.

[*A distant trumpet winds. It winds again*]

Theo.

There is a horn blowing.

Pompey

It is blowing like a death-horn.

Domi.

It is a Roman call.

In Cæsar's camp. [Domitius *flings aside the canvas.*]

[320]

It is the "Prepare to March." He is in retreat. His huts are burning. They are winding out upon the road there. They are floundering up the pass. Two thousand horse could ruin them.

POMPEY

Ruin is not my province. Let them destroy themselves. They are wandering out into the wilds without heart, without hope, without plan. That is the forlornest march ever called by trumpets. There is death in every heart already. Well. We shall follow.

Call the chief centurions.

[THEOPHANES *goes to the door, to the* Sentry *without*]

[*Going to the body.*] And to-night we shall be marching from this poor earth, pursuing Cæsar, marching to many trumpets, under the stars, singing as we march. I shall end Sulla's war, now. But we will kill the rebellion, remember, not those Romans.

[*The* Chief Centurions *enter*]

A trumpeter there. Strike camp. Prepare to march. [*A* Centurion *going out, calls.*]

Take up the body.

1ST CENTURION

Man is a sacred city, built of marvellous earth.

2ND CENTURION

Life was lived nobly here to give this body birth.

3RD CENTURION

Something was in this brain and in this eager hand.

[321]

4TH CENTURION

Death is so dumb and blind, Death cannot understand.
[*They lift the bier.*]
  Death drifts the brain with dust and soils the young limbs'
    glory.
  Death makes women a dream and men a traveller's story,
  Death drives the lovely soul to wander under the sky,
  Death opens unknown doors. It is most grand to die.

        [*They go out, followed by* POMPEY]

[*Now without comes a shaking blast from a trumpet. It is
taken up and echoed by many trumpets, near and far, blowing the legionary calls, till the air rings.*]

CURTAIN

SCENE II

The same. Taper light. Dawn later. POMPEY *writing. Enter*
                  LUCCEIUS

LUCC.

Not in bed, Magnus?

POMPEY

I have had evil dreams.
Are you from Rounds?
Is all quiet?

                  LUCC.

Yes.
There is a light near Cæsar's camp. They are burning their
dead.

Our scouts took two lancers. They say that Cæsar's men are dying. Of fever and hunger.

POMPEY

Yes. He must surrender within a few days. And so they are burning their dead?

LUCC.

Yes.

POMPEY

Now we have Rome to settle. [*Pause.*]
I lie awake, thinking.
What are we, Lucceius?

LUCC.

Who knows? Dust with a tragic purpose. Then an end.

POMPEY

No. But what moves us?
I saw a madman in Egypt. He was eyeless with staring at the sun. He said that ideas come out of the East, like locusts. They settle on the nations and give them life; and then pass on, dying, to the wilds, to end in some scratch on a bone, by a caveman's fire.

I have been thinking that he was wise, perhaps. Some new swarm of ideas has been settling on Rome. A new kind of life is being born. A new spirit. I thought a year ago that it was crying out for the return of kings, and personal rule. I see now that it is only crying out for a tyrant to sweep the old life away.

Rome has changed, Lucceius. Outwardly, she is the same, still. A city which gives prizes to a few great people. A booth where the rabble can sell their souls for bread, and their bodies

[323]

for the chance of plunder. Inwardly, she is a great democratic power struggling with obsolete laws.

Rome must be settled. The crowd must have more power.

Lucc.

[*Surprised*]. That would be a denial of your whole life, Magnus.

You have been crushing democracy for forty years.

Pompey

I have crushed rebellions. I mean now to crush their cause. There must be a change. A great change.

[*Enter* Metellus, Domitius, Lentulus]

Lucc.

[*Giving paper*]. This is my report. [*He salutes and goes. At the door he pauses, looking out.*] The pyre is still burning. They must be dying like flies. [*Exit.*]

Met.

[*As the* Generals *sit facing* Pompey]. Cæsar has sent to me privately, Magnus, to beg me to ask terms from you. I sent back his letter without comment.

The war is over; but we are not yet secure. We shall have to garrison the provinces for some years with men whom we can trust.

Spain and Gaul are arranged for among ourselves. It is the lesser appointments. Magnus, I want your voice, on behalf of Lucius Tuditanus. I was thinking of sending him as my deputy into Asia.

Pompey

Is that the soldier Tuditanus, who did so well under you? [*To* Domitius.]

DOMI.

No. His nephew.

MET.

He's a young man on my personal staff.

POMPEY

Has he qualified for the prætorship?

MET.

No. Not in the strict legal sense. But he was of the greatest use to me in Asia. He would be competent.

POMPEY

In what way was he of use to you?

MET.

In the collection of tribute, when they disputed our assessments. They hoped to wrangle in Court, without paying, till Cæsar saved them. Tuditanus stopped that. He judged the claims on the spot, and the tax was paid, or distrained, there and then. Often the patrols did not have to unsaddle. And as we needed the money quickly, the system was of great use to me.

POMPEY

Yes. But the law is plain, Metellus. A prætor and a prætor's deputy represent Rome. It is a responsible office. They judge and govern in Rome's name. Men must be trained for it. What has Tuditanus done, besides this tax-collection, that the laws should be broken for him?

LENT.

His father has made many sacrifices for us.

[325]

POMPEY

There is a growing belief in Rome that a sacrifice should be a good investment. Anything else?

MET.

He is one of those brilliant young men, of proved loyalty, for whom we ought to provide. I recommend him to you.

POMPEY

That is much in his favour. But I want proof that he can govern. Tell me, Metellus. Where has he shown administrative talent?

MET.

He has not shown it. He is a man whom we ought to bind to us. He would soon learn. We could give him a staff of old soldiers, to steady him, at first.

POMPEY

Has he any power of command? Where has he served?

DOMI.

He was in the horse for a time, in Lycia.

POMPEY

[*To* METELLUS.] What recommended him to you?

MET.

Never mind the merit. I am contending for the principle, that our friends must be rewarded.

POMPEY

Yes. But prætorian power. No. He must qualify.

[326]

Lent.

Before you reject him, will you not see him? Metellus and Domitius would not recommend him without grave reason. I might say, without urgent reason.

Pompey

I want an imperative reason. Without that, it would be a gross act of favouritism. And illegal. As for the results, we have seen such prætors. We should have a rising, and possibly a frontier war. No. Tuditanus cannot be prætor.

Met.

Remember, Magnus. Tuditanus is one of many. Others are in the same position. With a right to expect employment.

Pompey

Peace will try their quality.
There are men with Cæsar with a right to expect employment.

[*The* Generals *look at each other and sigh*]

Domi.

There is another point. We are going back to Rome. Rome is in a rebellious, unsettled state. We must secure ourselves.

I ask that every man of any standing in Rome be brought to trial, even if he have remained neutral. If the rebels have attacked authority, the neutrals have ignored it. And both must suffer. Rebellion must be stamped out. [*Gives paper.*]

The four hundred men in this list have actively helped the rebellion. There can be no question of trial for them. I ask that they be put to death.

POMPEY

That is out of the question. War will end when Cæsar sur-
renders. I cannot allow reprisals. I want Rome settled.

LENT.

Perhaps you will explain how you plan to administer Rome.
When we return.

MET.

[*Softly.*] There will be an amnesty for offences committed?

POMPEY

Yes.

DOMI.

You will pardon these rebels?

POMPEY

If they submit.

LENT.

[*Slowly.*] Will you allow them to help in the reconstruction?

POMPEY

[*Hotly.*] Yes. Power is in too few hands. There must be a
change in Rome. I would have these four hundred firebrands
made Senators, to help us make the change wisely.

MET.

So.

DOMI.

Magnus. There is only one way of settling Rome. By showing her who is master in a way which she'll remember.

[328]

Lent.

Any dallying with these rebels will leave us where we were before. Hated, and flouted by the rabble, and in danger from it. Losing our privileges, one by one. Losing our possessions and our power. Magnus, I would ask you to weigh this proposal very carefully. It affects the future of the patrician idea.

Pompey

And of Rome. What kind of future do you expect from a massacre like this? I will tell you what you will get. You will drive these four hundred firebrands into the Provinces, where it will take five years of war to crush them.

No. I'll go back with peace. Not a man shall be touched.

Lent.

Before we go back with peace, we must end the war. I have had letters from Rome.

Popular voice in Rome says that we have feared to risk a battle. That the war drags on, when it could be ended in a day.

That we dare not kill these representatives of the people.

That is a dangerous spirit in a city which we are about to rule. That spirit can only be broken by decisive success. We must go back with victory. A battle is certain victory to ourselves. We ask you to give battle.

Met.

We have asked this before, without success. We ask it now, feeling it to be a grave need. Lentulus has mentioned it as a political expedient. I add to that this, that our treasury is nearly empty. We have no means of raising more money. We have drained Spain and Asia for years to come. And your

inactive plan of campaign has killed our credit. We must fight.
We cannot afford to keep the field for another month.

POMPEY

Cæsar cannot keep the field for another week.

DOMI.

Cæsar will drag on, day by day, till the corn is ripe. It is
not many days now to harvest. You let his men get a full pro-
vision and you will see how long they will keep the field. I
could break that impostor's strength with the horse alone.

POMPEY

I can break his strength without risking a life. I will not
give battle. Be thankful that we can end such a war with so
little bloodshed. [*The* Generals *rise.*]

DOMI.

You are the oldest, Lentulus.

LENT.

It may lose us votes, remember. You are the most popular.

MET.

Perhaps I should do it. I am related.

POMPEY

What do you wish to say?

MET.

Magnus. I have to speak to you.
You love power too well.
Your command ends with the war.

You have tried to prolong your command by neglecting to end the war.

But the war is over.

You plan now to retain command while you impose your will upon the State. That is a menace to the Republic. We have been forced to convoke the Senate to discuss it.

The Senate has sanctioned the appointment of Tuditanus, and the list of the proscribed. It also commands that you give battle to Cæsar. [*He gives a paper.*]

[POMPEY *walks up stage slowly, then down. He stands at table, fronting them.*]

POMPEY

What do you expect me to say, Conscript Fathers? That I refuse to obey this order?

I could refuse.

If I were Cæsar, or Lentulus. Or you, Domitius, or Metellus. I should refuse.

And my soldiers, or Cæsar's there, would work my will on a Senate which had so insulted me.

But I am Pompey the Great. I am bound by my military oath.

Do not think to humble me. Death is a little thing to the loss of conscience.

Death is easier than life to me.

But even if I die, Rome will be a prey to unscrupulous men. There is no hope for Rome. She ends here. Disaster begins.

But for me, you would now be beggars at Cæsar's doors. I saved Rome from Cæsar.

And now Rome is to beg her life from you. You have used Pompey the Great to ruin her.

But you have first to fight for her.

You shall give your sin a dignity, by risking your lives for it. [*He strikes the gong.*]

[*Enter an* Aide]

[*To* Aide.] Give the signal for battle. [*Exit* Aide.]
You have your will, now.
This is the end.
And at the end, think what it is which you destroy.
Rome is nothing to you. Only the reward of greed, and hate, and pride.
The city where justice was born.
Look beyond your passions, at what Rome is. It is the state of Rome, not passion, which concerns us now.
A little while ago she was a market-town, governed by farmers. Now she rules Europe.
And in herself no change. Cramped still. Fettered. The same laws. The same rulers. Like iron on her heart.
And forty years of civil war. All my life. A blind turbulent heaving towards freedom.

[*Without, a confused noise as of many men stirring from sleep. Shouted orders are clearly heard above the murmur.*]

THE ORDERS

Fall in. Dress. Cohort. By the right. Cohort, to the left, wheel. Eyes left. Cohort. Fifers, three paces to the——Attention, etc., etc., Cohort. Salute, etc.

[*In a moment's silence a trumpet blows outside the tent. Cheering.*]

POMPEY

Five minutes ago I had Rome's future in my hand. She was wax to my seal. I was going to free her.

[332]

Now is the time to free her. You can tear the scales and the chains from her. You can make her a State so spendid that Athens would be a dust-heap to her.

You will not.

You will drive her back three centuries, so that you may wreak your passions on her.

Go on, then. Destroy her. Or be destroyed.

Whether you win or lose, Rome ends.

[*A pause. Orders without*]

ORDERS

The cohorts will advance in——Cohort, halt. Ground arms. Attention. Form four deep. Attention. By the right. Quick march. Cohort. Cohort. To the left. Turn.

DOMI.

What orders have you?

[*For the next minute or two a noise of troops moving*]

POMPEY

You have fought this battle many times in your hearts. [*He flings the doors wide, showing a bright dawn.*] Now you will fight it in earnest. You will fight the wild beasts whom I could have starved like beasts.

Go to your divisions.

[*The* Generals *go out silently.* POMPEY *stands by the table*]

ORDERS

Cohort. Halt. Ground arms. Attention. Form four deep. Cohort. Left turn.

[333]

[*Enter* PHILIP. POMPEY *does not look at him. Fifes of a cohort pass*]

PHILIP

Do you want me, my lord?

POMPEY

[*Turning.*] Can you sing, Philip?

PHILIP

Sing, my lord?

POMPEY

Yes.

PHILIP

I don't know, my lord.

POMPEY

What was that song we had? That night. In the Asian wars. When we broke Mithridates?

PHILIP

[*Hesitating.*] I don't know whether I can, my lord.

POMPEY

Sing.

PHILIP

I'll try, my lord. [*He repeats.*]
Though we are ringed with spears, though the last hope is gone,
Romans stand firm, the Roman dead look on.
Before our sparks of life blow back to him who gave,
Burn clear, brave hearts, and light our pathway to the grave.

[334]

THE TRAGEDY OF POMPEY THE GREAT

POMPEY

Take my purple, Philip. [*He flings his purple aside.*]

A CENTURION

Eyes left. Salute.

A COHORT PASSING

Hail! Pompey. Imperator. [*Trumpets.*]

CURTAIN

ACT III

The Poop of a Lesbian Merchantman of the First Century B. C.

On each side, the bulwark of a ship, painted green. There are gaps, or gangways, in these bulwarks, so that people may go down the ship's side into boats.

At back of stage, the poop-rail, also painted green. A wooden belfry with a bell stands upon the middle of the poop-rail.

On each side of the bell is a ladder leading down to the main deck. Gaps in the poop-rail allow people to reach the poop by these ladders.

Above the deck, sloping from amidships like a tent, is an awning of blue and white baftas. This awning has a flap, which falls at back of stage, hiding the poop from the main deck. On both sides of the stage the awning is secured by stops to guys above the ship's bulwarks.

In the centre of the stage (if the theatre stage is so built) is a hatchway, surrounded by a raised white rim or coaming. This leads down to the cabins.

Behind it is a mast (painted "mast colour") which rises up through the awning.

Round the mast is a square of timbers, like a stout fence. These are the bitts, to which the running rigging is belayed.

Stout ropes and blocks lead along the mast.

Attendants, Sailors, *etc., etc., keep always to the starboard side, out of respect to* POMPEY, *who uses the weather, or honourable side.*

At the rising of the curtain Captain *is standing by poop-rail, looking at the men at work forward. The* Boy *holds up the awning so that he can see under it.*]

[336]

THE CHANTYMAN

[*Heard off, amid a click of pawls.*] Old Pompey lost Pharsalia fight.

THE SAILORS

[*Heaving at the forward capstan.*]
Mark well what I do say.

THE CHANTY

Old Pompey lost Pharsalia fight.

THE SAILORS

And Cæsar now is the world's delight.
And I'll go no more a-roving,
　　With Pompey the Great.
　　A-roving.　A-roving.
Since roving's been my ru-i-n,
I'll go no more a-roving
　　With Pompey the Great.

THE MATE

[*From far forward.*] Avast heaving. Walk back. [*Pause.*]
Unship your bars.

THE CAPTAIN

That'll do, boy. [Boy *drops awning.*] Now we're riding to a
single anchor.

THE BOY

Yes, sir.

THE CAPT.

[*Kindly.*] D' you know what little port that is yonder?

THE BOY

No, sir.

[337]

THE CAPT.

That's Pelusium, in Egypt. This is the Nile.

THE BOY

Is this where the King of Egypt lives, sir?

THE CAPT.

[*Pointing.*] Over yonder. Where all those soldiers are. That's where the King of Egypt is. Young King Ptolemy, who Pompey sent the letter to, after Cæsar beat him.

THE BOY

Why does Pompey come to him, sir? He's only a boy.

THE CAPT.

It was through Pompey he became king. And there are lots of Pompey's old soldiers yonder. An army of them.

THE BOY

What a lot of ships, sir.

THE CAPT.

[*Anxiously.*] Ye-es. A lot of ships.

THE BOY

They must be men of war, sir. There's a bugle. Oh, look, sir, at those big galleys. Hark at the bugles. [*Bugle-calls off.*] Is that to call the slaves, sir?

THE CAPT.

[*Looking under the sharp of his hand.*] Is that a boat putting off from the flagship? That big galley nearest to us?

[338]

The Boy

Yes, sir. Don't they pull well, sir? They're coming to us.

The Capt.

Quick. Get the red side-ropes rove.
[*The* Boy *reeves side-ropes, which he takes from locker by the
gangway.*]

The Boy

[*At his work.*] They're hailing us, sir.

A Cry

Ship ahoy! Ahoy, you!

The Capt.

Hulloh!

A Cry

What ship is that?

The Capt.

The *Fortune*. From Cyprus.

A Cry

Have you Lord Pompey aboard you?

The Capt.

Yes. Lord Pompey's aboard us. Down below. [*Pause.*]

The Boy

They seem to be talking together, sir.

A Cry

When did you leave Cyprus?

THE CAPT.

[*Humbly.*] At noon, sir, yesterday. [*A pause.*]

A CRY

D'ye hear there? You're not to send any boat ashore.

THE CAPT.

Ay, ay, my lord.

THE BOY

They're pulling back to the ship, sir.

THE CAPT.

[*Testily.*] Quick. Dip our streamer. Dip our streamer, boy.
Don't you know enough for that? [*The* Boy *runs aft and dips
the streamer.*] Again. Now. Once more. Here. [*He beckons.*]
Go below quietly, and see if Lord Pompey's stirring. [*The* Boy
goes down the hatch. The Captain *walks up and down, uneasily
looking at the distant ships.*] No. No. I don't like it. [*He
shakes his head.*] I wish we were out of it. [*Re-enter* Boy.]
Well, lad?

THE BOY

Yes, sir. Lord Pompey's up, sir.

THE CAPT.

Ah. [*Kindly.*] You'll be able to tell them, when you get
home, that you were shipmates with Pompey the Great.

THE BOY

Yes, sir.

THE CAPT.

That's what comes of being a sailor.

[340]

THE BOY

Please, sir.

THE CAPT.

Yes, boy.

THE BOY

What is the name of that mountain, sir?

THE CAPT.

That? That's Mount Cassius. There's a tale about that
mountain. Something about a king. Or some one to die there.
I forget. Here. What are they doing aboard those galleys?

THE BOY

They are filling full of soldiers. Soldiers are putting off to
them in boats.

THE CAPT.

[*Striking the bell once.*] Mr. Mate, there!

THE MATE

[*Below, out of sight.*] Sir.

[*Enter* MATE]

THE CAPT.

Oh, Mr. Mate. Here, boy. What are you listening at? Go
forward. And if you want to see your mother again, you pray.
Pray that King Ptolemy'll let you.

[*Exit* BOY]

[*The* Captain *speaks intently to the* Mate.] Look here. We're
done. Pompey isn't wanted here. Those eunuchs have put
the King against him. See those galleys? They're getting
ready to sink us. If you see one of them getting under way,

cut the cable. Don't wait for orders. Cut the cable, and hoist sail.

THE MATE

I'll make all ready, sir.

THE CAPT.

It makes your blood boil, though. A week back they'd have crawled all round Pompey for a chance to kiss his footman's boots. Now they're going to drive him out.

THE MATE

Well, sir. You can't expect gratitude from a king, they say. The world's wide. There's other lands besides Egypt. Egypt's got trouble enough, without Pompey. What did he come here for? That's what I don't see.

THE CAPT.

He's had a misfortune. One doesn't know where to turn when one's had a misfortune. And having a wife and that. Very likely he's beside himself, for all he doesn't take on.

THE MATE

He'd ought to have come with his fleet. That would have frightened them. Coming alone like this makes people think he's a beggar. D' you think they'll ram us?

THE CAPT.

I don't trust them.

THE MATE

The hands don't trust them, neither.

THE CAPT.

Ah! the growlers. What do they say?

THE MATE

They're saying they didn't sign on to be rammed.

THE CAPT.

They signed for what I choose.

THE MATE

Yes, sir. They're afraid of the soldiers and that.

THE CAPT.

They got sense. If I were Pompey, I'd run for it. A man with a wife like that didn't ought to seek trouble. Well. God send pay-day! Watch the hands and stand by. That's your job.

THE MATE

I'll make all clear, sir. Bosun, there!

BOSUN

[*Off.*] Sir?

THE MATE

Overhaul your gear. Have all ready for getting under way.

BOSUN

Have all ready, sir. I will, sir. [*Whistle.*]

THE MATE

[*Going.*] There's his steward, sir.

[*Exit*]

THE CAPT.

Steward.

PHILIP

[*Entering*.] Sir.

THE CAPT.

Oh! steward. [PHILIP *approaches*.] Look here, steward.
What's Pompey's object in coming here?

PHILIP

He's come to see the King.

THE CAPT.

Is he come to ask for shelter?

PHILIP

He's come to raise another army out of all his old soldiers
here.

THE CAPT.

He won't get any soldiers here. They're all at the wars.
The young King's fighting his sister.

PHILIP

That will be patched up. The young King thinks the world
of my master. He'll do what Pompey wants.

THE CAPT.

He hasn't answered Pompey's letter yet.

PHILIP

No?

THE CAPT.

We've been told not to send a boat ashore.

PHILIP

Well, all I know is, the young King longs to honour Pompey.
But for Pompey the old King would have died a poor flute-
player in Ephesus. You can see for yourself he's coming.
There's his state barge at the jetty. Look. They're out on the
roofs. There's music.

[*Enter* POMPEY]

THE CAPT.

[*Unconvinced.*] It may be as you say, steward. Ah.
[*He starts, salutes, and hastily crosses to the starboard, or lee
side.*]

PHILIP

My lord. Do you know what day it is, my lord?

POMPEY

What day is it?

PHILIP

The day of your triumph, my lord. Your Asian triumph.
Thirteen years ago.

POMPEY

Is it so long ago? That was a great day.

PHILIP

Yes, indeed, my lord, I'll never forget that day. We always
like to keep it up with a little something among ourselves.
We brought you a few figs, my lord. They're only Cretans.
[*He offers figs.*] Just in honour of the day, my lord. If you
would accept of them.

POMPEY

[*Taking and tasting.*] Thank you, Philip. [*To the* Captain.]
This old servant of mine is always bent on spoiling me.

[345]

THE CAPT.

Yes, my lord. So I see.

PHILIP

[*Going.*] I'm sure I hope to-day will be a great day too, my lord.

[*Exit* PHILIP]

POMPEY

It should be, Philip. [*He lays figs on weather fife-rail.*] Captain!

THE CAPT.

Yes, my lord.

POMPEY

Has any one come aboard for me?

THE CAPT.

No, my lord.

POMPEY

Thank you.

THE CAPT.

Beg pardon, my lord.

POMPEY

Well?

THE CAPT.

The flagship has ordered us not to send a boat ashore. I thought I ought to report it, my lord.

POMPEY

Thank you, Captain. A fine fleet here.

[346]

THE CAPT.

[*Meaningly.*] They seem to be getting their crews aboard.

POMPEY

What speed have those galleys?

THE CAPT.

Those there, my lord? They might make seventeen. That's
with good rowers. And dead calm. And the ships new out of
dock. In a wind like this, they wouldn't make more'n about
eight. They can't work their oars in a sea-way. [*Pause.*] Now's
the time, my lord, if you think of putting to sea. By and by,
may be, they'll be able to stop us.

POMPEY

Thank you, Captain.

THE CAPT.

I'll report any boat, my lord.

[*Exit*]

[*Enter* CORNELIA]

CORN.

Has the King sent?

POMPEY

No.

CORN.

No answer?

POMPEY

Not yet.

CORN.

Can he know we are here?

[347]

POMPEY

Yes. He will come. He will come in person.

CORN.

Why has he not come already?

POMPEY

It is early.

CORN.

Do you think it is safe to wait? It is ominous. This silence. And all those ships. And the people crowding on the roofs. What if the King be against us?

POMPEY

He cannot be. Do not be afraid.

[*Enter* THEOPHANES]

THEO.

Magnus. They have sent an order. We are not to send a boat ashore. They are plotting something.

POMPEY

If they were plotting, they would ask us to come ashore.

CORN.

But why should we not send a boat, if they are friendly?

POMPEY

The King will be coming in person. Then there was plague in Cyprus. We have not got a clean bill.

CORN.

But to be ordered.

Theo.

The Admiral should have come.

Pompey

This is a merchantman. We are not under Roman colours.

Corn.

The Captain there is anxious. Look at him.

Theo.

Ask him.

Pompey

It is necessary for the world that I see King Ptolemy.

[*The* Captain *flings down the halliard coil and goes below*]

Strange. Is there any Cassius with Ptolemy?

Corn.

Lucius Cassius is dead, surely.

Theo.

There's Quintus Cassius. But he is in Spain.

Corn.

Is there not Cneius Cassius? He was legate in one of Cæsar's legions?

Pompey

Cneius? I thought he was killed?

Theo.

I could find out. Sextus would know.

Pompey

No. Do not wake him. It is absurd.

CORN.

Why do you ask?

POMPEY

When I was in Africa, at the time, an old woman bade me beware of Cassius. I have not thought of it for thirty-four years. An old black hag. Sitting in the sun, there. By the ruins of Carthage. Geminius was riding with me. She hobbled up on a crutch and plucked at my rein. "Young captain. You beware of Cassius. You that ride so proud, beware of Cassius. The sand is falling."

CORN.

Why should you think of that now?

POMPEY

Because I am going to victory, as I was then. [*The* Hands *come aft.*

THE MATE

[*Following.*] Get down off the poop. If you want anything, send a man aft.

1ST HAND

Begging your pardon, your honour. We want to speak.

2ND HAND

We mean to speak.

3RD HAND

We want to know why we're brought here.

4TH HAND

And how long we're to stay here.

[350]

2ND HAND

He's been beaten.

4TH HAND

He's got no friends. Our lives are as good to us as his is.

THE MATE

Down off the poop! Down with you! Bosun, there! [*Struggling.*]

POMPEY

What is the matter? [*Struggling ends.   Pause.*]

1ST HAND

Begging your pardon, your honour. We wanted to see the Captain.

POMPEY

[*To the* Mate.] What is their grievance?

THE MATE

Some more of their fancies, my lord. [*To the* Hands.] Get over to leeward.

POMPEY

They seem a good lot. What is it?

THE MATE

Oh, the Captain'll soon settle it, my lord. [*To the* Hands.] You wait.

[*Exit by hatch to find* Captain.   *Pause.*   POMPEY *takes a half turn, and then speaks.*]

POMPEY

[*To* Hands.] Of what do you complain?

[351]

1st Hand

Begging your pardon, you honour. We'd rather wait for the Captain.

Pompey

What is wrong, though? Tell me.

1st Hand

I'd rather not say, my lord.

Pompey

[*Takes a half turn, and speaks again.*] Come. What is the trouble? Is it the food? Or the drink?

1st Hand

Begging your pardon, your honour. We don't like the look of things.

Pompey

What things?

1st Hand

Begging your honour's pardon, the ships there.

2nd Hand

They're getting ready to sink us.

Pompey

Why do you think that?

3rd Hand

You can see the soldiers going aboard them, can't you?

1st Hand

[*To* 3rd.] Here now. Here.

[352]

3RD HAND

[*To* 1ST.] What's wrong? It's the truth. Isn't it?

POMPEY

So they are going aboard to sink us? Why should they sink us?

3RD HAND

Because you're aboard us. [*He stands out.*] You're not wanted here. You're no good to Ptolemy. Cæsar's the man, now, not you. You're no more than what we are.

[*To the* Hands.] And we're to be drowned, are we, because his mightiness that was is worth more dead than alive? He's down. He's no one. He's had fellows die for him for forty years. It's time he learned what it feels like himself.

4TH HAND

That's what I say.

3RD HAND

Come on!

2ND HAND

Man the halliards.

3RD HAND

We'll carry you to Cæsar. And sell you.

POMPEY

Stand back!
You say that the soldiers are coming to sink us?
There are five thousand troops there, and fifty ships.
Are they all coming to sink us?
It seems a large force to sink one ship, manned by such a company.

[353]

3RD HAND

Here. Look here!

1ST HAND

[*To* 3RD.] You'll get us hanged.

2ND HAND

Give him sheet.

4TH HAND

How about us? That's what I say.

POMPEY

If I am still so terrible, I must save you. I will go to the flagship yonder. Man your boat.

3RD HAND

You will go to the flagship?

1ST HAND

[*Alarmed.*] Look at her. There.

4TH HAND

Look.

2ND HAND

Look at her. She's got her oars out.

1ST HAND

She's coming. We're gone up.

3RD HAND

Then he'll go first.

1ST HAND

[*Holding him.*] No, you don't.

[354]

[*Enter* Captain]

THE CAPT.

She's coming, my lord. Shall I cut? We might do it, even now.

POMPEY

She is not coming. And if she were, what is death?

THE CAPT.

Hard times for the widow, my lord.

POMPEY

[*To the men.*] Leave the ropes.
Do you think the soul can be quenched with water? Or cut with swords? Or burned?

3D HAND

I know my body can, my lord.

POMPEY

You do well to fear death. Go to your place.
[*Musingly.*] If death can crush what comprehends heaven? Why! We are in a bad way, Captain.

[*The* Hands *file off, quietly.* POMPEY *looks down on the main deck. The* Captain *stands apart anxiously watching the flagship.* CORNELIA *and* THEOPHANES *eye each other.*]

CORN.

Is the flagship coming?

THEO.

She is ready to come.

[355]

CORN.

To sink us?

THEO.

She could sink us.

CORN.

I cannot bear this.

[POMPEY *turning, walks towards them*]

THEO.

We ought to have gone to our fleet. We're helpless like this.

CORN.

Magnus. This isn't what we planned.

POMPEY

Let me reassure you. Egypt is friendly to me.
I saved her independence. I made the elder Ptolemy King.
The young King is my ward, bound to me by intimate ties.
Those troops are veterans of my Asian Army.

THEO.

The young King's at his wits' end with civil war. How can
he begin a war with Cæsar?

POMPEY

Cæsar will begin a war with him whether he takes me or re-
jects me. Cæsar wants Egypt, as Ptolemy very well knows.

CORN.

[*Bitterly.*] And we are suppliants to him. We Romans. To
whom they should strike their flags. [*After a pause, quickly.*]
See if they refuse to salute us.

[356]

THEO.
We should know what to expect then.

CORN.
Oh, let us be certain. Hoist your colours.

POMPEY
It is not time yet. I will hoist them when the watch ends.
[*The* Captain *strikes the bell once*]

THE CAPT.
One bell, my lord.

POMPEY
The watch is nearly out?

THE CAPT.
Nearly, my lord. Will you hoist any colours, my lord?

POMPEY
My consular colours.

THE CAPT.
I'm only a merchantman, my lord. If they should refuse
to salute, my lord?

POMPEY
You will go alongside the flagship there, and order her to
salute.

THE CAPT.
[*Going.*] I am all ready to get under way, my lord. Bosun,
there! Stand by. Mr. Mate. Boy, there!

[*He goes to the break of the poop and looks down on main deck.*]
Are your colours bent on, Centurion?

CENTURION

[*Off.*] Tell him, yes.

BOY

[*Off.*] All ready to hoist, sir.

THE CAPT.

[*Coming to* POMPEY.] All ready, my lord. Will you make
eight bells, my lord?

POMPEY

When it is time. [*He paces leisurely.*]

THEO.

Have you your tables?

THEO.

Yes.

POMPEY

I shall want you to take notes.

[*To* CORNELIA]

What was that passage about the soul? We were reading it
that day at Alba, when the women brought you their first-
fruits? Our first year. We were in the garden. You were
reading to me. There was a verse about the soul.

CORN.

The upright soul is safe?

[358]

POMPEY

Yes. That was the verse. I have always loved Alba. I was there as a child. We were happy there, that year.

CORN.

Very happy. And that day. The doves came, picking the spilled grain. And at night there was a moon.

POMPEY

All the quiet valley. And the owls were calling. Those little grey owls. Make eight bells, Captain.

[*The* Captain *makes it. The* Bosun *pipes the colours up*]

THE CAPT.

Not so fast there, boy.

[*Eight bells is echoed over the harbour from ship to ship.* POM-PEY *and* THEOPHANES *raise their right hands. Perhaps* COR-NELIA *ought to veil*]

THEO.

The flagship is hoisting her ensign. [*Bugles off.*]

CORN.

Will she salute? Will she salute? There.

THEO.

There. She dips it.

CORN.

They all salute.

THEO.

Then we are safe.

[359]

POMPEY

That is settled, then. I am to be received. The King expects
me.

THE CAPT.

I beg pardon, my lord. I think his Majesty the King is
coming off to fetch you. The barge is putting off, my lord.
[*Approaching.*] No, my lord; it is not the King, it is one of the
pearl-boats, my lord, which work the pearl-beds here.

POMPEY

Something of the kind. What do you make of her?

THE CAPT.

They pull very badly, my lord. They pull like soldiers.

POMPEY

They are soldiers. I see the gleam of armour.

THEO.

Seven soldiers.

THE CAPT.

Am I to let them alongside, my lord?

POMPEY

Wait.

THEO.

Has he sent a boat like that for you?

CORN.

You cannot go in that old boat.

[360]

THEO.

Magnus. There is some treachery.

CORN.

Cneius. It is a dreadful risk. To stay.

POMPEY

It is necessary. I must carry this thing through. You would rather I ran the risk than let the world become—what it will become.

CORN.

Much rather.

POMPEY

You will understand, then.

THE CAPT.

They are hailing, my lord. Would the lady go below a little? They might fling a dart on board.

CORN.

The air is fresher here.

SEPT.

[*Off.*] Hail! Pompey. Imperator.

THE CAPT.

We could still run for it, my lord.

POMPEY

We must not show that we mistrust them.

[361]

SEPT.

[*Off.*] Hail, Pompey, Imperator!

POMPEY

Have your men ready to salute.

SEPT.

[*Off.*] In bow.

CORN.

Cneius. Cneius.

POMPEY

There is no danger. Have you the little book with my speech
to Ptolemy?

CORN.

Here it is.

SEPT.

[*Off.*] Toss your starboard oars. Way enough.

POMPEY

Company there. Salute.

THE CAPT.

The call, there.

[*Enter* SEPTIMIUS, *a Roman military tribune, with* ACHILLAS
EGYPTIAN, *both in military dress. The* Bosun *pipes the side
for each of them.*]

POMPEY

[*Advancing.*] You come from King Ptolemy? [SEPTIMIUS
salutes, ACHILLAS *bows.*]

ACHIL.

From King Ptolemy. He sends you royal greeting.

[362]

POMPEY

He wishes to see me?

ACHIL.

He wish to see you. To be your friend.

POMPEY

Shall I bring the ship alongside the quay there?

ACHIL.

There is much mud and sandbanks. There would be no water for this galley. You have to take a boat.

POMPEY

[*Glancing at ships.*] Your fleet is getting under way here?

ACHIL.

[*Shrugging his shoulders.*] Ah? Will you come into my boat?

POMPEY

She is not a very handsome boat.

ACHIL.

No? It is bad weather sometimes.

POMPEY

[*To* SEPTIMIUS.] I think I should know you, my friend. You and I have served together? [SEPTIMIUS *nods, but does not answer.*]

Where was it? I know your face. [*No answer.*]

A long time ago. Eighteen years ago. In the war against the pirates? [*Pause.*] Was it not? [*No answer.*]

[363]

You commanded a company in my guard. [*Pause.*] You did something? You burnt a ship one night? You paddled out alone and set fire to her? I remember you. I gave you a sword. You are wearing it now.

SEPT.

[*Turning to the boat, muttering to himself.*] I'm as good a man as you are.

ACHIL.

You come in my little boat. I take you to the King. The King is your friend. Lovely lady, the King want to see him.

CORN.

Yes.

POMPEY

I will follow you. Go down into the boat.

[ACHILLAS, *bowing, goes to gangway, where he stands, looking aft.*]

POMPEY

Now.

THEO.

Magnus. You mustn't go.

CORN.

Cneius Cneius. What do they mean?

THEO.

You mustn't go, Magnus.

POMPEY

My beloved! You must stay here. You must not come.

CORN.

My darling! What are they going to do?

[364]

POMPEY

What God wills.

Theophanes. If this is the end, I wish it to be the end. Those arrangements of the fleet. Cancel them. You understand. Go to Cato. Tell Cato to submit to Cæsar. War will only mean more bloodshed. He cannot stand against Cæsar. I could have.

Scipio's daughter. Make your father submit to Cæsar. Keep my sons out of it. Tell them. End the war. Life is very grand but there is something behind it. Something which strikes a mean. I had my hand on it. Come. Courage. These are Egyptians. [*To* CORNELIA.]

Captain. You must sail. Stand by.

What else is there? Asia. Theophanes. Asia must submit. Send to the Kings. The world must make what terms it can. This is all in the event. If this is the end. You understand? If not, you know my orders.

Philip. Scythes. Cotta. Go down into the boat.

PHILIP

My lord. I've served you a long time, my lord.

POMPEY

What is it, Philip? [COTTA *and* SCYTHES *go.*]

PHILIP

My lord. My old, beloved lord.

POMPEY

Why, Philip. We are the only ones left. We are two old Sulla's men. Have you my cloak in the boat?

PHILIP

Forty years, my lord.

POMPEY

The broidered one. [*To* CORNELIA.] Your gift. Come. Carry it down, man.

PHILIP

I wish it was to begin all over again.

[*Exit*]

ACHIL.

Will you come into the boat? The King is waiting.

CORN.

Cneius. My husband. My husband.

POMPEY

God only lends us.
If the King keep faith. We shall have time. Time for what we must imagine. If not. We know our love. The gods treasure you. [*He goes towards gangway.*]
Remember, Captain.
Theophanes. If I fail, you must warn Lentulus.

[*He goes to gangway. The* Bosun *starts to pipe the side.* POMPEY *turns to the* Boy. Bosun *stops his pipe.* POMPEY *takes figs from fife-rail and gives them to the* Boy.]

Can you eat figs? [*The* Boy *mumbles.*]
What is your name? [*The* Boy *bursts into tears.*]

ACHIL.

[*At gangway.*] Give me your hand. I take your hand down.

POMPEY

[*Pausing in the gangway and looking back. Sadly. To* THE-
OPHANES.]

"Into a tyrant's court the truly brave
Goes proudly, though he go to die a slave."

[*He goes down. The* Bosun *pipes the side*]

SEPT.

[*Coldly.*] Back your port oars. Shove off. Give way together.

THE CAPT.

[*Softly to* Mate.] Go on there. Man your halliards.

THE MATE

Take the turns off. Stretch it along. Softly now. Stand by.
[*The* Seamen *coming behind* CORNELIA, *man the halliards.
The* Chantyman *stands on the bitts. All look after the boat.*]

THE CHANTY

There's a lot of troops ashore.

THE MATE

S's't.

CORN.

They are not talking to him.

THEO.

He is reading his speech. [*Pause.*] He organises everything.
Cæsar improvises.

CORN.

There they go out of the sun.

[367]

THEO.

The hill casts a long shadow.

CORN.

What is the name of the hill?

THE CAPT.

Mount Cassius, lady.

THEO.

[*Quickly.*] They are coming with banners.   Look.

CORN.

He is safe.

THEO.

There comes the King. Hark! Trumpets. They're saluting.
He is standing up to land.

CORN.

Ah! Swords. He is stabbed.

THEO.

Ah! you gods.   You gods!

CORN.

Oh! He is killed! He is killed! He is killed! [*She collapses.*]

THEO.

[*Covering his eyes.*] The devils! The devils!

THE MATE

They stabbed him in the back.

ANTISTIA

It's ebb-tide now, my beauty.

THE CAPT.

[*Yelling.*] Cut the cable. [*Chopping forward.*]

A VOICE

All gone, the cable.

THE MATE

Let fall.

A VOICE

All gone.

THE MATE.

Sheet home. Hoist away.

THE MEN

Ho. [*They haul.*]

THE CHANTY

Away ho! [*The* Men *haul.*]
[*He intones in a clear loud voice. The* Seamen *sing the chorus, hauling.*
[*This song is sung like an ordinary halliard chanty. The chorus is to the tune of the old chanty of "Hanging Johnny." The solo will be intoned clearly, without tune. It goes to fast time, the chorus starting almost before the soloist ends his line. The* Men *must haul twice, in the proper manner, in each chorus. The hauling will have for natural accompaniments the whine of the three-sheaved block, the grunt of the parrels and the slat from the great sail.*]

THE CHANTY

Kneel to the beautiful women who bear us this strange brave fruit.

THE MEN

Away, i-oh.

THE CHANTY

Man with his soul so noble: man half god and half brute.

THE MEN

So away, i-oh.

THE CHANTY

Women bear him in pain that he may bring them tears.

CHORUS
THE CHANTY

He is a king on earth, he rules for a term of years.

CHORUS
THE CHANTY

And the conqueror's prize is dust and lost endeavour.

CHORUS
THE CHANTY

And the beaten man becomes a story for ever.

CHORUS
THE CHANTY

For the gods employ strange means to bring their will to be.

CHORUS
THE CHANTY

We are in the wise gods' hands and more we cannot see.

CHORUS

So away, i–oh.

A VOICE

High enough.

THE MATE

Lie to. [*The* Seamen *lay to the fall.*] Make fast.
Coil up.

A VOICE

All clear to seaward.

THE CAPT.

Pipe down. [*The* Bosun *pipes the belay.*]

CURTAIN

EPILOGUE SPOKEN BY COTTA

Pompey was a great Captain, riding among Kings, a King,
Now he lies dead on the sand, an old blind tumbled thing
Fate has her secret way to humble captains thus
Fate comes to every one and takes the light from us
And the beginning and the end are darkened waters where no
    lights be
But after many days the brook finds ocean
And the ship puts to sea.

NOTES

On the Appearance of Pompey

PORTRAITS exist of Cneius Pompeius Magnus. The most important of these is a marble bust at Copenhagen. Several likenesses are to be found on the gold and silver coins struck by his son, Sextus, in Spain. Plutarch says of him that, "being come to man's state, there appeared in his gesture and behaviour a grave and princely majesty. His hair also stood a little upright, and the cast and soft moving of his eyes had a certain resemblance (as they said) of the statues and images of Alexander the Great." This resemblance may still be traced.

At the time of his murder he was fifty-eight years old, a powerful, very active man, in the prime of life. His bust, evidently done towards the end of his life, shows that his hair, which was thick, coarse, and worn rather long, still tended to stand a little upright. The head is of great breadth at the eyes. The brow is low and lined with three deep lines of wrinkles going right across it in irregular M shape. The eyebrows are well marked: the supra-orbital ridge is heavy. The nose is full and strong, with the broad base which is so good an index of intellectual power. The septum is of great breadth. The mouth is of that kindly tightness which one sees in the portraits of some of our Admirals. Below the mouth is a deep horizontal dent. The chin is not cloven. The face is lined a good deal. A deep straight wrinkle runs from each side of the nose to the puckered angles of the mouth. The eyes are crowsfooted. There are no indications as to the colour of the hair and eyes. The shape of the head suggests the brown or fair type of man. At the time of his death he was perhaps grizzled.

No known portrait exists of any of the other characters. Metellus came of a family once distinguished for pointed noses, Domitius of a family once famed for red hair. Cornelia was famous for a grave and gentle beauty. She was young, though already a widow, when Pompey married her, a few months before the civil trouble began.

On the Fate of the Persons in this Tragedy

Philip. After religiously burning his master's body on the seashore, disappears from history.

Metellus Scipio. Fled from Pharsalia to Africa, where he carried on the war until 46 B. C., when he was defeated by Cæsar at Thapsus. Flying from Africa by sea, in bad weather, he was forced to put into the port of Hippo, where one of Cæsar's fleets lay at anchor. A battle followed. He is said to have drowned himself shortly before his ship was sunk.

Cn. Pompeius Theophanes. Returned to Italy, and was pardoned by Cæsar. He attained great fame as a writer. After his death the Lesbians paid him divine honours. His son held office under Augustus.

Marcus Cato. After Pharsalia, joined Scipio in Africa, and held command under him. He killed himself in Utica, shortly after the battle of Thapsus, so that he might not live to see the final extinction of liberty. His son was killed at Philippi, "valiantly fighting against Augustus," four years later.

Lucius Domitius Ahenobarbus. Was killed (some say by Mark Antony) either in the battle, or in the rout, of Pharsalia, at which he commanded the great brigade of horse, on the left of Pompey's army.

Marcus Acilius Glabrio. Continued in Cæsar's service, and rose to be governor of Achaia.

Lucius Lucceius. Returned to Rome, and received Cæsar's pardon. He was praised by Cicero for the excellence of his historical writings.

Lucius Afranius. After Pharsalia, joined Scipio in Africa, and held command under him, till the battle of Thapsus. While riding through Mauretania, on his way to Spain, after that disaster, he was ambushed and taken by Cæsar's lieutenant, P. Sitius. A few days later, the troops of Sitius killed him in a camp riot.

Lentulus Spinther. After Pharsalia, fled to Rhodes, where he was refused permission to land. He set sail again "much against his will," and either "perished ingloriously" or disappeared from history.

Achillas Egyptian. Was killed by Arsinöe (Ptolemy's sister) and the eunuch Ganymed in the year after Pompey's murder.

On the House of Pompey, After the Murder

Cornelia. After seeing her husband killed, fled to Cyrene, and thence to Rome, where, in time, Pompey's ashes were brought to her. She is said to have buried them "in a town of hers by the city of Alba," in Liguria.

Cn. Pompeius Magnus, the Triumvir's eldest son, by his third wife, Mucia, held Corcyra for a time, showing courage and bold strategic ideas. On hearing of his father's death, he went to Spain, where he raised a great army. He was defeated at the bloody battle of Munda, in the year 45. Soon after the battle, he was betrayed, taken and killed. His head was carried to Seville and exposed there to the public gaze.

Sextus Pompeius Magnus. The younger son (also by Mucia) continued the war in Africa, with Cato's party, till after the battle of Thapsus. He then joined his brother in Spain. After

Cæsar's murder, he was proscribed by Octavian, and took the seas, with a fleet, burning, sinking and intercepting commerce, till Octavian came to terms. On the recommencement of war between them, his fleet was beaten by Octavian's fleet under Agrippa. After trying vainly to beat up a force in Asia, he was taken and put to death at Miletus (probably by the order of Mark Antony) in the year 35. He left a daughter whose fate is uncertain. She was with him in Asia in 36.

Pompeia. The daughter (also by Mucia) married Faustus, the son of Sulla, who was killed with Afranius in the mutiny of the troops of P. Sitius, in Africa in 46. She afterwards married L. Cornelius Cinna. It is not known when she died; but it is certain that she predeceased her brother, Sextus. She had a son by Cornelius Cinna, who came to be Consul in A. D. 5. What became of her children by Faustus is not known.

And all their passionate hearts are dust,
And dust the great idea that burned
In various flames of love and lust
Till the world's brain was turned.

God, moving darkly in men's brains,
Using their passions as his tool,
Brings freedom with a tyrant's chains
And wisdom with the fool.

Blindly and bloodily we drift,
Our interests clog our hearts with dreams.
God make my brooding soul a rift
Through which a meaning gleams.

Feb. 8, 1908.   *July 5, 1909.*

THE FAITHFUL

A TRAGEDY IN THREE ACTS

To
MY WIFE
THIS BOOK IS AFFECTIONATELY INSCRIBED

NOTE: This play is written to be played uninterruptedly, with out more break in the action than is necessary to get the actors off the stage and to raise the screen or curtain dividing the scenes.

There are only two scenes: one the front part of the stage, left quite bare, without decoration, but with a screen, set, or backcloth at the back, representing a Japanese landscape, with hills and water, all wintry and severe; the other, the back of the stage, visible when this screen is lifted, a room in a Japanese palace, very beautiful, but bare, save for a few flowers and a picture or two.

A few minutes may elapse between Acts I and II, and a slightly longer wait between Acts II and III.

PERSONS

ASANO, A Daimyo.
KURANO, his Counsellor.
HAZAMA.
SHODA:
KIRA, A Daimyo.
SAGISAKA, his Counsellor.
KAMEI, A Daimyo.
HONZO, his Counsellor.
A YOUTH of Kira's palace.
A WOMAN of Kira's palace.
THE ENVOY.

A POOR GIRL.
LADY KURANO.
A CAPTAIN of Kira's guards.
CHIKARA, Kurano's son.
FIRST RONIN.
SECOND do.
THIRD do.
FOURTH do.
FIFTH do.
A HERALD.
Guards, Nobles, Attendants, Ronin.

In Act I, Scene I, throughout Act II, and in Scenes I, II, and IV of Act III, the scene is: An open space near ASANO's palace.

In Act I, Scene II and in Act III, Scene III, the scene is: A room in Kira's palace.

TIME: Acts I and II, 10th March, 1701.
Act III, 10th March, 1702.

THE FAITHFUL

ACT I

SCENE I.—*The outer scene.* ASANO *alone, dawn. A shaft of light strikes colour.*

ASANO

[*Kneeling.*]   Light that my soul has followed, bless this beloved land, where I work with my men to make life nobler.   For now my work here is threatened by an evil man, who draws nearer daily, violating Right and Law.   [*He rises and stands listening.*]   Kurano.

KURANO

[*Off.*]   Is that you, Asano?

[KURANO *enters*]

ASANO

Yes, my dear friend, I have waited for you; I need not ask your news, you bring no good news; I see that in your face.

KURANO

No; no good news.   The Judges decided against us.

ASANO

You bring yourself at least.   Does your wife know?

KURANO

Yes.   I have sent to tell her.   The men are here, if you will speak with them; they all look to you to save them.

[381]

Asano

Let them come in. Do they guess that we have lost?

[Kurano *lifts a hand to the men*]

Kurano

Yes. They are all afraid of Kira. Come in, there.

[*The men come in and crowd about the lower steps*]

Voices

Asano! Master Asano! Save us and defend us, beloved master. Lord Kurano, beseech our master to help us!

Kurano

Still! Let the head man come forward. Stand there, Hazama. Our master will speak to you.

[Asano *comes forward*]

Voices

Master Asano! Master Asano! Defend us, master!

Asano

Friends and fellow-workers, it is now twenty years since I came among you on the death of my father. You know how, in that time, we have worked together, making this province one of the most fruitful, and quite the happiest, in the Empire. If I have failed in this or that, I know that I have won your friendship, and that you have been happy under me. Latterly, as you know, our happiness has been marred by the actions of an ambitious man, whom we now know as Lord Kira. Some of you can remember when that lord was a little boy, the son of a steward, in the house of old Lord Ashiza, who petted him for

[382]

his cleverness. As you know, presently, when he grew up, he ousted the old lord and took his province. Since then, all of you have seen his treacheries bringing him nearer to this valley of ours, till at last nothing but the hills kept him from us. Last week Lord Kira claimed the hills and occupied them with hired troops, so that we could no longer pasture there. I made my protest against the seizure. Lord Kurano here has just returned from the Courts where the protest has been heard. He will read the Judges' finding.

VOICES

Ah, our master has saved us!

HAZAMA

Silence, silence!

KURANO

The Judges have decided that the protest lodged by Lord Asano cannot stand, and that the head of the valley claimed by Lord Kira is, truly, Lord Kira's property, together with its inhabitants and their possessions. And to this they set their seals. [*A moan passes over the crowd.*]

HAZAMA

But the head of the valley is free land, between two lordships. It has been free for centuries. It cannot be Lord Kira's.

KURANO

The Judges have decided that it is.

FIRST RONIN

And all that mountain pasture, and the glen where our river rises, is to be his?

KURANO

Yes.

HAZAMA

So. Now he is at our throats.

ASANO

It is bad news; but not hopeless. We have failed in these Courts; but Lord Kira is not here yet. We may still stop him. We must turn, now, to our work. Meanwhile do not quarrel with Kira's men, whatever the provocation, and above all trust me, and be of good hope. After all, a way may be found. Dismiss, and to work, Hazama.

HAZAMA

We thank you, master Asano. God knows we trust you.

VOICES

Thank you, master.

HAZAMA

Dismiss now to work, as the master bids.   [*They go out.*]

KURANO

What hope have you, then?

ASANO

None.

KURANO

None?

ASANO

Only a faith, and that is shaken, that the triumph of the wicked is a short one.

KURANO

It was a wicked judgment; the Judges were bribed.

ASANO

It seems that Kira is to have this province. We shall be his next prey. And I have been thinking through the night how much this place means to me. I see that all this will have to end. Our life here and all that we have tried to do is at Kira's mercy. We muster some seventy men and boys; Kira since his marriage has a thousand. What can we do?

KURANO

Rebel and die.

ASANO

Yes, we could do that. But I want what we have sown to live. You know how my ancestors first came here. They were driven from home and roved till they reached this glen, where they could live at peace. I shall do that, Kurano. I shall give up and go, with all my people.

KURANO

Where to?

ASANO

To the outer islands.

KURANO

And leave this a prey to Kira?

ASANO

It is that already.

KURANO

Without a protest?

ASANO

What other protest can I make? My men are like my sons, they shall not be trampled out by Kira. I will carry them out of his reach.

KURANO

And when would you go?

ASANO

Soon.

KURANO

It will break your heart to leave this.

ASANO

Never mind, if I save my men from Kira. I only hesitate for your sake, for you have a wife and son, with a right to something better than exile.

KURANO

There is a kind of exile which is a grand career for any wife or son. . . . But, Asano, I say that you must not abandon this place, but meet Kira with arms, and bring it to civil war here. No one has dared that yet, so Kira has prospered. He is not a robber; he is nothing so noble; he is a knave. If you fight him he will draw back and it will come to the Commander's ears, and justice will be done.

ASANO

What justice, Kurano? What justice should I get in any Court in this land?

KURANO

The justice that every man like myself does you with his whole heart.

Asano

My dear Kurano, what Court in the land would not decide for Kira, the ready and the lucky, rather than for me, the friend of man? Kira would ask nothing better than for me to attack him. I am suspect, an innovator, an unorthodox. Every knight in the land would be glad to see me ruined. Besides . . . the worth of the law has been proved already in yesterday's case. My instinct tells me to withdraw, with all who stand by me.

Kurano

My instinct tells you to stand firm.

Asano

That course needs your power, which I have not got.

Kurano

Here it is, by you.

Asano

We must live by our own laws, Kurano. No angel is given two messages. I shall warn my people to-night that we shall abandon these old homes of ours. Leave word with Hazama that they muster.

Kurano

It will be a terrible night to your friends.

Asano

I expect the parting to have every circumstance of pain.

Kurano

You spoke a moment ago as though you were hated and Kira loved. Surely you must know that Kira has made enemies wherever he has gone.

Asano

He has made slaves, Kurano. His enemies are dead or beggared.

Kurano

He is feared, then. All who fear him would rally to the first man to stand against him.

Asano

Some things are given to me, Kurano, to know burningly. I know that Kira has a conquering star, and none can stand against him yet. His cup is not full. We will go into the wilderness with what we believe.

Kurano

You are making a mistake, Asano.

Asano

I see this too clearly for that.

Kurano

You are despairing.

Asano

I neither despair nor fear: I see.

Kurano

You take the men's view. They think that Kira is a power. They will find out their mistake too late.

Asano

They will have their freedom at least.

KURANO

Perhaps. I will tell Hazama to muster them after work to-night. They seem merry yonder. Listen! there! There agian.

[*A sound of clapping and cheering draws slowly nearer*]

ASANO

There is little cause for rejoicing in this place.

KURANO

What can they be cheering for?

VOICES

Victory. Asano. Victory. Saved. Victory.

ASANO

Can they have been fighting Kira's men?

KURANO

I hope so. Hark!

[*The* Men *appear*]

VOICES

Victory. Master Asano, they are ruined. Kira is ruined.

[*The* Men *crowd up*]

ASANO

How is Kira ruined?

KURANO

Keep back. Keep back. Let Hazama come forward. Let the head man speak; silence, the others.

Asano

What news have you, Hazama?

Hazama

Master Asano, we left you, even now, feeling that Lord Kira was at our throats; we had little hope but to be slaves, and worse than that for some of us. We went away in despair, Master Asano, and now a blessing has come upon us.

Asano

Can the decree be annulled, Kurano?

Kurano

No. What blessing, Hazama? How has a blessing come?

Hazama

We had gone but a little way, to the cross-roads by the bridge, when there came the noise of a horse and a man galloped up, a tall man, in a broidered cloak, riding a stallion which was all great flecks of foam. And when he pulled up, the wind blew the cloak back and we saw all gold, and never once for thirty years has the like been seen here. He was a trumpeter.

Kurano

Is this one of their visions?

Asano

I do not understand. What trumpeter?

Hazama

A trumpeter from the Presence. He blew a great blast on a trumpet, and cried out that we were to prepare.

Then he said if any of us had a complaint to make, or a petition to give, or suffered from any wrong, or were in fear or misery, we were to take heart.

KURANO

Yes?

HAZAMA

Because the very Presence has sent an Envoy here to right all troubles, master, and now Lord Kira will be driven back and we be at peace again.

VOICES

It is blessed news, master.

ASANO

Thank you, Hazama. Since the Envoy has come from the Presence, a thing unknown in our time, we may be sure that injustice will be redressed. Where is the Envoy?

HAZAMA

He is in the province already, master, and his Court is to be held to-day.

ASANO

Thank you. Let this news reassure you. Return now to your work, and be thankful to that August One who watches even over us, in this far corner.

HAZAMA

We are very mindful of Him, Master Asano.

VOICES

We give thanks to Him for this doing of justice.

[They go out.]

ASANO

This alters everything. I shall go at once to the Envoy's Court and appeal against Kira.

KURANO

I will come with you. Perhaps the Court has heard of Kira and decided to check him.

ASANO

You are too hopeful, Kurano. I only hope for a little crumb of justice in this question of the hills.

KURANO

Will you speak to the men to-night, notwithstanding?

ASANO

I will wait till I know what the day brings forth.

[*Enter* SHODA]

SHODA

Have I the honour of speaking to Lord Asano?

ASANO

I am Asano.

SHODA

I come from the Envoy now visiting this province to tell you that you are to be specially honoured by him.

ASANO

The Envoy's wishes are a law to me, and his honour more than I deserve.

SHODA

You have been appointed to be the Envoy's host when he holds his Court to-day.

ASANO

That is an honour indeed, and a very grateful pleasure.

SHODA

I am happy that my message pleases you. The Lord Kamei who is, I believe, your friend, will act with you and share your task.

ASANO

That will add to my pleasure. I have long known Kamei.

SHODA

The Envoy wishes me to say that he looks forward with much happiness to so pleasant a means of meeting you, of whom he has so often heard praise.

ASANO

I hope that my welcome will not be unworthy of so generous a lord. Before you go, will you not rest in my house a little?

SHODA

I cannot, thank you. The ceremony will begin so soon. I must return.

KURANO

Is not the ritual of receiving the Envoy a difficult one?

ASANO

I know nothing of the ritual.

Shoda

That difficulty has been foreseen and arranged for. Your friend Lord Kira, will instruct you in the ritual.

Asano

Lord Kira?

Shoda

Lord Kira, yes. He will receive you at any hour, the earlier the better, since the ceremony will be held at noon. He is expecting you now.

Asano

Where is he waiting for us?

Shoda

At his palace. The Envoy's reception will take place in Lord Kira's palace.

Asano

We will wait upon Lord Kira.

Shoda

I shall look forward to meeting you there after the ceremony. Good-bye till then.

Kurano

Good-bye. [Shoda *goes*.]

Asano

So Kira is to teach us the ritual, and I am to receive the Envoy in Kira's palace. The issue is joined indeed.

Kurano

It could not fall out better. You will front Kira and accuse him in his own house, before all the nobles of the province.

ASANO

I am troubled though.   I am to be his pupil.

KURANO

I shall be with you.   Come.   The chess-board is set.

ASANO

Still, I an troubled.   I feel that Kira has contrived this, for reasons that I cannot see.   I wish that this had not happened.

KURANO

You will only meet Kira officially, for a prescribed ceremony.   You will not even be the only pupil, for Lord Kamei will be learning with you.

ASANO

I have misgivings.

KURANO

All great things come from misgivings.

ASANO

Come then.   It is time.   Even at our wisest Fate uses us; and I shall be with you.

[*A messenger runs in.*]

THIRD RONIN

Lord Kurano.   Lord Kurano.   Your lady.

KURANO

What?   What is it?

[395]

THIRD RONIN

Your lady has fallen, Lord Kurano, on the palace steps.

ASANO

Is she killed?

THIRD RONIN

Please God, no, my lord. But she calls for you and they think her dying.

ASANO

You must go. I will go on alone to Kira.

KURANO

If I can come, I will follow you.

ASANO

I trust you will find all well. Go now.

KURANO

Take me to where she is. [*Turning.*] Asano, promise me one thing.

ASANO

What?

KURANO

That you will be on your guard with Kira; that you will not let yourself be led away by him.

ASANO

I am playing for all these souls, Kurano. But who can promise for himself?

KURANO

You can and must. Do you understand? He may provoke

you. Whatever the provocation, be calm. May the gods guard you, Asano.

ASANO

They guard us. You, too.

KURANO

Please Heaven. I have misgivings now. I wish I were coming with you.

ASANO

We are being played by the gods. Go, now, quickly.

KURANO

Yes. Pray the gods I may follow quickly.

ASANO

Now hurry. I shall be late. [*They part and go off right and left.* ASANO *turns.*] Kurano. Good-bye, Kurano.

[*He watches* KURANO *go*]

CURTAIN

SCENE II.—*The inner scene*

KIRA

God of my fortunes, who hast brought me from being the steward's son to be Lord Kira. Now that the last enemy, Asano, is within the net, grant me thy intellectual power, that I may strike him to the ground. [*Comes forward.*] Then with jewels and dominations I shall go on. My power will stretch to the sea. There is no drunkenness like power. Sagisaka.

[SAGISAKA *enters*]

SAGISAKA

My lord.

KIRA

Now the sun rises, friend.

SAGISAKA

Yes, my lord.

KIRA

You see you were wrong. That stroke on the valley-head prospered.

SAGISAKA

They will appeal, my lord.

KIRA

Yes, but meanwhile they have to learn the ritual. Have they come yet?

SAGISAKA

Asano and Kamei have come. They are outside.

KIRA

Tell me more of Kamei.

SAGISAKA

An honest, blunt man, wealthy, too; he has a pearl fishery.

KIRA

He is not a friend of Asano's?

SAGISAKA

They are said to be friendly.

KIRA

Nothing in the nature of allies?

SAGISAKA

No.

KIRA

Let us see these pupils. [SAGISAKA *opens the door.*]

[*Enter* KAMEI, HONZO, *and* ASANO]

KIRA

Who are you? Are you Lord Kamei?

KAMEI

Yes.

KIRA

Who is with you?

KAMEI

My attendant, Honzo.

KIRA

And this is Lord Asano. Is anyone with you?

ASANO

No, Lord Kira.

KIRA

You have come to me to learn the ritual for the reception of the Emperor's Envoy. I have to tell you that the Envoy is even now within this palace, and that this is therefore a sacred place. I need not remind you that a place so hallowed exacts a reverence. My duty prescribes that I declare this room hallowed. Whoever breaks its peace, by violent act or oath, by blow or by the drawing of a weapon, is liable to the punishment of death, with confiscation of goods; so the Emperor's edict prescribes. You understand?

KAMEI

Yes.

KIRA

You, Lord Asano; do you understand?

ASANO

Perfectly.

KIRA

You have a look as though you did not understand so perfectly. Sagisaka.

SAGISAKA

My Lord?

KIRA

Are not these pupils very late?

SAGISAKA

They appeared to think not, at the door, my lord, but they are late, some twenty minutes.

KIRA

It is very annoying, that there should be so little care to be punctual. Give word for my cordial to be brought. [SAGI-SAKA *goes to the door.*] Why do you stand, sir, so near to the pupils?

HONZO

I am in attendance upon Lord Kamei.

KIRA

Your place is near the door, till you are wanted.

HONZO

I am sorry, my lord, I did not know. [*The cordial enters.*]

KIRA

And why do you come unattended?

ASANO

Lord Kurano, who was coming with me, was detained.

KIRA

What detained him?

ASANO

An accident to his wife.

KIRA

Give me the cordial there. [*Drinks*.] Sagisaka.

SAGISAKA

My lord?

KIRA

Has any apology been received from this gentleman, for coming alone?

SAGISAKA

No, my lord.

ASANO

If an apology is necessary, let me state my regret now. Nothing but this sudden accident would have kept Lord Kurano from being present. I still hope he may be here.

KIRA

Yes. But how am I to know that this accident is not merely an excuse to be away?

ASANO

I have the honour to tell you.

[401]

KIRA

Can you vouch for the accident or have you only heard of it?

ASANO

I heard of it, from a man on whose truth I can depend.

KIRA

"Truth" and "depend." And I have to depend on your dependence in condonation of your fault, which is tantamount to an impiety. Why did you bring no other friend, when you knew that Lord Kurano could not come?

ASANO

As I said, Lord Kira, I still hope that Lord Kurano may come here in time.

KIRA

You were not here in time yourself. You have been guilty of great disrespect, both in coming late and in coming alone. Remove these cups. Ah, Sagisaka.

SAGISAKA

My lord?

KIRA

What is the other person's name?

SAGISAKA

Kamei, my lord.

KIRA

Kamei. What made you late?

KAMEI

I was not late, Lord Kira.

[402]

KIRA

You will not improve your case by denial. You have heard this gentleman say that you are late.

KAMEI

He is not a gentleman.

SAGISAKA

They came on foot to the gate. The porter took them for beggars.

KIRA

I have heard, and the Envoy has heard, of new opinions in this province, of a want of respect for sacred things, of contempt for order, and distaste for duty. I grieve to find evidence of all these things in your behaviour to-day. You come late, you come improperly, unattended, dusty, and inclined to rudeness. The Envoy will be pained to hear my report of you.

KAMEI

Lord Kira, we have come to learn the ritual from you. If, as you say, we are late, it might be well if you would confine yourself to that.

KIRA

You will remember this person's remarks.

SAGISAKA

Yes, my lord.

KIRA

I will read those letters if you will bring them to me. [*Reads.*] You may take this one, Sagisaka. [*Gives letter.*] This needs no answer. Asano, I have a letter here from my steward. He complains that in spite of the Judges' verdict yesterday your men still persist in occupying my pasture.

ASANO

Lord Kira, your steward is mistaken.

KIRA

That is not possible. Here is his letter.

ASANO

Do you depend upon his truth?

KIRA

I do.

ASANO

And I am to depend on your dependence in an accusation of the kind? Well, Lord Kira, all my men, without exception, have been in attendance at my house through the night.

KIRA

You will have to prove that.

ASANO

As you please.

KAMEI

Lord Kira, I have no concern with your private quarrels with Lord Asano; it is very painful to have to listen to them. I take it as a gross breach of privilege that you refer to them at all in your present position. I must ask you to perform the duty, for which I am in attendance; otherwise I must withdraw, to claim the respect not yet offered to me.

KIRA

As my pupil, you have neither the right to make remarks nor the power to withdraw. Within this Court you attend my instruction, at my pleasure, and obey my will at my bidding; that is your province as pupil; I, as teacher, will attend to mine. If your gross ignorance and crass conceit mislead you, let me set you right; for I, here, Lord Kamei, represent a sacred Envoy, and will brook no babbling from a gray-haired country clown.

HONZO

For God's sake, stop him!

ASANO

Be quiet, Kamei; be quiet.

KAMEI

This man sat with my lackeys.

ASANO

I know, I know, but you are in his power if you stir.

KAMEI

The dog! The dog! I have seen him eat broken meats after the feast. I will not be quiet.

KAMEI

You shall, Kamei, you shall not ruin yourself.

KIRA

Sagisaka.

SAGISAKA

My lord?

KIRA

Request these people to be silent.

[405]

Sagisaka

Be silent, you, and you.

Kamei

What do you bid me?

Kira

[*Rapping with his fan*]. Be silent, please. Prepare yourselves to learn the ritual.

Lord Kamei, you are the elder of my two pupils?

Kamei

Yes.

Kira

Come forward, please. [Kamei *advances*.]

It is with your goodwill that you come to learn this ceremony?

Kamei

What do you mean by that question? I am here.

Kira

Do you come with your goodwill?

Asano

Answer, man, answer.

Honzo

Say, yes, master, or it will be ruin, ruin.

Kira

Will you two, to whom I am not speaking, keep farther back? Must I repeat my question, Lord Kamei? There is a prescribed form which I have to follow. I ask you, do you come here of your own will, freely?

Asano

Say yes.

Kamei

Yes, I do.

Kira

Come nearer to me, Kamei.

Kamei

I am here, Lord Kira.

Kira

Kneel down, kindly. [Kamei *kneels*.] Fasten my shoe for me.

Kamei

Perhaps I do not understand you, quite.

Kira

The clasp of my shoe is loose, I ask you to clasp it.

Kamei

Ask me?

Kira

I tell you.   Fasten it.

Kamei

You tell me to fasten your shoe?

Kira

Yes.

Kamei

Then—— [*The door at the back opens with a clang.*]

[407]

[SHODA *appears*]

SHODA

Pardon my intrusion upon this office. I had the misfortune to interrupt you, Lord Kamei. The Envoy requests me to desire your immediate presence, Lord Kira, if you will be so good as to go to him.

KIRA

Thank you. I break up this Court. Come, Sagisaka.

[KIRA *and* SHODA *go out*]

SAGISAKA

Stay, you, till my lord returns. [*Exit.*]

HONZO

Intolerable. It was intolerable.

KAMEI

That is the end, however.

ASANO

Kamei, you have been wonderful.

KAMEI

He went too far, Honzo.

HONZO

My lord, I thank God you kept the peace.

KAMEI

I shall keep it no longer. Give me that dirk you wear.

[408]

HONZO

What are you going to do, my lord?

ASANO

Do not give it, Honzo. Kamei, you have been right, up to this very last. We have only to keep calm through this; we can appeal to the Envoy.

KAMEI

What has the Envoy to do with this, Asano? This concerns my personal honour. The upstart told me to clasp his shoe-buckle. Give me your dirk, Honzo. [*Snatches the dirk.*]

HONZO

My lord, my lord.

ASANO

No, no, Kamei, no; you cannot claim a precedence. This concerns us three.

KAMEI

You were not told to handle his shoes. You are not an old man who has seen this dog fawning at his lackey's pantry for scraps and gobbets. You are a young man, with work, and you are an old man with sons. I am only an old man with a memory of what was, and I am going to kill that man.

ASANO

Kamei, Kamei, can you not see that a riot is what Kira wants? We two are his last rivals here. He has contrived all this to trap us; it is death if we lift a finger. If we endure this till the Envoy comes, we can appeal, and Kira will be degraded. Give me that dirk, for all our sakes.

KAMEI

Not I, Asano.

HONZO

Lord Kamei.

KAMEI

[*Putting them aside.*] My mind is made up.

HONZO

Master Kamei, I have served you many years now. I carried you when you were little, when I was a lad, pikeman to the Emperor. I promised the old knight, your father, that I would mind you, and I have, master, many's the time, and your sweet lady, my mistress, and the young knights, your sons. This lord is right, Master Kamei, it is a trap to bring you to death. I saw it in his look directly he began. I saw him smile when he touched you. Lord Kamei, it is not only your death that would follow if you struck him, but the beggary of your lady and her babes; and this lord is right, that you should bear till the Presence comes.

KAMEI

I will not bear.

HONZO

Then it is for me to save you, Lord Kamei; I will kill Lord Kira.

KAMEI

Please keep from me. If death is the penalty, I am ready for death.

Lord Asano, Honzo; I am grieved if I have spoken rudely to you. I count upon you not to interfere. Take these trappings, Honzo, and the purse. [*Gives things.*] Honzo, please go to the door, and tell me if Lord Kira is coming back.

HONZO

[*At door*].   He is in the corridor, talking to a woman.

KAMEI

Is his guard there?

HONZO

No.   Ah!

KAMEI

Is he coming?

HONZO

Yes.

KAMEI

Alone?

HONZO

No, the girl too.

KAMEI

On which side?

HONZO

The right.

KAMEI

I'll stand here, then.

HONZO

[*Speaking through.*]   God deliver us.   God deliver us.

KAMEI

Stand away, Honzo.   Keep behind me.

HONZO

This is the end of it all; the end of everything.

KAMEI

Be quiet.   Come, Kira.

[411]

HONZO

He's at the door.

KAMEI

Hush! Listen!

HONZO

Hark!

KAMEI

Quiet, Honzo.

ASANO

What is it?

KAMEI

He has gone past, I think.

HONZO

Please God.

KAMEI

Look, Honzo, softly.

HONZO

[*At door.*] He is there.

KAMEI

Where?

HONZO

[*Pointing.*] There.

KAMEI

Just outside?

HONZO

His hand upon the latch.

KAMEI

Then make your peace, Kira.

[412]

KIRA

[*As he half opens the door.*] That must wait till to-night.

A WOMAN'S VOICE

Yes, but there is another thing.

KIRA

What can that be?

VOICE

No, that shall wait till to-night, too.

KIRA

No, you must tell me. [*Closes door again.   The* Voice *laughs.*]

KIRA

[*Off.*] You will not escape like that.

KAMEI

Kiss your farewell to her.

HONZO

They are moving down the corridor.

ASANO

She is singing.

KAMEI

Look, Honzo.   Look.

HONZO

They are there.   She is gone now.   He is coming.

[413]

KAMEI

Quickly, then, behind me; farther back.

ASANO

Now.

HONZO

Here.

[SHODA *enters behind them quietly and goes to* KAMEI]

KAMEI

[*Thinking that he is* HONZO]. Keep away, Honzo. Keep from me. I warn you. [*Turning.*] Who is this? Who are you? Ah, Lord Shoda.

SHODA

Lord Kamei, may I have the pleasure of waiting on you to your robing-room?

KAMEI

Ah, have I to robe?

SHODA

If you will forgive the trouble. You, too, Lord Asano.

ASANO

We have not yet been taught the ritual.

SHODA

That will be taught when you are robed. Will you come, then? These ceremonies are tedious; but the Envoy keenly looks forward to meeting you. This will be the way. Perhaps this gentleman will wait [*indicating* HONZO].

[*He takes out* ASANO *and* KAMEI]

[414]

HONZO

[*Kneeling.*] You gods who have granted me this moment's truce, help me to save my master.

[*Enter* SAGISAKA. *The two eye each other*]

SAGISAKA

Well, fellow?

HONZO

Look.

SAGISAKA

What?

HONZO

This. It is my master's purse.

SAGISAKA

I suppose money is a rare sight where you come from?

HONZO

[*Jingling money.*] Could you get me a moment's private talk with Lord Kira, here, now, this very instant?

SAGISAKA

For you? What if I could?

HONZO

[*Jingling.*] This . . . to begin with.

SAGISAKA

Let me see it.

HONZO

When Lord Kira is here.

SAGISAKA

I want more than that.

HONZO

You shall have more, if you will bring him at once.

SAGISAKA

What do you want Lord Kira for?

HONZO

I will tell him when he comes.   Only bring him.

SAGISAKA

I must have something to tell him.

HONZO

Say I must speak to him.

SAGISAKA

Must? Must speak? Well . . . [*Going.*] But if you want him like this; no [*stops*]. I have myself to consider. I cannot fetch him till you have made it worth my while.

[*Enter* KIRA]

KIRA

Fetch whom?

HONZO

Lord Kira, will you grant me the favour of a moment's talk?

KIRA

A moment's talk?

SAGISAKA

He has been troubling me, my lord, with a great deal of nonsense about talking to you. He is foolish.

HONZO

It is for Lord Kamei, Lord Kira.

KIRA

For Lord Kamei? Lord Kamei can speak for himself.

HONZO

I am his treasurer, Lord Kira.

KIRA

Yes? What then?

HONZO

Might we be alone, Lord Kira, for a moment only?

KIRA

Go, Sagisaka.

SAGISAKA

[*Passing* KIRA.] Have a care, my lord; he may be planning you a mischief for what you said to his master.

KIRA

What? You think that?

SAGISAKA

There is a strange look in his eyes.

[417]

KIRA

There is. You, man; put down that cloak you are carrying. What weapons have you in your sleeves?

HONZO

None, my lord.

KIRA

Feel him, Sagisaka.

SAGISAKA

There is nothing, my lord. What have you done with your dirk?

HONZO

I lost it.

SAGISAKA

Yes, where you lost your wits, I think.

KIRA

Leave us then, Sagisaka. [*Exit* SAGISAKA, *back*.] Well, treasurer.

HONZO

Lord Kira, where we live we are not used to Court ceremony, so we sometimes offend. My master has asked me to say this, lest you should be annoyed at our country way. He, I mean we, have put you to a great deal of trouble in this matter of the ritual. If we might make some return, without offence, as a sign of how much we feel it; if you would not misunderstand.

KIRA

I shall not misunderstand a kind thought.

HONZO

We have heard that you collect jewels, Lord Kira.

[418]

KIRA

I have a few jewels.

HONZO

We in the country are sometimes able to help in the matter of jewels, what with the mines and the pearl-fishery. Lord Kamei thought that perhaps you might like to see these pearls.

KIRA

These are black pearls.

HONZO

Yes, your lordship might call them black. We . . . we . . . we did not like to set them . . . as your lordship's taste is so well known. . . . If you would accept them from Lord Kamei, it would be a pleasure . . . as a return for your kindness, Lord Kira.

KIRA

This is very handsome of Kamei. I shall be very pleased to have them. They are very fine. There are few things so rare. I shall set them . . . how shall I set them?

HONZO

If your lordship cares for these things, Lord Kamei will be pleased to show you his collection.

KIRA

That is a pleasure we must arrange. Your name is Honzo, I think. I thank you, Honzo. But I think your master must be robed and we must proceed. Will you withdraw through that door, Honzo, while we go on? I thank you. I shall thank your master.

[HONZO *goes actors' left.* KAMEI *enters actors' right*]

KAMEI

Now, Kira.

KIRA

No, Lord Kamei, let me be beforehand with you. See. I fling down my sword. I kneel to you. Listen. I ask your pardon for my rudeness.

KAMEI

You ask my pardon?

KIRA

Yes, for my gross insolence; I ask it kneeling. . . . My dear lord, let me congratulate you. You stood the test superbly.

KAMEI

You explain yourself.

KIRA

You do not know these rituals.

KAMEI

No. Nor wish to know more.

KIRA

You will perhaps understand, when I tell you that the early part of the teaching is designed to test the pupil's loyalty, his reverence for an Envoy's person, which it is important to know. You were wonderful. There can be few more loyal subjects than you. The Envoy, who was listening, was most pleased with you. And now you must forgive me, and allow me to say how pained I was to insult you in that way. Come, you must shake hands, and to-night you must honour me, you must be my guest.

KAMEI

Well. Say no more. There is my hand. You certainly put me to a test.

KIRA

Yes; it is a test. Sometimes in these rituals men who have not your marvellous forbearance are brought to the brink of murder.

KAMEI

Self-control is a great gift.

KIRA

To tell the truth, the test to-day was more strict than usual; for, between ourselves, there has been talk of disloyalty, new ideas, irreverence, in this province, and the good wheat is being sifted.

But, come, that unpleasantness is over. The ritual is simply this. Come with me here. [*Leads him actors' left.*] Your place will be here. You will be told when to come forward. Then you will . . . [*Whispers.*] You understand?

KAMEI

Is that all?

KIRA

Yes. I leave you now. And let me thank very you warmly for your charming conduct and willing pupilage. [*Shakes his hand, leaves him in prompt wings and returns to central stage.*] Sagisaka.

SAGISAKA

My lord.

[*Enters*]

KIRA

See that Lord Kamei's men are treated with every care.

SAGISAKA

Yes, Lord Kira.

KIRA

Has Lord Asano's friend come, this Kurano?

SAGISAKA

No, my lord.

KIRA

Is he in sight? Look and tell me.

SAGISAKA

There is a horseman on the road, riding fast.

KIRA

How far is he?

SAGISAKA

Three minutes; four . . .

KIRA

Is it likely to be Kurano?

SAGISAKA

It might be.

KIRA

Kurano is the wise man of the two; he is a man of sense?

Sagisaka

He is said to have more than his master.

Kira

I can wait three minutes. Put these pearls in the treasury. See that man Honzo well cared for; specially well.

Sagisaka

Yes, my lord.
Have you as much time to spare as you think, my lord?

Kira

I can wait two minutes more for Kurano.

Sagisaka

That horseman does not seem to be coming here, my lord; he is turning off at the cross-roads; he is going towards the hills.

Kira

Is anyone else in sight?

Sagisaka

No. Very far away there is a horseman.

Kira

How far?

Sagisaka

Just come in sight, my lord, and walking.

Kira

That would be ten minutes?

[423]

SAGISAKA

Quite, my lord.

KIRA

I cannot wait so long. I must go on. Let the other come; Asano.

[SAGISAKA *goes actors' right and opens door.*]

SAGISAKA

Will you come in?

[ASANO *enters.* SAGISAKA *goes out back*]

KIRA

Your friend has not come, Lord Asano.

ASANO

I am grieved. I fear his wife is badly hurt.

KIRA

I am sorry.

ASANO

I will tell him of your sympathy.

KIRA

What is that?

ASANO

I will tell him of your sympathy.

KIRA

Ah, yes.
But I regret his absence for another reason, which has nothing to do with an accident to a woman.

[424]

Asano

Indeed.

Kira

I presume that I may count upon his coming later?

Asano

I cannot answer for him.

Kira

I presume that I may count upon someone coming on your behalf, if not now at least in connection with your visit?

Asano

No one will come on my behalf, Lord Kira.

Kira

It is a great pity that Lord Kurano is not here; I fear you do not understand me.

Asano

I understand you perfectly well, Lord Kira. You are hinting that you would like a bribe. I tell you frankly that you hint to the wrong man. I would not make you a present if you held my life in your hand. Now teach me the ritual, as you are bidden, and let me hear no more of hinting and presuming. You pollute this place and degrade your office.

Kira

You misunderstand, Lord Asano; but you are right, we will proceed to the ritual. Come with me here. [*Leads him actors' right.*] Your place will be here. You will be told when to come forward. Then you will . . . [*Whispers.*] Do you understand?

ASANO

From here?

KIRA

Yes.

ASANO

It is not easy to do.

KIRA

Surely.

ASANO

Can I not rehearse it?

KIRA

The ceremony must begin. I will leave you here. [*He remains alone on the stage; goes slowly back*.] Sagisaka.

SAGISAKA

[*Entering*.] My lord?

KIRA

The hosts are instructed in their duty.

SAGISAKA

The Envoy is ready to proceed, Lord Kira.

KIRA

As he pleases.

[*Kneels*. SAGISAKA *goes out*, NOBLES *enter*]

Be humble and prepare for the glory that has come among us.

[*The* ENVOY *enters*]

VOICES

We give thanks for this mercy vouchsafed.

[426]

The Envoy

May peace be here; may righteousness be done here.

Kira

Be it again declared, that he who breaks the peace or does unrighteousness within these walls, dies, as an outlaw, with the greater and lesser confiscations.

Voices

Be it enacted as it is declared.

The Envoy

Who welcomes us in this holy place?

Kira

Those whom the Presence has honoured, if it be so willed.

The Envoy

It is so willed.

[*The door, actors' left, opens.* Kamei *appears and performs his rite properly.*]

Kamei

I have the honour to welcome you.

The Envoy

[*Raising him to the seat at his right.*] We thank you for this welcome, which we well know proceeds from love.

Few things are so pleasant to us as this evidence of love for Him whom we all serve, and the knowledge that all which you do for ourselves, great though it is, in the saving of pain as well as in the warmth of welcome, would be done in far fuller measure for Him, were He to be here.

Nor is it less pleasant to see again old rites and customs feelingly observed, and to remember the beautiful meaning hidden in them by the reverence of our fathers, by whom we live. For what we do here keeps alive what was passionate in the thought of our fathers; a thankful and holy task, which none but an impious man would slight or bring to mockery.

It is so willed.

[*The door (right) opens.* ASANO *enters, advances on his knees, stumbling in his robes, and takes the* ENVOY's *hands. The* NOBLES *laugh.*]

THE ENVOY

What is this outrage?

KIRA

What has possessed you, Asano?

THE ENVOY

Do you do this to insult me?

ASANO

Insult you? I do not understand.

KIRA

This is monstrous.

ASANO

I did as I was bid, my lord. [*Looking round, he sees all the* NOBLES *tittering.*] You planned this, Kira, to shame me.

KIRA

Do not aggravate your offence, Asano. Hold him, he will kill the Envoy.

[428]

Asano

You shall not live to boast of it. [*Draws dirk and strikes at* Kira.] Die, you.

Nobles

Part them; quick, part them.

Kamei

God, he has killed him.

Asano

There, Kira.

Sagisaka

No.

Asano

Yes, I say.

Sagisaka

Let go. I have you. Drop the dirk. Wrest it from him.

A Voice

You shall not.

A Voice

I have it. No, Lord Asano, come.

Kira

Oh! remember, remember; this is a holy place.

Kamei

Lord Kira is bleeding.

Kira

Never mind me, look to the Envoy. He stabbed at the Envoy.

Kamei

Hold him, he is fainting.

[429]

A Voice

Fetch water. He has been stabbed to the brain.

Kamei

Lean on me, Lord Kira.

The Envoy

Is he dead?

Kamei

Blind with the blood, I think, my lord. It is a cut along the brow. Have you a cloth? The cloth, there!

A Voice

This is a terrible thing, Lord Asano.

The Envoy

Little did I think that I should live to see new principles lead to so blasphemous a sacrilege. I suspend this Court. Let the wound be dressed. How bad is the wound?

Kamei

A shallow cut, my lord.

A Voice

The knife must have slipped, or it would have killed him.

The Envoy

See to it, Shoda. Where is this man?

Kira

My lord, although his aim was to make it seem that I had not taught him the ceremony, and afterwards perhaps to kill me, I make no charge against him. He has been at law with me and is prejudiced and passionate; I think not really wicked. As far as any injury has been done to me, I ask for his pardon, my lord.

The Envoy

That well becomes you, Lord Kira. I wish that I could grant a pardon. Take him, Shoda, before the cut stiffens.

[Kira *is led out*]

This outlaw, now. It is Asano, is it not?

Asano

Yes, lord.

The Envoy

Asano, if you are not still blind with passion, listen to me. Perhaps even now you do not understand your position.

Asano

I understand it.

The Envoy

That I am thankful for; because you stand upon the brink of ruin.

I wish that, as Lord Kira asks, it were possible to pardon you. But society is held together solely by the chain of order, and to weaken a link of that chain is to bring in chaos. Think of what you have done, and of what you have outraged, but do not think, for a moment, that your sin can be lightly punished.

Asano

The net was set for me and I am caught. I am too wise, my lord, to appeal against the machine of this world, against the strong, unscrupulous man and old custom. I have outraged both. But I should not have outraged either had not some-

[431]

thing higher been outraged, something here in me. Well, you have me.

THE ENVOY

You do not realise your offence, Asano. Your sin is that of blasphemous, sacrilegious passion, shedding blood upon consecrated ground. I will consider your case. Remove him. Bring him to a sense of how he stands. Stay, Lord Kamei.

[All go, save KAMEI*]*

He is an intemperate man, I fear. Do you know him?

KAMEI

He is a gentle, quiet man, my lord.

THE ENVOY

He is a free thinker, they tell me.

KAMEI

I cannot answer for a man's thoughts, my lord.

THE ENVOY

You can deplore what they lead to, I hope.

KAMEI

My lord, we are all subject to passion. Kira so insulted me this morning, that I was on the verge of killing him.

THE ENVOY

The verge is the line between man and devil, and men keep within it. Leave me. [KAMEI *goes. A pause.*]

A YOUTH *enters*

[432]

THE YOUTH

I beg pardon, my lord.

THE ENVOY

What is it?

THE YOUTH

I was to cense the room, my lord. [*A pause.*]

THE ENVOY

Boy.

THE YOUTH

Yes, my lord.

THE ENVOY

Do you believe in God?

THE YOUTH

Yes, sir.

THE ENVOY

Would you forgive a man who had broken the peace in the
house of God?

THE YOUTH

Broken it, my lord?

THE ENVOY

Yes, drawn a knife there and tried to kill a man.

THE YOUTH

It would depend on what the other man had done..

THE ENVOY

Say that the other man had insulted him and made a mock
of him?

THE YOUTH

That's a hard case, my lord.

THE ENVOY

Would you forgive him or would you put him to death?

THE YOUTH

My lord, it's a hard case; I would forgive him.

THE ENVOY

Why?

THE YOUTH

No man would do a thing like that unless there was excuse.

THE ENVOY

So you would forgive him. Freely?

THE YOUTH

As I would hope to be forgiven myself, my lord.

THE ENVOY

Ah! Will you find Lord Shoda for me? He is outside there. [*The* YOUTH *goes. Pause.* SHODA *comes.*] Shoda, I have considered this case. Order the other ministrants to leave the precincts.

SHODA

Very well, my lord. Shall I bring the prisoner to you?

THE ENVOY

Not yet. See that Lord Kamei goes.

SHODA

I will, my lord.

THE ENVOY

When you go, please order the room here to be laid with mattings. [*Exit at actors' left.*]

SHODA

I will give order, my lord.

[*The* YOUTH *enters to cense the room*]

THE YOUTH

[*Censing.*]

> One and two and three
> Sweet spirits sweeten me;
> With thy precious grace
> Be about this place;
> Let Fate with the dark star
> Be . . .

[*Enter* KURANO *at back*]

KURANO

Is the Court broken up?

THE YOUTH

Sir?

KURANO

Is the Court broken up? Are they dining?

THE YOUTH

One went there, my lord, to that room, and the other lords went there; but I do not know, my lord, I am not one of the household.

KURANO

Ah! [*Enter, back, two men, with white mattings, who cross to front and prepare the seppuku.*] Where is the Court now? Can you tell me? [*The men do not answer.*] What is this? [*Enter* KAMEI.] Ah, here is Kamei. Is the Court over?

[435]

KAMEI

Yes, it is. Your friend, Asano, has done a mad thing.

KURANO

What?

KAMEI

He was mad, Kurano. He performed the ceremony like a madman and the people laughed. He drew his dirk and struck Kira in the face.

KURANO

Then Kira taught him the wrong ritual.

KAMEI

That is incredible.

KURANO

Things are, till they happen. What is being done?

KAMEI

I do not know. I have been ordered to go.

KURANO

Is he in arrest? Of course he is. Where is Kira?

KAMEI

Gone to have the wound dressed.

KURANO

Which way, though?

KAMEI

You cannot set upon Kira in his own house.

KURANO

He must set this right. You boy, where is Kira? I should

have been here from the first: my wife's unhurt. I galloped to catch you, but the horse went lame. Which door, you, to Kira's rooms? Lord Kira's rooms?

The Youth

One of these doors, my lord. I do not know which.

Kurano

Come, Kamei. We must find either Kira or the Envoy. Come. [*He goes to door at back, just as it is flung open. Enter the* Envoy, Shoda, Asano *under guard*, Sagisaka, *and* Nobles.] My lord, I beg for the privilege of a moment's speech with you.

The Envoy

I have a painful duty here, sir, which makes it impossible.

Asano

I am condemned to kill myself, Kurano. I am going to death, now, for striking Kira.

Kurano

Good God! My lord, I protest against this sentence.

The Envoy

You protest?

Asano

Kurano, do not ruin yourself for my sake.

A Guard

Come, sir; stand aside.

Asano

I am ruined and the estate confiscated; that is enough. Let the ruin end with me.

[437]

Kurano

My lord, I appeal. Any crime is sometimes justified, and I appeal now for my friend. The whole ritual was irregular, he was unattended, I was not with him.

The Envoy

He is condemned for sacrilege, Kurano.

Kurano

My lord, I know. But I know this man. He could not have committed sacrilege. I say that Kira wilfully taught him the wrong ritual to make him a mock; and that was the only sacrilege committed here, and in striking Kira he punished it. I claim a reversal of your sentence and judgment on Kira.

The Envoy

Arrest this man. No, no, loose him. Stand from him.

Have you any evidence to support your statement against Lord Kira?

Kurano

None, my lord. Only my knowledge of my friend and Kira's hate.

The Envoy

Sacrilege is a sin against the Divine; the question of human provocation does not apply. I am being very merciful to you, Lord Kurano, because I am an old man and know the value of life. Do not force me to remember that I have a peculiar power.

I uphold the sacredness of my master, and administer His law, as an old man soon to be judged himself.

Will you be silent here, in this place of death, or must I take order?

KURANO

Nothing that I say, or do, can save my friend?

THE ENVOY

Nothing.

KURANO

I have duties to the living, then.   I will be silent, my lord.

ASANO

May I speak with him?

THE ENVOY

It is not usual to grant speech.

KURANO

It is not an usual case, my lord.

THE ENVOY

You may speak for one minute, then.

ASANO

Alone?

THE ENVOY

The minute has begun.

KURANO

My dear man.

ASANO

Well, Kurano, the gods make pawns of us.

KURANO

Kira taught you the wrong ritual?

[439]

ASANO

Yes.

KURANO

You will not go unavenged. And the confiscation? Who takes the land?

ASANO

It will go to the Crown, I fear. I pray Kira will not get it. I have played badly for those who trusted to me.

KURANO

This is the gambit only. What can I do for you or say for you?

ASANO

Nothing; I know you'll do everything. There is one thing——

KURANO

What?

ASANO

That woman whom I hoped to marry. No. She belongs to the past. I can think of nothing.

KURANO

There is no need where one loves.

ASANO

There are strange thoughts rising in me about the ways of the gods.

Kurano, one thing . . . about Kira. You spoke of vengeance . . . before that . . . Listen. Try to stop the confiscation.

[440]

THE ENVOY

The minute is past.

ASANO

Remember, Kurano, before all that . . . appeal . . . get
the inheritance for my brother.   Remember.

A GUARD

Come this way, Lord Kurano.

KURANO

I will remember.   [*He is led off.*]

ASANO

Sometimes, in wintry springs,
Frost, on a midnight breath,
Comes to the cherry flowers
And blasts their prime;
So I, with all my powers
Unused on men or things,
Go down the wind to death,
And know no fruiting-time.

[*He kneels on the white mat and takes up the dirk*]

CURTAIN

ACT II

SCENE—*The outer scene*

A VOICE

Lord Asano is long at his honours. Is that he?

A VOICE

No, not yet.

VOICES

No. Hazama has gone up the road to see if he is coming. He must be here soon.

FIRST RONIN

The Envoy may have kept him.

A VOICE

There. There he comes. He is coming.

VOICES

Welcome home from your honours, Lord Asano.

SECOND RONIN

It is not he; not yet; but he cannot be long.

FIRST RONIN

Very often the Envoy keeps them.

VOICE

Whatever honour he wins they will not honour him as much as we do.

SECOND RONIN

He has been our guardian and our friend.

A VOICE

How long it seems.

FIRST RONIN

Sometimes the Envoy feasts them; in fact, usually.

A VOICE

Here is Hazama.   He is coming.

VOICES

Asano, welcome!

VOICES

Where?   Show me.   I see Kurano.

VOICES

Welcome!

[*Enter* HAZAMA]

Welcome!   Welcome!

HAZAMA

No, no! no, no!   Hush!

VOICES

Asano!

HAZAMA

Quiet!

VOICES

Asano.   Welcome!   Welcome!

HAZAMA

Hush.   Quiet!   Still!

[443]

Voices

Asano. Asano!

Hazama

It is not he, I tell you. It is Lord Kurano.

Voices

Kurano! It is Kurano. Welcome. Kurano. Kurano!
Carry him. We'll carry him home.

Hazama

Still, everybody!

Voices

Here comes Kurano, etc.

[*Enter* Kurano]

Hazama

Here comes Lord Kurano. Welcome him home to us.

Voices

Kurano. Welcome back to us, Lord Kurano!

Kurano

Stop this noise. Have this noise stopped, Azama.

Voices

Kurano and Asano forever. Welcome! etc.

Kurano

Let them, for God's sake, stop. Silence, I say.

Hazama

Still, still! Still a moment!

[444]

Voices

Friends forever. Our friends forever. Hush. Quiet.

Kurano

Come round me here.

Voices

He has something to say.

Third Ronin

Would you taste our wine, lord?

Hazama

Wait till he has spoken.

Kurano

Kneel down.

Hazama

What is it, master?

Kurano

Your master Asano is dead.

Hazama

For God's sake, master!

Voices

Dead? In God's name! Our master? What killed him?

A Voice

What was it he said? I did not hear.

A Voice

That our master Asano is dead.

[445]

FIFTH RONIN

O desolation!

FIRST RONIN

That death should happen like this, going to an honour!

HAZAMA

If I might ask it, master, how did he come by his end?

KURANO

By a knife.

FIRST RONIN

By an accident, then, was it?

KURANO

No.

THIRD RONIN

Was no one there? Did no one see?

KURANO

I saw. There were many looking on.

HAZAMA

Was he murdered?

KURANO

My friends, he was condemned to death. He killed himself.

ALL

Oh! Oh, God!

KURANO

This is the knife. This, here. This killed your master.

[446]

VOICES

Look, if there isn't his blessed blood on it. O Master Kurano!
Poor soul. Poor blessed saint!

HAZAMA

My master that raised me, done to death like a thief!

KURANO

Done to death, by Kira. Goaded to it. Hounded to it till
it passed bounds, when he struck Kira and was condemned.

HAZAMA

Kira is dead, then?

KURANO

No, alive; scarcely hurt.

HAZAMA

Then come, all of us, we'll burn him in his house.

KURANO

Wait. That could only be death. Kira has borrowed guards.
His house is surrounded by them.

HAZAMA

We will wait till the guards are gone.

KURANO

You see this paper? You hold an Envoy sacred?

VOICES

Yes, indeed.

[447]

Kurano

This is an Envoy's decree. I am charged by the Envoy to read it to you. I will read it:

"These are to declare that anyone who endeavours in any way to avenge Lord Asano or to hinder the transfer of the estate will put himself without the law and will be punished by instant death, with confiscation of goods."

You see, nothing but ruin can come of any protest or act; nothing but death; and you are married men, with wives and children, or young men with parents to keep. If you lift a finger to avenge our friend, it can only wreck yourselves and them. You must submit.

Voices

We had rather die. No, no! We will not submit.

Kurano

I knew him well; better than you. He was very dear to me. You have your wives and children to think of. You must remember those; they have a claim upon you. But to me, he comes first.

A Voice

And to us, master.

Kurano

No, no! You must remember what I have read to you, and the ruin of your families.

Voices

We're ruined as it is. Kira shall die. Die, now. Lead us against him, you.

We can never be in better state to avenge him.

[448]

KURANO

No, No! Wait. Before we deal with Kira we must fulfil Asano's dying wish.

VOICES

What was that, master?

KURANO

To save the estates for the rightful heir.
I can only appeal for that if you obey this edict. [*Murmurs.*] You must obey it.

VOICES

We will not.

KURANO

It is his last word to me.

VOICES

We must kill Kira.

KURANO

You cannot kill Kira. We may stop his getting these estates, which you may be sure he aims for. And there is another thing. A shameful thing. [*Murmurs.*] Our master is denied burial. [*Cries.*] He is sentenced to a criminal's grave. If we can stop the confiscation, we may remove that slur, too. Wait till these appeals are judged, before you think of revenge. But more news comes. . . .

[*Enter* FOURTH RONIN]

VOICES

Who is this? It's the widow's boy from up by the ford. What is it?

FOURTH RONIN

Lord Kurano.

Kurano

Yes. What?

Fourth Ronin

Our Lord Asano is killed and all our land is to be Kira's.

Kurano

Yes.

Fourth Ronin

Kira's guards are moving in from the valley-head already, to turn us out. Hundreds of them are coming. Look there, lord, you can see the flames. They have burnt my old mother's house. They have orders to burn every house and occupy the whole province. There are horsemen with them, herding the stock; they are taking and destroying everything.

Kurano

It has begun, then.

Fourth Ronin

They are going to scatter us so that we shall not avenge our master.

But that is nothing, Lord Kurano. I was in a barn, among the straw, and I heard the troopers talking. They are coming for you, they said, for you are the leader.

Kurano

Are they going to kill me?

Fourth Ronin

They said they were going to make sure of you. They will kill you if you show a sign against them, Lord Kurano. I have run to beg you to hide.

KURANO

I will not hide. But you see now, you see how little hope there is.

But in the few moments left to us, before we are scattered, shall we not make a pact together, that we'll avenge our friend?

VOICES

Ay, we will. We will indeed.

KURANO

Let me trap no one. There will be no feasting in this fellowship; only a wandering in the cold, perhaps for months, and death at the end, according to this decree. Understand solemnly that the man who puts hand on mine marks himself for death.

VOICES

We will come, Lord Kurano.

VOICES

We know what the end will be.

VOICES

One has to pay a price in this world. We are ready to pay this, Lord Kurano.

KURANO

Come about me.

Here is the relic of our friend. Let us swear together, on this relic, to avenge his death.

VOICES

Yes, master.

KURANO

I speak, then, for each man here. I will avenge your death, Asano, lord and master, on the person of Kira Kots'ke, or die in the task, and to this I consecrate my life. Will you swear to this?

VOICES

I swear. I swear. So be it. I swear. I, too, swear. I make oath to this. I put my hand to this. May my name perish if I fail in this. I swear. I, too, swear. I vow this solemnly, Lord Asano. I swear, etc.

KURANO

Now swear, too, that you will avenge him only as I bid you, and when I bid you.

HAZAMA

You are our captain, Lord Kurano.

VOICES

We swear that we will obey you faithfully.

KURANO

Then it will not be, and must not be, till after the suits are heard.

All is done, then; but to say good-bye. We have no home here, henceforth; we are ronin and wanderers.

Scatter, now, through the province, wander and wait; that is all that we can do; his spies will be on us.

Now comes the bad time when you will be tried, and I have only one word to say to you: Endure. Endure all things, all things; lest we lose our revenge.

HAZAMA

And you, Lord Kurano, Kira will want to kill you.

KURANO

Yes, he will want to kill me.

HAZAMA

Will you stay here, lord, when his soldiers are coming?
Come with us, master, for safety's sake.

KURANO

I have my own part to play here.
Dismiss, then. And believe nothing that men say of me.
But, I give you no hope, remember; nor any word but endure. Perhaps some day he will dismiss his guards . . . and
then . . . justice may be done . . . if there is justice. Now
go.

[*They go out, leaving him alone. The* GIRL *remains*]

KURANO

What are you?

GIRL

Nobody.

KURANO

What is your name?

GIRL

Wild Cherry.

KURANO

What are you doing here?

GIRL

I came over for the feast.

[453]

KURANO

There will be no feast.

GIRL

I hate Kira.

KURANO

It is very wrong to hate people.

GIRL

You don't see them so close as I do.

KURANO

True.

GIRL

I like wine.

KURANO

There is plenty here. Drink.

GIRL

I like you.

KURANO

How old are you?

GIRL

Old enough.

KURANO

You ought to be with your lover, child.

GIRL

Ah! I've a lover, haven't I?

KURANO

Was your lover killed?

[454]

GIRL

Yes, Kira hanged him. I'd have been married but for that. Now I don't much care.

This yellow wine is nice.

KURANO

You good gods.

GIRL

You'll get past that stage. Was it a friend of yours that was killed?

KURANO

Yes.

GIRL

Was that through Kira?

KURANO

Yes.

GIRL

We ought to be friends, we two. You take it too seriously; I did at first. What is the use of sorrowing? It won't bring him back. Had your friend fair hair?

KURANO

No, girl; dark.

GIRL

Mine was fair. This was some of it. Of course, I'm the lowest of the low, but I've always kept some of it; then one doesn't feel so low.

KURANO

I shall kill Kira.

GIRL

I thought I would at first; but one cannot kill Kira. Be-

[455]

sides, what is the use? It won't make it any better. Nothing makes it better, except wine. They do charge us for wine. You ought not to complain; you have all this for nothing.

KURANO

Give me some.

GIRL

I'll try some of the red.

I'm sorry about your friend. It makes one so savage and all the time one is so helpless. Here's a lady.

KURANO

It is my wife. Sit still. Give me some wine.

GIRL

Now I shall get beaten and then they'll fine me especially if my sash is torn.

KURANO

Hand me that bowl; thank you.

LADY K.

Kurano.

KURANO

What do you want with Kurano?

LADY K.

Who is this?

KURANO

My sister.

LADY K.

What has happened?

KURANO

Asano is killed.

[456]

LADY K.

I felt that it would end like that. Thank God, it was not you.

KURANO

Do not thank God yet. Why did you lie to me?

LADY K.

When did I lie to you?

KURANO

This morning. You lied and made others lie.

LADY K.

This is a strange language. I do not understand. What do you mean, Kurano?

KURANO

You sent word to me this morning that you had fallen on the steps?

LADY K.

I did fall.

KURANO

And that you were dying.

LADY K.

No. My message was simply "Come. Come quickly."

KURANO

The messenger said that you were dying.

LADY K.

I do not know what the messenger may have said.

KURANO

You scared the messenger.

[457]

LADY K.

He was concerned for me. Were not you?

KURANO

Too deeply—God!

LADY K.

What is the matter, Kurano? Why do you speak to me in this way?

KURANO

You were not hurt this morning?

LADY K.

I was hurt and shaken, and I am faint and sick still.

KURANO

Not to that point.

LADY K.

Will you not even ask me how I am?

KURANO

No.

LADY K.

Oh, you are cruel to me.

KURANO

Do you know that if you had not recalled me, I should have been with Asano to-day? And then all this would not have happened, and he would be alive now.

LADY K.

That is ignoring Fate. Who can measure causes and results?

KURANO

I can measure that.

LADY K.

Your place was beside your wife, Kurano.

KURANO

Only while my wife is worthy. No, do not weep, do not cry out; I know you. Your fall was a trick to keep me.

LADY K.

Can you think, after twenty years, that I should stoop to trick?

KURANO

Yes.

LADY K.

Is it not rather terrible to you that a woman should be forced to trick, after twenty years?

Listen, then. I did trick. I did it to save you. I knew where Asano was dragging you in his mad opposition to Kira. I knew that he would ruin himself and you, too, and that to-day would decide it. So I saved you, Kurano.

KURANO

And my friend lies down in the dust.

The blood runs along the ground and soaks in, and then the brain cannot think and the hand cannot do, and twenty years' work is a memory. You killed Asano and do not even know what he was.

LADY K.

I loved Asano. I loved your friendship with him. I know how you have worked together. I knew his nobleness. But

I knew that if he were twenty times as noble he would still not be worth your little finger. You are too generous, Kurano, where you love, and too blind.

KURANO

Asano is blind. [*He rises.*]

LADY K.

What are you going to do, Kurano?

KURANO

Drink.

LADY K.

Will you not take me home?

KURANO

I have no home. The "mad opposition" is over now; Kira is master here. Do you hear, you, who admired Kira so? Go and make your peace with him. I am going.

LADY K.

Where?

KURANO

Where beaten men go.

LADY K.

I am your wife, Kurano.

KURANO

You were.

LADY K.

I am your wife; more than that, I am your loving wife. Dear, I am all shaken and strange. Say a kind word to me.

You will, I know you will; you would never do an unkind thing.

I know that I am nothing beside Asano; but now that he is dead, I could help a little. I want the world to know how noble and wonderful my husband is.

KURANO

Those are words; drink, and a dirk in the ribs, are my future.

LADY K.

Then I had better go and drown myself.

KURANO

It would be better.

LADY K.

Oh!

KURANO

I am giving you good advice. You're harmless, as women go, what is called virtuous, loving, wise. Go and drown yourself. Kira is coming. Asano was all that, yet it ended in him killing himself. You virtuous are lost in such a world. Go drown or drink; then you'll be spared things.

LADY K.

That is not the language we have faced the world with these twenty years. Dear, do not drive me away like this. Let us face it together. I do not mind for myself, but you are lost somewhere and I want to be by you. You cannot put twenty years' life together so lightly aside. Think of our children and our times together. Dear, I beg you not to put me away. I am ill, dear, and faint, and I cannot bear this. We'll plan what we can do against Kira. This is so unfitting, it is breaking my heart.

Kurano

Drink this, then, and forget it; drink.

Lady K.

It is not a little thing that you are putting away, Kurano.

Kurano

I am thirsty, and I am weary of you; besides, this is my sister.

Lady K.

I will not interrupt you, Kurano. [*Exit.*]

Girl

Was that really your wife?

Kurano

Yes, poor soul.

Girl

You oughtn't to have driven her away, like that.

Kurano

Why, the thing has come to an end.

Girl

Still, she hadn't hurt your friend, had she?

Kurano

She? No.
It is twenty-one years, to a day, that we first joined hands. [*He covers his face.*] Now I shall not see her again.
Stand up there, you, and tell me what you see?

Girl

Nothing but the fields.

[462]

KURANO

Look along the road, towards Kira's country.

GIRL

Yes, there is something burning. It is moving.

KURANO

Those are torches. I thought he would be coming soon. It is Kira coming to take possession here.

GIRL

Is that beast coming here?

KURANO

Yes. Give me some more wine.

GIRL

I'm afraid.

KURANO

Drink. It is not so bad, this life of ours, while one has this. Can you dance?

GIRL

Not if Kira is coming here.

KURANO

I can dance. I've a good mind to try. I can dance stately dances and gay dances; and I can sing.

GIRL

Don't you anger Kira.

KURANO

I tell you I can sing. I'm going to sing.

GIRL

Don't, I say, don't. You don't know Kira. He is terrible.
You take me away somewhere. It will be death if you stay
here talking all this folly.

KURANO

Why do you make that noise when I say I'm going to sing?
You have never heard me sing. The roses turn to me, when I
sing. The birds in the air turn. There was a song I made
when my friend came home; that was the friend who was
killed. But I won't sing that, that was too sad; I want a
merry song; for what is the use of being sad? Come you and
sing.

GIRL

You are mad.

KURANO

Listen to me, now. Is not this well sung?

> Fate with her changing tune
> Keeps her appointed time,
> Her ever breaking thread,
> For ever spinning.
> We, who are singing, soon
> Will cease to rhyme,
> Our moment will be sped. . . .

What comes next? Hark! Did you hear footsteps?

GIRL

It's the torches. Don't let them catch me here.

KURANO

Sit still and drink. Come here to me.

GIRL

No, I'm going, I'll not stay. You don't know what soldiers are.

KURANO

You are my dear and my delight and now we will sing together.

> Yellow wine in a silver bowl
> Is true contentment to the soul.
> A dancing girl with brilliant eyes
> Is true contentment to the wise.
> O friends, rejoice, for man is meant.

[*Enter* KIRA's *guards with* SAGISAKA]

SAGISAKA

This is the man we have come to see.

KURANO

Who are you and what do you want? Let me finish my song?.

> To, what is it, man is meant?
> To dance and sing and be content.

This is my sister. You haven't told me yet who you are.

SAGISAKA

Pay attention to all he says, Captain. You know me well enough.

KURANO

I do. You are Lord Kira's wife.

SAGISAKA

I——

KURANO

Are not you?

SAGISAKA

No, I am not.

KURANO

I get puzzled, seeing you so much together. This is very excellent wine.

SAGISAKA

I did not come to drink, Lord Kurano.

KURANO

It's the most innocent of the vices.

THE CAPTAIN OF THE GUARDS

Is this the man?

SAGISAKA

Yes.

CAPTAIN

He seems a drunken fellow.

SAGISAKA

He is less drunken than he seems.

CAPTAIN

I am not sure. Come and drink, come and drink, my friend. There is nothing like drink.

KURANO

You're a reasonable being. It is the one friend. Here's one for you.

Is that your friend?

CAPTAIN

Yes.

KURANO

He is an ugly one.

CAPTAIN

He was kicked in the face by a mule when he was young.

KURANO

Do not make fun of me.

CAPTAIN

It is the truth; isn't it?

SAGISAKA

But now I do the kicking.

KURANO

I don't like you.

SAGISAKA

That's unfortunate, for you'll perhaps see a good deal of me in the near future.

KURANO

Shall we drink together?

SAGISAKA

No.

KURANO

Then if you won't drink you're a dog and an unbelieving dog and the mule shewed sense. What do you come here for, if not to drink?

CAPTAIN

Humour a drunkard.

[467]

SAGISAKA

I come to take over these estates, which are forfeited by that friend of yours.

KURANO

Is your friend Kira going to have them?

SAGISAKA

Yes.

KURANO

Is Kira in want of a man, for I shall be out of employment.

SAGISAKA

Kira does not employ drunkards.

KURANO

Who says I am a drunkard?

CAPTAIN

Never mind what my friend says. He does not know you.

KURANO

Do you dare to call me a drunkard?

SAGISAKA

I'll dare more than that, when this first month is over.

CAPTAIN

He calls you a gentleman.

KURANO

So I am a gentleman.

CAPTAIN

We are all gentleman.

[468]

KURANO

Don't let him call me a drunkard then.

CAPTAIN

Come, we are all friends; and this is your sister.   Is your name Cherry?

KURANO

Her name's my sister.

CAPTAIN

I had a sister like her once.

KURANO

Then you had more than you deserve.

CAPTAIN

I had.   She cost me six months' pay.

KURANO

I like you.   We shall be friends.   Shall we make him drunk?

CAPTAIN

No, it would kill him.

KURANO

Never mind.

CAPTAIN

It would be difficult.

KURANO

No.   We would throw him down and pour the wine down his throat.   Shall we?

CAPTAIN

Yes.   Yes.

KURANO

You take his heels.

GIRL

Yes.

KURANO

We will.

CAPTAIN

Yes, but wait a moment.

KURANO

No, not wait.

CAPTAIN

Yes; first let us all three be drunk.

KURANO

Roaring drunk?

CAPTAIN

Roaring and raging drunk.

KURANO

All be drunk.

I'll be drunk. You'll be drunk. She'll be drunk. We'll be drunk, you'll be drunk, he'll be drunk. We'll all be drunk. Let us see who'll be drunk first. Here's yours, here's yours. I don't want to be drunk, I want to dance. Kira is coming here, so we shall be friends, you and I will be friends.

You think I've been against Kira; I'm his best friend and your best friend, so let us dance.

SAGISAKA

You shall dance to-morrow.

KURANO

I want to dance now. My sister will dance with me.

[470]

GIRL

Oh, loose me, do! I'll get fined ever so if the stuff is rumpled.

KURANO

I tell you, we will dance. Come here. We will move those mats to one side. Are you coming to dance?

CAPTAIN

Yes; dance, yes, as soon as ever you have moved the mats.

KURANO

I like you. Are you a good dancer?

CAPTAIN

Not so good as you.

KURANO

I am a good dancer, am not I?

CAPTAIN

Excellent. Let me see you dance the sword dance.

KURANO

Shall we pour the wine on our heads first?

CAPTAIN

No, afterwards, when we are hot.

KURANO

But we will?

CAPTAIN

Yes. Oh yes.

KURANO

Yes, we will pour the wine on our heads. We are going to pour the wine on our heads.

SAGISAKA

I would.

KURANO

[*To* GIRL]. I'll pour it on yours and then we'll dance. Sometimes I am sad, for all my merrymaking. It is not such an easy world. There is a fellow, Death, who is a danger, if one could find him. I had a friend once; my head is all in a whirl; a very dear friend; I could weep when I think what happened to him. It was Death who took him away. I would like to go to look for Death.

CAPTAIN

Your sister will bring you to him.

KURANO

Yes, so they say; all have told me that.

I will go look for Death, for Death is everywhere,
Putting his hands on friends and dulling women's hair.
Death took away my friend; and I have prayed for years,
But Death has paid no heed. Death does not yield to tears.

CAPTAIN

Death is like that.
You should drink again.

KURANO

There is no wine strong enough. But we will find him, some day.

SAGISAKA

He may be nearer than you think.

KURANO

You look like a friend of his. I have known wise, beautiful people; but Death did not care. [*To* GIRL.] We will go away, we two; I do not like these people; they think only of themselves. We, who have lost friends, are in another world.

We know how many miles the soul can tread,
We who go seeking signs from dear companions dead.

Come, girl, we'll go. Poor child, you are cold. We'll knock at the doors for shelter. [*Exit.*]

CAPTAIN

There is no doubt about him, poor fellow.

SAGISAKA

I am not so sure.

CAPTAIN

He is both drunk and mad.

SAGISAKA

I would like to see him sober.

CAPTAIN

I was sorry for him. This death of his friend has turned his brain.

SAGISAKA

It had better remain turned. Did you feel that he was drunk?

CAPTAIN

Yes.

SAGISAKA

And mad, you said?

CAPTAIN

Yes, both.

SAGISAKA

He is an object of pity, a martyr. He is dangerous, so.

CAPTAIN

He could be shut up, if he should become that.

SAGISAKA

That would make him still more a martyr.

CAPTAIN

What is he doing, now? I cannot see.

SAGISAKA

He'll come back. Captain.

CAPTAIN

Yes?

SAGISAKA

I believe he is pretending.

CAPTAIN

He pretends unusually well, then.

SAGISAKA

Captain, can you take a hint?

CAPTAIN

Yes.

SAGISAKA

He would be better out of the way.

CAPTAIN

I've no orders about that; that is life and death.

SAGISAKA

Kira would be grateful.

CAPTAIN

I've no means of knowing that.

SAGISAKA

I will answer for so much.

CAPTAIN

Do you order me to kill him?

SAGISAKA

Come, these are harsh words, Captain; "order" and "kill."

CAPTAIN

It's a harsh subject.

SAGISAKA

Supposing he were to talk in his cups, excitedly, provocatively. . . . Or rave against us . . . inciting to riot. . . .

CAPTAIN

Well, what then? I could only arrest him for . . . being drunk . . . or out of his mind.

SAGISAKA

Of course. . . . What more could you do? You would arrest him.

CAPTAIN

That would not help you.

SAGISAKA

Supposing he were to resist arrest, to struggle with you, or to try to get away?

CAPTAIN

The guard would bind him.

SAGISAKA

If he were violent. One of them might . . . in self-defence?

CAPTAIN

I see what you mean.

SAGISAKA

Kira would not forget it.

CAPTAIN

You want him killed?

SAGISAKA

It would be easier with him away.

CAPTAIN

I see.

SAGISAKA

Kira is thinking of putting you in command here.

CAPTAIN

Ah!

SAGISAKA

Can I trust you to carry out Kira's wishes?

CAPTAIN

The man is only a madman. He is harmless.

SAGISAKA

Madmen are not harmless, and I do not believe that he is
mad.

CAPTAIN

Drunken, then.

SAGISAKA

He is neither one nor the other. He is pretending.

CAPTAIN

If he is pretending, I will see to him.

SAGISAKA

You promise?

CAPTAIN

Yes, but that is not pretence. Watch him there as he comes.

SAGISAKA

I shall watch him very narrowly.

CAPTAIN

What is he saying?

SAGISAKA

Some folly. If I lift my hand like this, it will be a sign; and
then you will kill him.

CAPTAIN

If he is pretending, yes; right; but this poor fellow is not
pretending.

[*Enter* KURANO *with* GIRL]

[477]

Kurano

This is she. This is she who makes us mad. Look at her, she has driven me mad; it is in her eyes. It is bad when we are young, for then they smile, and we tear at the world's throat, and throw ourselves away, and all they want is vanity. If mirrors could speak, men would never be troubled by them. Look at her. All this beautiful bait to catch the little foolish fish in man.

It is beautiful, those eyes and the mouth, and all the curves, and the ears and the pretty teeth. Men have thought of these things going to death; thought of them with prayers. [*To* Captain.] Look at her. Is not she a beautiful thing? You've prayed to this in your time.

Captain

Ay, in my time.

Kurano

And you?

Sagisaka

Kurano, leave off pretending that you are mad and listen to what I have to say to you.

Kurano

Do you believe in the gods?

Sagisaka

I am not deceived, Kurano.

Kurano

If you believe in the gods you should be thankful.

Sagisaka

Give heed, Captain. Why?

[478]

KURANO

Because your mother played false with a millstone.

CAPTAIN

What makes you think that?

KURANO

It may have been flints; but it was something hard; and so you were spared feelings. You were never driven mad by one of these things. You never will be; this does not stir you. Be glad; they are fatal things. When we grow up they twine round us and fawn and purr and clog us to a standstill. They call themselves our mates. O heaven! that a thing so empty should have such power upon men. Do you see this head, how beautiful it is? Is not it wonderful, poised on the throat like that? Look how the flesh dimples, and then these shadows, and the red lips that the worm will eat, and these eyes that glitter so and tell her brain about us. Did you ever cut open such a head?

SAGISAKA

No; did you?

KURANO

With my mind. There was nothing there. I was puzzled at that.

SAGISAKA

Captain.

CAPTAIN

Do you know where you are, Kurano?

KURANO

Yes. At a very interesting point. I was saying that I was

puzzled. Then I saw that these things are parasites, who suck their lives from ours. Our life gives them life. Our imaginations give them a mind, they have none of themselves. There is nothing in them. They are only shells and coffins where we bury our best thoughts. They turn them to dust and give back nothing. Why should we deceive ourselves about them? Can you tell me why?

CAPTAIN

It would take a wiser man than me to answer that.

KURANO

Yet you and that fellow there rule the world.

SAGISAKA

We will not wait for any more, Captain; this is not madness.

CAPTAIN

It is an odd kind of talk.

SAGISAKA

Kill him when he comes back to us. I will keep his attention.

CAPTAIN

It is not like mad to me, it is more like one of these frenzies.

SAGISAKA

Well, end it. Kill him.

CAPTAIN

I have half a mind. Kurano; do you see the house on fire?

KURANO

Do not. Do not. You are always interrupting. I am going to sing to you.

Once, very long ago,
When there was still the sun,
Before these times, before
The light was darkened,
One whom we used to know
Made life most noble; one
Who would have changed the world
Had people hearkened.

It was a dream.   Perhaps
Time drugs the soul with dreams
To all but blind desire
For high attempt;
Then the intense string snaps;
The project seems
A hearth without a fire;
A madness dreamt.

SAGISAKA

I think that decides it.   Now, Captain.

KURANO

[*To* SAGISAKA.] What can it decide?   Do you think I blame
you?   You are stupid, you are vulgar, you play into life's hands.
It is life that I blame, life is the enemy—life, who takes my
friend and leaves you, the usurer, and you, the bully, and you,
the doll.   Come on then, for I will fight with life till I drag him
from behind his veil.   He is behind you and behind you and
behind you and I will have him from his hiding-place.   No,
you shall not escape.   I will have you.   Out of my way.   And
you, the doll, the clog, to be left when my friend is taken. . . .
[*He beats them with a cloak.*]   No.   No.   Forgive me.   I am not

settled in my wits. You had better give me wine. For I'm going to law, and must have my wits about me. Wine will steady me. I fill to you and to you and to you, and then I fill to myself. Then we will drink and fall asleep.

CAPTAIN

There can be no mistaking that.

SAGISAKA

I was wrong. He is mad.

CAPTAIN

A raving madman.

KURANO

[*To* GIRL.] We'll drink and sing:

> Wine is a strong drink
> Beauty is a stronger
> Grief makes a man think
> And makes the day longer.

So give a man beauty, and give a man wine,
And drink to your true love while I drink to mine.

[*Falls asleep on the ground, spilling the bowl*]

SAGISAKA

[*Kicking him.*] So much for Lord Kurano.

CAPTAIN

It is a pity. There was something in some of what he said. He has been a fine man; a soldier they said?

SAGISAKA

Yes.

CAPTAIN

We come to strange ruins. Perhaps he would be happier if
I were to end him.   Let sleepers be; sleep is better than nothing.

[*Enter* KIRA *with* HARIMA]

KIRA

What news of Kurano?

SAGISAKA

There.

HARIMA

Drunk?

SAGISAKA

Drunk and raving.   His brain is turned.

KIRA

Turned?   Are you sure he is not pretending?

CAPTAIN

He is not pretending, Lord Kira.

SAGISAKA

I suspected him, but this last has convinced me.

KIRA

It falls out luckily.

SAGISAKA

I was not sure . . . whether to kill him in any case.

KIRA

No, no, no; nothing of the sort.

[483]

SAGISAKA

He said something of going to law.

KIRA

Well, we must humour him.   All else goes well?

SAGISAKA

All the men of the estate have scattered; this blow has destroyed them.

KIRA

A higher power has been in this.   It is a mercy from above.

HARIMA

True.

KIRA

Come, we will celebrate this happy day fittingly; meanwhile let us give thanks at the temple.

[*Exeunt* KIRA, SAGISAKA, CAPTAIN]

HARIMA

[*Lingering.*]   Sot and coward!   Beast.   You called yourself Asano's friend.   Pah, you drunkard.   May your own friends let you die so.

[*Kicks him and exit.   A moment passes; a distant bell strikes.*]

KURANO

[*Rises.*]   So there is mercy for the madman, none for the wise man, it seems.   Now, you blind wolves, you shall see whether I have forgotten.   Thus! thus!

[*He tears his robes across*]

CURTAIN

[484]

ACT III

SCENE I.—*The outer scene.* THE HERALD. KURANO *in the background.*

THE HERALD

Comrades, imagine that a year has passed.
    Asano's men have not avenged their lord.
They have been wanderers, houseless to the blast,
    Keeping most bravely to their plighted word,
Biding revenge, until the Courts declare
Whether Asano's brother may be heir.

To-day the Judge has uttered his decree
    That Lord Asano's castle fief and lands
Are forfeit to the Envoy and shall be
    Given forever into Kira's hands;
For Kira's plans have thrived. The Court intends
To crown him Duke before to-morrow ends.

This news so fills the Ronin with despair
    That seventy men desert Kurano's band,
Making all hope of vengeance empty air;
    Since the remainder cannot hope to stand
Against the thousand guards in Kira's pay,
Kurano's planned revenge is swept away.

Here in the snow, alone with cruel thought,
    He thinks of his dear comrade tricked to death,
Kira in pride and vengeance brought to naught,
    And justice by decree made empty breath.

[485]

Friendship and justice, hate and vengeance fail;
Nothing remains, but love that cannot quail.

His son is coming, bringing bitter news;
Life has no pity on the men who lose.

[*Exit* HERALD]

[*Enter* CHIKARA]

KURANO

Chikara, is that you? Come, boy, I have news to tell you.
We have lost the suit of the inheritance.

CHIKARA

I expected that, father. Kira is the law here now.

KURANO

Yes, he is. . . . But you are shaking; what makes you so
white, boy?

CHIKARA

Nothing, father. Have you had good sales to-day, father?

KURANO

No, boy; none yet.

CHIKARA

Are you selling toys to-day, father?

KURANO

Not toys, dear lad; toys are luxuries. I sell vanities; they
are necessaries. But you tremble like a leaf. . . . What is it?

CHIKARA

It must be the cold, father.

[486]

KURANO

You must have my old cloak, Chikara.

CHIKARA

Then you'll be cold.

KURANO

No, I am too hot. I have been excited. Let me put it well round you.

CHIKARA

Thank you, father. What has made you excited?

KURANO

Thoughts.

CHIKARA

Were you thinking what night it is, father?

KURANO

No, boy. What night is it?

CHIKARA

It is a year to-night since we left home. The men are meeting to-night. They mean to keep the year. Will you go, father?

KURANO

No, boy, I do not think to go.

CHIKARA

How strangely you answer, father.

KURANO

Do I? Well . . . my thoughts are strange.

[487]

CHIKARA

Father, may I say something?

KURANO

Yes, boy.

CHIKARA

Will you give up the drinking and singing?

KURANO

Why, boy?

CHIKARA

Father, it cuts me to the quick to hear the men about you; they say you have forgotten our master.

KURANO

I have not done that, Chikara.

CHIKARA

I am sorry, father.   Father.

KURANO

Yes?

CHIKARA

If Kira were to die, from some illness, should we all go back home and be knights, as we were before?

KURANO

If he were to die, boy; have you heard that he is ill?

CHIKARA

One hears all sorts of things, father, and fears all sorts of things.

[488]

KURANO

Kira is cunning; he would like us to fear all sorts of things. But what is the matter, dear lad? Your brow is burning. You are ill?

CHIKARA

I am not, father. I was only thinking, that if he were to fall ill and die, it would be a bad thing.

KURANO

Yes; that would be a bad thing.

CHIKARA

I think it would be terrible, father.   [*He breaks down.*]

KURANO

Ah, boy, this is the world we used to read of together.

CHIKARA

Have you heard about mother, father?

KURANO

No, boy; never since.

CHIKARA

Father, I would give anything that you had not sent her away.

KURANO

My lad, we are not like other people, who can enjoy themselves. We were born knights, with duties.

CHIKARA

You know she has killed herself. She said there was a woman's way of being faithful. She would not keep you back?

[489]

Kurano

No, boy. She would not keep me back. She would not keep you back. So, she is dead. Chikara, my boy.

Chikara

Yes, father?

Kurano

Once a woman of our ancestors was defending a doorway with her husband against the enemy. She was shot in the breast with an arrow. She cried to her husband, "Never mind me. But use my body as a shield and keep the door." So he did.

Chikara

Was she killed, father?

Kurano

As far as such souls die she died.

Chikara

You never told me that tale before, father.

Kurano

No, we told gentle tales, in the evening bell-time. Did I ever tell you of Choryo?

Chikara

No, father. Who was he?

Kurano

A knight like us, lad. A lord killed Choryo's friend; it was Choryo's duty to avenge him. But the lord camped with his army, with soldiers all about him. Chotyo was alone, but for his son.

Chikara

Did they do anything, father?

Kurano

They crept into the lord's camp at night, right up to his tent, through all the guards.

Chikara

Did they kill him?

Kurano

No, boy, they were caught, and put to death, like thieves.

Chikara

O father!

Kurano

That is why they are remembered, perhaps. They are in the stories.

Chikara

I believe you are making up these tales, father.

Kurano

I've been thinking in these last hours, boy. The world talks much about brotherhood; it is nothing to fatherhood. It is a proud thing to be a knight, and to have my son beside me.

Are not you very proud to wear a sword, Chikara?

Chikara

Yes, father.

Kurano

All the evil in the world is at the mercy of a sword.

Chikara

Why do they let Kira wear a sword, father?

Kurano

Evil can be very strong when knights forget their oaths.
Kira is to be made Duke to-morrow, and to have our lord's estates.

Chikara

Are we going to kill him then, father?

Kurano

No, boy; I am afraid not.

Chikara

Father, dear.

Kurano

Yes, my dear lad.

Chikara

The men say a terrible thing about you.

Kurano

What?

Chikara

That you care for the drink more than for fighting Kira.

Kurano

Yes; they may say that. Do you think that?

Chikara

No, father.

Kurano

Ah, lad, I've been trying to blind Kira. The drink was nothing but a blind.

Chikara

You have blinded the men, father.

[492]

KURANO

Does it make any difference?

CHIKARA

It makes all the difference.

KURANO

You are wrong, boy.

CHIKARA

If I am wrong, will you meet them to-night and tell them?

KURANO

How your voice rings, lad, and only last year you were playing at school. Do you remember?

CHIKARA

Yes, with old Daigaku.

KURANO

Now you are alone with me.

Listen, Chikara, there has been a break in the League; over seventy have left us.   It is all over with the League.

CHIKARA

Yes, father.

KURANO

I cannot trust the others now. Our duty rests on us two. Do you understand?

CHIKARA

It is on us two, father.

KURANO

We must take desperate risks, like Choryo. Will you come, now?

[493]

CHIKARA

Where to, father?

KURANO

To Kira's palace.

CHIKARA

Yes, father.

KURANO

There will be many workmen about, getting ready for to-morrow, perhaps we shall be able to get in. Do you know Kira?

CHIKARA

No, father.

KURANO

He is a tall man, very noble-looking, with grey hair. He is restless and has quick eyes and a great voice. He is very glorious in his dress. But you will know him by one thing; he commands.

CHIKARA

Yes, father.

KURANO

If we get in, perhaps we shall only see, only spy out the land, see the guards.

CHIKARA

Yes, father.

KURANO

But Kira walks sometimes in the courtyard.

CHIKARA

Yes, father

KURANO

There is a kind of god, boy.

[494]

CHIKARA

Yes, father.

KURANO

If we see Kira, if we get near him, keep my left side and back.

CHIKARA

I will, father, while I live.

KURANO

You are like your mother, boy. She was a very noble woman, Chikara. She told me strange things, once, long ago. Come, now.

Sing as we go, lad.

CHIKARA

Sometimes, when guests have gone, the host remembers
  Sweet courteous things unsaid.
We two have talked our hearts out to the embers,
  And now go hand in hand, down to the dead.

CURTAIN

[SCENE II.—*The* RONIN *grouped in the dark in the snow, moaning to themselves.*

FIRST RONIN

Has Lord Kurano come?

SECOND RONIN

No.

FIRST RONIN

Are all the others here?

[495]

SECOND RONIN

All who are coming.

FIRST RONIN

Friends.

SECOND AND THIRD RONIN

Let our friend speak.

FIRST RONIN

Asano's men.

FOURTH AND FIFTH RONIN

Quiet! Quiet!

FIRST RONIN

This is the last meeting of our League. Our brotherhood of misery comes to an end. [*A moan passes over the crowd.*]

We have starved and wandered as Kurano bade. Each in his way we have all prepared for an attack on Kira, but to-day, as you know, three-fifths of our men have left us; all hope of revenge is gone. Our share in the preparations was to supply swords. Here they are, all that we have. We starved and begged and dug in the fields to buy them. We shall not want them now. So . . . let them lie. [*Flings them down.*]

SECOND RONIN

I and my fellows had an easier task. We had only to spy on Kira. We know Kira's palace as we knew ours. These plans are our share. But we shall not want them now. Lie there with the swords. [*Flings them down.*]

THIRD RONIN

It was our task to supply armour. This is what we made. We made it, after work, in the fields, in the cold nights, out of whatever we could get, broken metal and leather; rusty with the snow, too. Since it will not be used, no matter. Ground arms, with the rest.

Fourth Ronin

Our band swore to get hooks and ladders in case we should scale Kira's palace. Here they are; the best we could get. Heap them down. We shall never climb by them.

Fifth Ronin

I and my fellows made these lanterns in case we should make a night attack. They will not light us to any revenge. They may lie dark. [*Flings them down.*]

First Ronin

We have been a year in the rice plots, as farmers' men.

Second Ronin

We have been joiners and beggars and fruit-sellers.

Third Ronin

We have been wanderers, glad of broken meats at the door.

Fourth Ronin

We have been fishermen at sea.

Fifth Ronin

We have been dogs in the kennels, outcasts.

First Ronin

And whatever we have been, these things were made at the risk of our lives, when it was death by decree to plot revenge or speak revenge.

Second Ronin

We might have spared ourselves the pain.

First Ronin

Not ourselves. Our wives and children might have been
spared. My wife came to me, she had stabbed herself in the
breast. She said: "You are a knight. You must avenge your
lord, not think of women."

> Her beauty died there.
> My guest went from my fireside.
> Our talk, our friendship,
> Broken, unfinished,
> The best things unsaid.

Second Ronin

I had no wife. I was to have been married before the ruin.
But I had to think of my lord, not of marriage. I never saw
her again. The girl has gone now, ruined, too; and whether
she is dead or in a teahouse I shall never know.

Third Ronin

I had no wife, nor lover, I am a widower. I had a little son.
They told me he was lying on the flowers. I brought him in to
the shed where we lived, we had no proper home. He had
killed himself that I might be free to kill Kira. His little hands
were clenched on the dirk.

Fourth Ronin

My father and mother had a right to peace, after eighty
years. But they were afraid that they might be a burden on

[498]

me, while I had my duty to my lord to do. They killed themselves.

And all these lives go for nothing.

FIFTH RONIN

Those losses were beautiful, you can be proud of them. Kira
brought other losses on me. I saw my children starved to
death.

> We lay on the reeds
> In the marshy places.
> They cried for food,
> For the sweet cakes of old.
> "Father, father,
> I am so hungry!
> May I have a rice-cake?
> I have had no rice-cake
> All to-day."
>
> All around
> Were the marshy places.
> They cried for food,
> Those sons of mine.
> "Father," they said,
> "Will it soon be food-time?
> Can you feed us, father?"
> I told them, "No."
> And then they cried.
>
> Kira it was,
> The great Lord Kira,
> Who burnt our home
> And drove us forth.

THE FAITHFUL

It was his deed
That starved my children,
My little sons
In the wild swan's lair.

We cannot kill him,
We cannot harm him,
We cannot rob him
Of a moment's pleasure,
The unatoned blood
Cries unheeded.
We are poor men
Lost in the snow.

FIRST RONIN

That is a true song, brother; we are lost indeed.

SECOND RONIN

Kira triumphs.

FIFTH RONIN

He drinks with his dancing women, he is made Duke.

THIRD RONIN

He will be harsher to us now.

FOURTH RONIN

I thought the gods checked pride, but evil like Kira's checks the gods.

FIRST RONIN

Since all is useless, we will burn these things and dissolve the League.

[500]

SECOND RONIN

There is nothing else that we can do.

THIRD RONIN

Heap them together.

FOURTH RONIN

Pour the oil upon them.

FIFTH RONIN

These were the deserters' banners; they had better burn.

FIRST RONIN

So, pile them, and good-bye to revenge.   Would the deserters were burning with them!

VOICES

Burn, with our hopes, to ashes, all is past,
The waiting in the snow,
The year-long pain,
The faith that equal justice falls at last.
We may depart, but not with hope again.
So burn, so perish, as the fire drives,
Our hope, our love, our service, all our lives.

[*Enter* KURANO *and* CHIKARA]

VOICES

You come too late, Lord Kurano; you should have come before, we are disbanded.

KURANO

Not yet, not for a moment.   There are things I wish to say to you.   Tread out the fire.   Come nearer.

[501]

FIRST RONIN

What have you to say to us, Lord Kurano?

SECOND RONIN

You can say nothing, but that we are ruined while Kira is triumphant.

KURANO

I have just come from Kira's palace.

THIRD RONIN

What did you see there?

KURANO

Preparations for to-morrow; a muster of the guards.

FIRST RONIN

What then?

KURANO

Kira came out.

VOICES

Ah! the accursed!

KURANO

He had gifts for the guards for guarding him. This was in the courtyard. I was watching through the gates. The gates have been gilded for to-morrow, they are like gold. There were a thousand guards, in armour.

VOICES

We know their strength, too well.

KURANO

I had not seen them march before. They marched past Kira to salute, till the courtyard shook. They sang, too, rank after rank, a song in praise of Kira. "Aha, Aha, Kira." They came staight towards me; the dust in the court was like smoke.

[502]

They came straight to the gates. The gates were opened and they came through, horsemen and swordsmen, with fifes and banners. They still sang to Kira: "Bow down to Kira, to Kira the Duke." There were ten picked companies marching there. They thought I was a beggar at the gate, they flung money to me. They all came glittering out, singing their song about Kira in his glory.

When they had all come out, the gates were closed, and presently a little old man came out and locked them and a boy brought rice and flung it to the pigeons, and then it was sunset, and the gilders packed their tools and went home, and twilight came and a star, and they brought lanterns then and hung them in the courtyard so that one saw shadows, and they lit the cresset on the gate so that it was all wavering light.

Presently it began to snow, and the snow came down and down, but I stayed on by the gate in a kind of dream, for things came into my head about my friend, my friend Asano. He came into me here next my heart, talking to me. "Kurano, Kurano, and all my men of old time, fellowship goes on after death, dear brothers, in its struggle against wrong."

And I fell into a kind of dream about the Envoy, who is to make Kira Duke, being the man who condemned Asano a year ago; and I thought, "Yes, the Envoy is coming, and the palace is a sacred place and so Kira has dismissed his guards."

YELLS

What? What?

KURANO

He has dismissed them till to-morrow, and on this snowy night, he'll be unprepared, and
We can attack him if you will.

[503]

Voices

Free? Free to attack him? The guards are gone. We can attack him.

Kurano

Yes, if you will. Will you?

Voices

Very well; we will; to-night.

Kurano

Let us arm, then. Chikara, boy, we are going to die in a few hours. They are excited now, and will be, for a time, but it may pass. I look to you to help me to keep them thus.

Chikara

Very well, father.

The Ronin

We are ready, Master Kurano.

Kurano

Now we will cast off our rags for death, and say our death-poems. This is the knife that killed our Master Asano. Let us consecrate ourselves to the washing of the blood away.

Chikara

I am the youngest, I will say my death-poem first: "Life is a banquet spread, but I cannot stay for the feast."

First Ronin

I will say mine: "To-morrow I shall be under the grass, but to-night I am a man and on to-morrow's morrow men shall talk of me."

Second Ronin

I will say mine: "Young men often die for old men, it is the way of the world. I am an old man dying with young men in the young man's cause, and I am happy."

Third Ronin

I will say mine:
"We are outlaws, going to die like outlaws.
"The flowers from our bones will be better laws."

Fourth Ronin

I will say mine: "Brave men going to battle for our land will stop to lay flowers upon our graves."

Kurano

I will say mine: "Evil is very strong, but men who will give their lives are stronger."
Let us go out into the night.

First Ronin

We should have a banner, master.

Kurano

[*Raising the dagger.*] This is our banner. Play music. March!
[*They go out to a droning oboe and the slow tapping of a drum. They begin a pæan.*]

Curtain

Scene III.—*The inner scene.* Kira's *palace.* Sagisaka. Kira.

SAGISAKA

Will you not rest, my lord? To-morrow's ritual will be long; you will be fatigued.

KIRA

Honours do not fatigue. About those tenants near the stream. See them all turned out to-morrow, and their houses pulled down. I mean to dam the river there and make a fish-pond.

SAGISAKA

If you made the fish-pond above, my lord, or shut them from the sea below . . . they would be forced out, without your sending a man.

KIRA

That may have served in the old days. I am strong enough now for directer methods. Have you had any news of Kurano since his suits were heard?

SAGISAKA

He has flung away his swords. He goes in rags like a beggar, they say; drunk in the kennel half his time; mad the rest.

KIRA

Ah! My plan throve, you see. Asano's men have quarrelled. Their quarrelling so soon perhaps seems suspicious?

SAGISAKA

I doubt their love for Asano; men hate philanthropists.

KIRA

It might have been better to have watched them more closely.

SAGISAKA

People so broken as Asano's will not be able to do much.

KIRA

I wonder if we were wise to dismiss the guards.

SAGISAKA

We should hear in time if there were any movement. We could recall the guards. They are only half a march away.

KIRA

True. Still. . . . It might be better.

SAGISAKA

I will write the order for them to return.

KIRA

Give me some wine, Sagisaka. [*Drinks.*] I will have up that woman from the village, the pretty one.

SAGISAKA

[*Writing.*] The one you saw this morning?

KIRA

The one with the broad brow.

SAGISAKA

You have an eye for them, my lord.

KIRA

She is here, I suppose?

[507]

Sagisaka

I will send her.

Kira

What is this?

Sagisaka

The order for the guards; if you will sign it I will send a
rider with it.

Kira

Now? It must be midnight. Whom would you send?

Sagisaka

A groom will take it.

Kira

It is a bitter night; still snowing. Do you know if the horses
have been roughed?

Sagisaka

They were going to rough them to-morrow if the frost held.

Kira

Send me the stableman to-morrow; the fool should have
roughed them to-day.

Sagisaka

We could rough one now if you would like the letter sent.

Kira

It is spoiling six men's sleep for the sake of one man's folly.
I will cast that man, and promote the other, the horse-breaker.

Sagisaka

Very well, my lord.

KIRA

What are the women like, down at the fishery?

SAGISAKA

There's a girl I would like you to see.

KIRA

A girl, eh?

SAGISAKA

She's a bright little thing.

KIRA

I would like to see her to-night.

SAGISAKA

She cannot be here till to-morrow.

KIRA

I will have the other then, for now.

SAGISAKA

Here are the sweetmeats.

KIRA

Thank you, Sagisaka.

SAGISAKA

I will tell the women to send her up.

KIRA

Yes. Good-night, Sagisaka. Oh, Sagisaka.

SAGISAKA

My lord?

[509]

KIRA

Take notes of this, please.

SAGISAKA

Certainly, Lord Kira.

KIRA

To-morrow, before everything, send out two whom you can trust to find out about Asano's men, what they are doing and what parties they are in.

SAGISAKA

I will see to it myself. Is there anything else?

KIRA

We do not renew Nekko's bond.

SAGISAKA

He is counting on us.

KIRA

I cannot renew; the man's a fool. There was another thing . . . it has slipped my mind. . . . Oh, about Kurano.

SAGISAKA

Yes, Lord Kira?

KIRA

We will have him here, where he can live with some dignity; after all the man is a gentleman, nobly born. I do not like to think of him as he is.

SAGISAKA

It shall be done, my lord.

KIRA

You disapprove?

[510]

SAGISAKA

No, my lord. What was that?

KIRA

What?

SAGISAKA

I thought I heard a tapping.

KIRA

It was the snow. That window often rattles in bad weather.

SAGISAKA

It sounded more like a branch.

KIRA

The yellow plum-tree, no doubt; it needs cutting back. [*Drinks*.] Do not send the girl yet. I want to finish that problem of chess. [*He takes chessmen.*]

SAGISAKA

Very well, my lord. I will go, then.

KIRA

Good-night, Sagisaka. Open the window, as you go, the room's too hot. Is it still snowing?

SAGISAKA

A little. The moon's up. I'll leave the window. [*Passing* KIRA.] I believe you should move the knight, my lord.

KIRA

Nonsense, Sagisaka; look where the castle is.

[511]

SAGISAKA

Well, good-night, my lord.

KIRA

Good-night. [SAGISAKA *goes and re-enters*.] Well?

SAGISAKA

Shall I send that order to the guards?

KIRA

To-morrow will do.

SAGISAKA

It shall go at sunrise.

KIRA

Are you anxious? Do you feel that the guards ought to be here?

SAGISAKA

One feels safer with them.

KIRA

Ah, we are safe.

SAGISAKA

I hope so, my lord.

KIRA

I know so. What is to hurt us?

SAGISAKA

I don't know, my lord.

KIRA

Nor I.

SAGISAKA

I am sorry to have disturbed you, my lord.

KIRA

Wait. Is my servant outside?

SAGISAKA

He is just outside the door.

KIRA

He will call when I am ready. Go to rest now; we shall have a hard day to-morrow. [*Exit* SAGISAKA.] [*To himself.*] If I move the knight, the castle takes it. What other move can the knight have? Not there. There. No. The king must move. [*A packet is thrown in.*] [*Quoting.*]

"Earth to the king is but a chessboard laid,
  With men and women waiting to be played."

[*A tapping.*] What is that? [*Goes to window.*] It rattles, yet the wind has fallen. [*Returning.*] What is this? [*Picks up packet.*] Did Sagisaka drop this? Was it thrown in? I cannot read it in this light. [*Comes forward to read.*] [*Reading.*] "Danger. Danger. Danger!" What danger? It is another of these madmen. Pah! [*Settling to his game.*] Now if I moved the pawn . . . the pawn is the key. . . .

A VOICE

Read it, Kira.

KIRA

What?

VOICE

Read it, Kira.

KIRA

Who said, "Read it, Kira?" [*Crossing to window.*] Can

any one be in the courtyard? It is all bright moonlight. I heard a voice.

I am sure I heard a voice. [*Goes to door.*] Ono.

SERVANT

Yes, my lord?

KIRA

Did you hear a voice just then?

SERVANT

No, my lord.

KIRA

There was a voice calling my name.

SERVANT

I heard nothing, my lord. It has been all quiet in the house.

KIRA

No one has been to the door?

SERVANT

No one, my lord.

KIRA

Do you see any tracks in the snow there?

SERVANT

It is all white, untrodden snow, my lord.

KIRA

Send two of the men round with lanterns to make sure.

SERVANT

Very good, my lord. Shall I bar the window, my lord?

[514]

KIRA

Yes, close the window; then go. [*Exit* SERVANT.] Strange. There was a voice. I am well; am I well? What am I to read? [*Opens and reads.*] "You are to be killed to-night. Hide. Hide." I am weary of these warnings. I will have them ended. It is strange that they still come. To-morrow I will root out those Asano people. [*Writes.*] There. There. Then these warnings will end. [*The little god on the bracket at the back of the stage falls and breaks*.] What was that?

[ONO *enters*]

ONO

Are you hurt, my lord?

KIRA

No. This fell.

ONO

May the gods turn it to our good. What made it fall?

KIRA

The support was rotten, look. It is broken to pieces.

ONO

May the gods have pity on us!

KIRA

Why do you say that? You are trembling.

ONO

This is the god of this house and it is broken.

KIRA

It is a piece of baked clay which fell on to a piece of stone.

[515]

Ono

It is your god and it is broken.

Kira

And what do you think that means?

Ono

May the gods prevent it being so!

Kira

What does it mean?

Ono

That your luck is passing.

Kira

So it is, Ono. Lord Kira is passing. To-morrow he becomes Duke and Overlord. To-morrow, did I say? No, to-day. What time is it?

Ono

On the stroke of twelve, my lord.

Kira

Did the watchmen find anything?

Ono

Nothing, my lord, all was quiet, but for one thing.

Kira

What was that?

Ono

The dogs were howling.

Kira

They were baying the moon.

Ono

No, my lord.

Kira

Then it is the frost; their drink is frozen.

Ono

They were baying at something in the air.

Kira

What?

Ono

Something over the house; a bird that was flying away.

Kira

It was an owl like yourself, Ono. Take these orders. They are to be in the Captain's hands by noon to-morrow. Is that woman ready?

Ono

Yes, my lord.

Kira

Go down with those orders and then send her up. [*Exit* Ono.] [*Picking up the shards.*] You have watched out your time. You have been with me since the beginning. Now we shall have a new one. A famous artist will make one all of gold, for Duke Kira. It will watch me go on, from power to power, Duke Kira, Prince Kira.

Prince Kira. [*Drinks.*] Why not?

[*The door opens and a woman appears*]

You are the Starblossom?

Woman

Yes, lord.

KIRA

Will you not put off that veil?

WOMAN

No, lord.

KIRA

Let me help you.

WOMAN

No.

KIRA

Do not shrink from me. I hear you have a very beautiful voice, a thrilling voice. These sweetmeats are for the voice. Will you not sing to me?

WOMAN

I cannot sing.

KIRA

Here is the viol. I am sure that you will play to me.

WOMAN

I am terrified, terrified.

KIRA

Take this viol, now, and let me hear your voice. You will spoil your singing if you are terrified. Look at these pearls, every word that you utter is a pearl; these shall be yours for one song. Your voice is cool and white; it is as beautiful as these pearls. There is the hand, now, on the strings; a touch and music comes. Sing me some song that means very much to you, some gentle song like your voice, a delicate song, like a touch upon the heart. You have suffered, to have such a voice; you have had a sorrow.

WOMAN

Yes, Lord Kira.

THE FAITHFUL

KIRA

Sing to me of that, if it is not too great a pain.

WOMAN

Are you Lord Kira?

KIRA

Yes.

WOMAN

They told me you were a devil.

KIRA

You see that they were wrong.   Please tell me of yourself.
Sing me this song of yourself.

WOMAN

It is not so very beautiful; but it is common enough.

KIRA

It will be human, then, if it is common.

WOMAN

It is human, if sorrow is human.

Queens long ago
Knew sorrowful days,
Seeing their husbands killed,
Their sons destroyed.
Death makes the full heart void,
The cold heart filled,
Those women knew Death's ways,
 I also know.

[519]

Father and mother gone,
He whom I loved, and now
My sons, my lovely sons,
My three bright boys
Killed, while the sunlight shone,
And blossom filled the bough;
I was so happy once
But Death destroys.

Yet, although Death is great,
Earth's many million tears
Move on the heart of things
Quickening a change to be;
And drop by drop the sea
Moans from its springs,
Its cry will reach God's ears;
Man has not long to wait.
Death is but tool to Fate.

The cup is brimmed in time and then it spills over.

KIRA

You are young to have sorrowed so.

WOMAN

There are younger ones who have sorrowed worse. If you
knew what goes on in this land of yours, Lord Kira.

KIRA

You were beautiful when you said that.

WOMAN

Was I?

[520]

KIRA

Very. Listen, will you tell me more, tell me of what goes on in this land of mine?

WOMAN

You do not want to hear.

KIRA

From you, I do. There is another thing I want to hear from you. [*The oboe and the drum far off.*]

WOMAN

Hark!

KIRA

You will not put me away like that, Starblossom.

WOMAN

There was a noise. There it is again.

KIRA

We will not mind the noise. I want to hear the music of your voice, saying something.

WOMAN

No, no, no!

KIRA

Say something sweet, Starblossom. What a beautiful name, it is beautiful like your voice. Will you say this thing, Starblossom, the little sweet word, while I hold your hands like this, and look into your beautiful eyes? [*The music loud, and voices.*]

WOMAN

What is it that I must say, Lord Kira?

[521]

KIRA

That you love me, Starblossom. How you tremble, little flower; how white you are!

THE PÆAN OF THE RONIN

The time dragged by till our hearts were broken,
    The time dragged by till we cursed the sun;
Now the hour has struck and the word is spoken.
    The time is fallen and the deed begun.

Asano. Asano. Over the wall with the banner.

KIRA

What do they say?

WOMAN

It sounds like rejoicing.

KIRA

Ah, yes. To-day I receive the Dukedom.

WOMAN

They are coming to cheer you.

A VOICE

Kira's men. Help me, Kira's men. Help me, I'm alone.

A VOICE

Guard the great gates. Shoot at the roof.

WOMAN

You must show yourself to them.

KIRA

You have not said that you love me yet.

WOMAN

Do you want me to?

KIRA

Yes, Starblossom.

WOMAN

You have not shewn that you love me.

KIRA

I will shew you, Starblossom.

WOMAN

[*Flinging.*] Fetch me my comb.

KIRA

These pearls will serve instead. [*Clasps pearls about her throat.*] Now you are prisoner, beautiful Starblossom.

A VOICE

I cannot. Look! They are all sticking in me.

A VOICE

O, I am killed . . . killed!

A VOICE

Die, you! Where is he? [*The Pæan in snatches.*]

WOMAN

Get away. Listen! Oh, what was that?

KIRA

What! What is this, then? [*Strikes gong.*]

WOMAN

They are fighting.

KIRA

[*Going to door.*] Where is Ono? Ono!

A VOICE

We are coming, Master Asano.

WOMAN

It is Kurano and his men, O God!

KIRA

Quiet, woman! I must think.

[*Enter* SAGISAKA]

SAGISAKA

Run, my lord. Get out of the house. It is Kurano. Run. Go, man. They've surprised us. Hide. Run. Go, you girl. Run.

KIRA

Yes.

[*Drops his white cloak and runs to the door right.* SAGISAKA *hides behind the door. The girl flies door left.*]

SAGISAKA

Can I get that knife before they come?

[*Crawls out, listens, and crawls back*]

KURANO

He cannot have escaped.

HAZAMA

I have looked. He was not there.

[524]

FIRST RONIN

None of us is much hurt. They made a good stand in the courtyard.

KURANO

Your cut about. Hara. Bind his head, Kodera. Come in here. He may be here. Come carefully. [*They enter.*]

HAZAMA

He is not here. This is a living-room.

SECOND RONIN

We have come the wrong way. Go back, master.

FIRST RONIN

There is his wine. He is not here. He has got away.

HAZAMA

I believe he has. Let us waste no time here. Come, quickly.

KURANO

Wait. What is this wrapping?

FIRST RONIN

A cloak. Some of their clothes.

KURANO

It is his cloak. Look at the purple edge.

HAZAMA

Master, we have not searched the stables. He may have taken horse by this. Run, you.

KURANO

Wait. This cloak is warm. He must be near. He must have been here within the minute. Come. We'll search this way.

SAGISAKA

[*Springing out.*] Not yet. [*He sends* CHIKARA *reeling.*]

HAZAMA

Ah, cockerel. [*Stabs him. The others go past.*]

SAGISAKA

I have got . . . one of you. [*Falls.*] Tell the trumpeter . . . tell the trumpeter . . . tell the trumpeter . . . to call . . . the call. [*Dies.*]

HAZAMA

They have him. [*Goes to door.*] Come this way, you Ronin. Come this way, Asano's men. Kira is taken.

[*A shout of joy. The* RONIN *flock in and line back of stage.* KURANO *and the others bring in* KIRA.]

KURANO

Take that body aside. [SAGISAKA *is drawn aside.*] Be quiet, please. Duke Kira, Overlord of this Province, Knight of the Sacred Presence, Chieftain of the Captains, Supreme Counsellor. We are the friends and servants of Lord Asano. who was done to death by you, a year ago. We come before you with a message from our beloved master and friend. [*He displays the dagger.*] We cannot rest till our master is avenged. We have the honour, Duke Kira, to request you to kill yourself, with this knife, duly prepared.

[*He kneels and offers the dagger. A long pause*]

The Ronin

[*Kneeling.*] We have the honour, Duke Kira, to request you to kill yourself. [*A pause.*]

Kurano

Duke Kira, in the name of our beloved master, and friend, we request you to kill yourself. [*A long pause. Drawing his sword.*] Justice must be done, then.

Curtain

Scene IV.—*The outer scene*

Kurano

Come this way. Come this way. It is but a little way. The word has gone to the Envoy. The order will come in a few minutes.

This is the grave. This is the holy place. We are all anointed and ready. We have kept faith this night, and it will soon be morning. Look, our lanterns are dim, and there is all the dew on the grass. This is Asano's grave. This little green heap where the little flowers grow. So now we have come here. Oh, the joy of being able to come! We are the happy faithful and the birds are beginning.

My beloved man, whom I knew, our master and friend, lying here under the grass, we come here on our knees, to say that we have kept faith. We have broken the chain and spilled the cup. He is dead, Asano.

Asano, beloved master, we offer you back this knife.

It was stained when you left it with us. We have cleansed the stain.

Take it from us, Master Asano, with our love and with our lives.

The Ronin

Gladly given, Master Asano. [*A trumpet winds.*]

Kurano

Now I receive the herald who will bid us come to you, Asano, in whatever windy place the dead know, to be with you forever. [*A trumpet winds.*]

[*The* Herald *enters*]

The Herald

Kurano and the retainers of Asano Takumi no Kami.

Kurano

We are here.

The Herald

I have a message for you.

That you are to kill yourselves here, on this spot for the murder of Duke Kira. [*He presents the order.*]

Kurano

We accept the order. You shall witness our obedience to it.

The Herald

I salute you, faithful ones.

Kurano

You trumpeters, who call the faithful to death in all the armies of the world, blow a long point

> That long-dead heroes
> Manning the ramparts of God
> May hear us coming,
> Baring our hearts to the sword
> For him we loved so.

Curtain

[528]

PHILIP THE KING

A PLAY IN ONE ACT

TO

MY WIFE

PHILIP THE KING

Philip

[*Kneeling*] Lord, I am that Philip whom Thou hast made
King of half the world. Thou knowest, Lord, how great a fleet
I have fitted out to destroy the English, who work evil against
Thee. Lord, I beseech Thee, keep that great Armada now,
as I trust, in battle on the English coast. Protect my ships,
O Lord, from fire and pestilence, from tempest and shipwreck,
and in the day of battle. Amen. Amen.

Lord, now that the battle is joined, grant us Thy victory,
I beseech Thee. Amen. Amen.

Lord, I beseech Thee to have in Thy special keeping my
beloved friend, Alonso de Leyva, now at sea with my fleet.
Guard his ways, O Lord, that so he may come safely home to
me. Amen. Amen.

Lord, of Thy mercy, I beseech Thee to send to me, if it be
Thy will, some word or message from my fleet, that I may
know Thy will concerning it, that my weary heart may find
peace. Amen. Amen. [*He rises.*]

[*Enter the* Princess]

Princess

Has no news come?

Philip

None yet.

Princess

Still nothing?

Philip

No.

PRINCESS

Two months now since they sailed and still no word.

PHILIP

The wind is foul; they cannot send.

PRINCESS
               I know.
And yet what tales, what rumours we have heard.
How the heart sickens for the want of news.
Is that a courier?

PHILIP
     No.

PRINCESS
          What if we lose?

PHILIP

Why should we lose?

PRINCESS
          Because of too much pride
Planning for glory not as scripture bade.

PHILIP

I am not proud nor hopeful, nor afraid.
But you are trembling, sweet, and heavy-eyed.

PRINCESS

I am afraid, for all night long
The spirit of Spain's committed wrong,
Nourished wherever a life was shed,
    Stood near my bed;
Amd all night long it talked to me
Of a trouble there is beyond the sea.

[534]

PHILIP THE KING

A trouble of war . . . I heard a horn
    Blowing forlorn,
And I knew that it came from far away,
From men of Spain in a pass at bay
Blowing for help; the beaten call
None heeds at all.
And now I fear that we have angered Him
    Who makes pride dim.

PHILIP

What we have done with our might
Cannot be hateful to God.
He speaks with dreams in the night
That the tired heart turn home
And an end of brooding come.
My heart has flushed in His praise,
The glow in my heart took sail
In a fleet that darkens the sprays;
Sacrifice may not avail,
But the uttermost gift is wise.

PRINCESS

Yes, I believe that; and the deed is grand—
It is a mighty blow to deal for God.
But in my ear there rings
Ill-omened words about the pride of kings—
"Pride is the evil that destroys a land."

PHILIP

Brooding and watching waste you, you must sleep;
The hand of God will bring us through the deep.

[535]

PRINCESS

Amen, my father, but my heart is breaking.

PHILIP

You are too young for heart-break; let it be.

PRINCESS

There was another fear which kept me waking:
Spain's unborn monarchs came by night to me,
Each holding fewer of the Spanish gems
Here and abroad, each weaker in the soul.
With wearier brows and dimmer diadems,
And feebler fingers giving up control,
Till, as it seemed, a hundred years from now,
An idiot child was all the might of Spain,
And English spirits beat them on the brow,
Robbing their gems and binding them with chain.
And Spain's proud flag was draggled in the sea.
And then these shapes lamented, threatening me;
Saying that we began Spain's downfall here—
So grimly, father, that I shook with fear.

PHILIP

Child, these are only dreams. I have learned this
Since I have been a king, that our concern
Is not with Hope nor Fear, but with what is,
Which, when we follow dreams, we cannot learn.
Be patient, child; besides, the wind has changed;
God's will must never find our hearts estranged:
The wind is north, the news may come to-day.
Ship after ship is running down the Bay
With news; God grant that it be happy news.

PRINCESS

Rest till it comes, dear father.

PHILIP

You can choose,
You who are young, whether to rest or no;
When one is old one sees the hours go.
Dear, they go fast from withered men like me.
You were my little daughter on my knee
When first this war with England was conceived.
Now you are this . . ., it would not be believed,
And nothing done, and still time hurrying by.
We are two grey old partners—Time and I:
Look at the work we do . . . you talk of rest.

PRINCESS

You call your Captains in and choose the best,
And make him do the work.

PHILIP

Ah, you're a Queen,
That is what you would do, but I am King.
Kings have no beauty to make duty keen;
They have to supervise with whip and sting.

PRINCESS

You do not whip men; you are good and mild.

PHILIP

Artists and Kings do what they can, my child,
Not what they would.   It is not easy, dear,
Working with men, for men are only clay,
They crumble in the hand, or they betray

And time goes by, but no results appear—
Your little hands have happier work than mine.
Ah, little daughter, childhood is divine.

PRINCESS

I am no child now that the fleet has sailed;
I was till then, but now I realize
What it would cost my father if it failed.

PHILIP

Yes, it has cost some life, this enterprise.

PRINCESS

But all you had to do was give the word.

PHILIP

Ah, darling, many thousand men have heard
Orders from me since this attempt began
Seventeen years ago.   Full many a man
Who helped the earliest outlines of the plot
Died at his unknown task suspecting not
What pattern his life's colour helped to weave.
Child, if I told you, you would not believe
How this idea has triumphed on unchanged
Past great commanders' deaths, past faith estranged,
Past tyranny and bloodshed and ill-hap,
Treachery striking like a thunder-clap,
Murder, betrayal, lying, past all these,
Past the grim days when feelings had to freeze
Lest the great King should drop his mask of lies
And hint his purpose to the thwarted spies,

Past half a world of men and years of thought,
Past human hope, to be the thing I sought.
Now that the dice are scattered for the stakes,
I half forget that old affront of Drake's,
By which this war with England was begun.
O child, the labour that must first be done
Before a King can act!—unending work.
All the long days of beating down the Turk,
Then when Don John had thrust the Crescent down
(You cannot know) he plotted for the crown;
Don John, my Admiral, plotted against me.
He would have sunk the English in the sea,
But since he plotted, that was ended too.
Then a great world of labour still to do,
The French to check, and then the Portuguese,
Clearing myself a pathway through the seas.
Then, when my way was clear, my Admiral died,
The Marquis Santa Cruz, the unconquered guide,
The greatest sea commander of known times.
Seventeen years of subtleties and crimes.

But it is done. I have resolved those years,
Those men, those crimes, those great attempts, those tears,
Sorrows and terrors of a twisted earth,
Into this fleet, this death, this Dragon's birth;
I who have never seen it, nor shall see.

Princess

I shall thank God that it was shown to me;
I saw it sail.

Philip

You saw my heart's blood, child.

PRINCESS

All a long summer day those ships defiled.
I never saw so many nor so grand;
They wandered down the tide and cleared the land,
And ranked themselves like pikemen, clump to clump.
Then in the silence came the Admiral's trump,
And from those hundreds of expectant ships,
From bells and cannonade and sailors' lips,
And from the drums and trumpets of the foot
Burst such a roaring thunder of salute
As filled my heart with wonder like a cup.
They cheered St. James's banner going up—
Golden St. James, whose figure blew out fair,
High on the flagship's mast in the blue air,
Rippling the gold. Then all the city bells,
Fired like the singing spheres some spirit impels,
Rang in the rocking belfries, the guns roared,
Each human soul there shook like tautened cord.
And to that Christian march the singing priests
Bore up the blessed banners. Even the beasts
Ramped at the challenge of that shouting crowd.
Then, as the wind came fair, the Armada bowed.
Those hundreds of great vessels, ranked in line,
Buried their bows and heaped the bubbled brine
In gleams before them. So they marched; the van,
Led by De Leyva, like slipped greyhounds, ran
To spy the English. On the right and left
By Valdes and his friend the seas were cleft;
Moncada's gallies weltered like a weir,
Flanking Recalde, bringing up the rear,
While in the midst St. James's banner marched,
Blowing towards England till the flagpole arched.

Onward they swept the sea, the flagship's side
Smoked from her cannon's hail; she took her stride,
Leaned and stretched forward.
                                    I was conscious then
That I beheld the greatest fleet that men
Ever sent seaward; all the world was there,
All nations that begem the crown you wear,
Pikemen of Rome, whose settled pikes had stood
Stern in full many a welter of man's blood.
Cunning Levantines, armed with crooked swords,
Venetians bronzed, the ocean's overlords,
Pisans and knights of Malta, Ferrarese,
Passionate half-bloods from the Indian seas,
Hollanders, Austrians, even English, come
To bring again religion to their home;
Spain too, our Andalusians, and the hale
Iberian Basquers used to hunt the whale—
The flower of the knighthood of the world
Mustered beneath the banner you unfurled.

        *   *   *   *   *   *

And that was but the half, for there in France
Was Parma's army ready to advance,
Death-coupled bloodhounds straining to the slip.
Waiting your navy's coming to take ship.
Father, such power awed me.

                        PHILIP
                                Time and I
Worked for long years.

                        PRINCESS
                        And when it had passed by
The bells were silent, and a sigh arose

Of joy in that fleet's pride, and grief for those
Who, even if all went well, had looked their last
On men and women who had made their past.
Then darkness came, and all that I could see
Was the horizon where the fleet must be—
A dimming skyline with a setting star.
It was as though they died; and now, who knows
What has befallen them, or where they are?
And night by sleepless night my trouble grows.
This daily silence has been hard to bear,
But now I dread news worse.

Philip

               We must prepare,
Hoping the best, but ready for the worst;
But patient still, for rumour must come first—
Rumour and broken news and seamen's lies;
Patience, expecting nothing, is most wise.
If God vouchsafes it, we shall hear to-day.
Lighten your heart, my daughter.

Princess

                   I will pray—
Pray for a Spanish triumph.

Philip

                Pray for me.
Pray for God's cause adventured on the sea.

Princess

I will; God help my prayer.

PHILIP

God help us both. [*She goes.*]

Lord, I have laboured long to keep my oath,
And since my loved one died it has been hard.
O Lord, my God, in blessed mercy guard
My only friend De Leyva, now at sea;
Keep him, O Lord, and bring him home to me.
O Lord, be thou his bulwark and his guide;
I am so lonely since my loved one died.

How splendidly the nations hold their way,
Marching with banners through the fields of Time!
Who sees the withered King weary and grey,
Prompting it all with secret lust or crime?
Who guesses at the heavy brain behind?
I am Earth's greatest man; the world is blind.

[*He droops over his papers. Starting up*]

I have still strength, and I must read these scrolls,
Or else all goes to ruin; I must read. [*He sleeps.*]

VOICES

Philip!

PHILIP

Who calls?

[*The* INDIANS *enter*]

VOICES

We are the Indian souls,
Loosed from the gold-mines where our brothers bleed.
We swell the tale of blood: we dug you gold;
We bore your burdens till we died of thirst;

We sweated in the mines or shook with cold,
Washing the gravel which the blast had burst.
We dived for pearls until our eyeballs bled;
You burned us till we told where treasure lay.
We were your Indian slaves, but we are dead;
Our red account is cast and you must pay.

A VOICE

Our lives paid for your fleet; you pay for us.
The unjustly killed restore the balance thus.

A VOICE

They flung my little baby to the hounds.

A VOICE

They took my daughter from me for their lust.

A VOICE

Even the weak are strong beyond life's bounds;
We myriad weak add power to the thrust.

VOICES

Philip! Philip! Philip!
We gather from over the sea
To the justice that has to be
While the blind red bull goes on.
Philip! Philip! Philip!
We who are ciphers slain
In a tale of the pride of Spain
Are a part of her glory gone.

A VOICE

We see them where our will can help their foes.

[544]

A VOICE

Quick, brother, quick! another galleon goes!
Waken those sleeping gunners by the fire,
Or she'll escape unracked. [*They fade away.*]

PHILIP

The voices tire.

They go. I dreamed. I slept. My heavy head
Is drowsed. What man is that?

[DON JOHN *appears, with* ESCOVEDO *behind him*]

VOICE OF DON JOHN OF AUSTRIA

I am the dead;

I am your brother, Philip—brother John.

PHILIP

You corpse-fetch from the unclean grave, begone!
I had no brother.

DON JOHN

Would you never had!

PHILIP

You were a landmark of my father's sin,
Never my brother.

DON JOHN

I was that bright lad,

Your father's son, my brother; I helped win
Great glory for you, Philip.

PHILIP

I agreed

To overlook your bastardy, my friend,
So long as your bright talents served my need;
But you presumed, and so it had to end.

[545]

DON JOHN

My talents served you well.

PHILIP

They did, at first.

DON JOHN

I won the Battle of Lepanto for you.

PHILIP

And afterwards you killed my troops with thirst,
Following a crazy scheme which overbore you.

DON JOHN

Not crazy, unsuccessful.

PHILIP

Poor vain ghost,
Poor flickering candle that was bright awhile.

DON JOHN

I was the man whom Europe worshipped most,
One with a mighty plan which you thought guile
Why did you kill me, Philip?

PHILIP

You betrayed me,
Or would have, traitor, had I not been wise.

DON JOHN

I was your board's best piece, you should have played me,
Now I am dead and earth in is my eyes.

[546]

I could have won you England. I had planned
To conquer England. I had all prepared
Ships, soldiers, money, but your cruel hand
Killed me, and nothing's done and nothing's dared.

PHILIP

You planned to conquer England and be King;
Those who obstruct my path I sweep aside.

DON JOHN

Brother, there is a time for everything;
That was the time for England, but I died;
Now you attempt too late,
The powers have closed the gate,
Destiny enters by another door,
The lost chance comes no more.

THE VOICE OF ESCOVEDO

Philip, he tells the truth. We could have won
England for you, we were no plotters then.

VOICES

Philip, you were betrayed, you were undone.
You had the moment, but you killed the men.

ESCOVEDO

The liar, Perez, tricked you. O great King!
We would have added England to your crown,
Now the worms cling
About our lips deep down.
You had me stabbed at midnight going home
That man of Perez' stabbed me in the back.

And then I could not stir, down on the loam;
The sky was full of blood, the stars were black.
And then I knew my wife and children waited
But that I could not come; a moving hand
Had interposed a something fated
'Twixt us and what we planned.

Don John

You had me poisoned in that Holland den,
Outcast, alone, without the help of men.
We planned a glorious hour
Hoisting the banner of Spain
On the top of London Tower,
With England a Spanish fief.
Life cannot happen again,
And doing dies with the brain;
Autumn ruins the flower
And after the flower the leaf.

Voices

Philip, Philip, Philip!
The evil men do has strength,
It gathers behind the veils
While the unjust thing prevails.
While the pride of life is strong,
But the balance tips at length,
And the unjust things are tales,
The pride of life is a song.

Philip

I kept my purpose while you lived.   Shall I
Be weaker, now that you are dead, you things?

What can such reedy wretches do but die
Standing against the purposes of Kings?

Don John

Do? We can thwart you.

Voices

       And we will, we will;
All Spain's unjustly murdered work you ill.
Gather against him, gather, mock him down.

The Voice of the Marquis of Santa Cruz

Scatter, you shadows, fly. Philip, great King.
You vultures gathered in an unclean ring;
Away, you shadows, scatter.
They are gone,
Philip.

      [The Marquis *enters]*

Who calls?

Santa Cruz

Master.

Philip

                Let me dream on.
Whose voice was that? It warned me of defeat.

Santa Cruz

I am that Santa Cruz who built your fleet,
And died to make it good. It was my child.
I call because my work has been defiled.

Philip

Why rail, uneasy soul?

PHILIP THE KING

Santa Cruz

If I had spent
Less life in that, I should be still alive,
Commanding what I built to my content,
Driving the English slaves as conquerors drive.
Why did you give away my splendid sword,
Forged by a never-conquered captain's brain,
Into the hoof-hand of an ambling lord,
Useless in all things, but to ruin Spain?
Would God I had but guessed it! Would my stars
Had shown me clearer what my death would bring,
I would have burned those galleons, guns and spars,
Soldiers and all, and so have stopped this thing.
And doing that I should have served you well,
And brought less ruin on this lovely land.
What folly from the unfed brain of hell
Made you promote that thing to my command?—
Folly from which so many men must die.

Philip

We stand against all comers, Time and I.
I chose the Duke because I wanted one . . .
Who . . .

Santa Cruz

Give no reason for the evil done.
Souls wrestle from the ever deedless grave
To do, not to hear reason. Oh, great King,
You still may save the ruin of this thing!

Philip

You speak of ruin. Tell me what you see.

[550]

Santa Cruz

Ruin that threatens, but need never be.
Be silent, Philip; listen while I tell
What you must do.

Philip

You are a voice from hell;
I will not listen to these obscene dreams.

Santa Cruz

Life is a heavy cloud, through which come gleams.
Oh, Philip, let me speak! Philip, I say,
One way can still be tried; I see the way.
You must do this, but listen.

Philip

I still doubt.

Santa Cruz

Listen, great King; the light is dying out.
You are fading from me, Philip; they are coming.
Before it is too late for ever send . . .

Philip

Send?

Santa Cruz

Yes.

Philip

To whom?

Santa Cruz

To . . .

Voices

Drown his voice with drumming;

[551]

Pipe with the Inca conch, the Indian flute.
What red flowers spring from this blood-sprinkled root!

PHILIP

What name was that you said?

SANTA CRUZ

Wait, Philip—wait;
They are so many and so full of hate.

VOICES

Call to your monarch, Marquis—call again.

PHILIP

Something he meant is knocking at my brain—
Knocking for entrance.   Marquis!

SANTA CRUZ

Philip! King!

PHILIP

What must I do?

SANTA CRUZ

Oh, fiends!

VOICES

Ah, conquerors, sing!
Now we have triumphed.

We have torn the flag.
Dance in a ring, victorious spirits, dance;
Brought to a byword is the Spanish brag,
And ruined is the grand inheritance.
Mourn, wretched Philip, for your plans are checked;
Your colonies defenceless; your sweet faith
Mocked by the heretics; your ships are wrecked;
The strength of Spain has dwindled to a wraith.

[552]

Aha! you beaten King, you blinded fool!
Scream, for the empire tumbles from your rule.

PHILIP

God will deliver me; you are but words
Called in the night-time by malignant birds
But who are you?
[*The figure of* DE LEYVA *enters*]

VOICE OF DE LEYVA

I am De Leyva, come
Out of the sea, my everlasting home,
To whisper comfort to my ruined friend.
Dear, I am dead, but friendship cannot end;
Love does not die, and I am with you here.
Often in sorrow you will feel me near,
Feel me, but never speak, nor hear me speak.
Philip, whatever bitter Fate may wreak
On Spain and you, remember I am here,
The dead are bound to those they held most dear.

PHILIP

Dreams of the night. I dreamed De Leyva came.

VOICES

Awake to hear the story of your shame.
[*They cry. A gun is shot off. Bells*]

PHILIP

[*Rousing.*] I dreamed I was defeated like those men
Whom I defeated; I have felt their woe.
What is this noise? A message?
Enter then.

PRINCESS

A prisoner comes with news of victory.

PHILIP

So.
Victory comes! We win!

PRINCESS

The fleet has won!

PHILIP

Thanks be to God on high.

PRINCESS

His will be done.

PHILIP

Lord, help me use this victory for Thy praise.
Lord, Thou hast burst this night of many days
With glorious morning and my heart is full.
O God, my God, Thy ways are wonderful!
Bring me the prisoner.

PRINCESS

He brought this letter.

[*An Englishman is brought in*]

PHILIP

You are an Englishman?

PRISONER

Yes, your Majesty.

PHILIP

This letter says that you can tell me how things have fared.
Tell me your story.

Prisoner

I was at sea, my lord, fishing, some fifteen miles south-west from Falmouth. We were not expecting the Spanish fleet, our cruisers had said it was not coming. It was hazy summer weather and early morning. We could hear that we were among a big fleet, and when the haze lifted your ships were all round us, so we were taken aboard an admiral's ship. A dark man the admiral was, with a very quick way; he was not the chief admiral, but an Admiral Recalde, with the rear-guard.

Philip

Where was the English fleet at that time? Was it expecting us?

Prisoner

No, your honour. It was windbound in Plymouth, unprepared, as I told your admiral. Then I was taken down below.

Philip

Did our fleet enter Plymouth, then?

Prisoner

No, my lord, and I could not think why, for the wind held and they had only to sail straight in. The day passed.

The next day there was firing, and I thought "The English have got out of the trap at least," but the firing died down, and I concluded the English were beaten.

Philip

Yes?

Prisoner

I thought the ships would put ashore then to take what they

had won, but they kept at sea some days, though there was firing every day, sometimes very heavy. They said they were burning all the English towns as they passed, and then going to France to fetch an army; and after some nights I was brought ashore in Calais to come to your Majesty.

PHILIP

What did you see in Calais?

PRISONER

It was a dark night, my lord, when they sent me in. I saw the road full of shipping, lit up like a town.

PHILIP

What was the feeling among you English prisoners? That the Spaniards had prospered?

PRISONER

Yes, my lord. You had reached your army, which was all your intent. You had only to take it across the Channel; the wind was fair for that.

PHILIP

So then you started for Spain. You know no more of what happened?

PRISONER

No, my lord, except that looking back from a hilltop, I saw a great glare over Calais.

PHILIP

Something was burning there?

PRISONER

It was the bonfires, my lord, to give them light; they were

embarking the army. Then in France later on we heard that
Drake had been sunk off Calais with fifteen ships. A man
said he had seen it. That is all I know, my lord.

PHILIP

What you say will be proved. You will be returned to England. Treat this man well. [*Exit* PRISONER.]

PRINCESS

Father, what blessed news!

PHILIP

We have not failed;
But then he hardly knew. The letter here
Shows that our navy partly has prevailed.

PRINCESS

The news has spread.

CRIES WITHOUT

Long live King Philip! Cheer!

CRIES

Cheer our great King! Long live our noble King.
Beat "Santiago," drummers.

PRINCESS

Hark! they sing.
The court is dark with people, but more come.

CRIES

Long live King Philip!

A GREAT VOICE

Silence for the drum!
And when the drum beats, we will lift our thanks
Till his heart triumphs.

[557]

Silence in the ranks!
Eyes front! O people, listen! Our attempt
Has triumphed more than our desires dreamt.
England is ours. Give thanks. Sound trumpets. Sing!

CRIES

Philip, Philip the King! God save the King!
Philip the conqueror! Philip! [*A strange cry.*]

PRINCESS

Oh, look! look! . . .
Just as they cheered, the palace banners shook,
They took it for a sign.
The guards are there,
Look, and the monks are forming in the square
Bringing the blessed relics. Oh, my dear!
I am so happy. Listen how they cheer.
Father, they're cheering because Spain has won.
All you have hoped and striven for is done.
I hardly dare believe it.

CRIES

Long live Spain.

PRINCESS

O, there are horsemen, I must look again!

CRIES

There is the Princess at the window. See?
God save you, little lady. Which is she?
There. Is the King there? No. He must be. Yes.
God save your Grace. He's there with the Princess.

PHILIP

Stand farther back; they saw you.

PRINCESS

Oh, not now!

They called "God save me," father; let me bow.

PHILIP

Bow, then, my dear.

CRIES

God save your pretty face.

PRINCESS

Father, do come, they want you.

CRIES

Bless your Grace.

God save the King—King Philip.

PRINCESS

Father dear,

They're calling for you; stand beside me here.

PHILIP

Not yet.   It is not time.

CRIES

Philip the King!

PRINCESS

Oh, father, come! It is a thrilling thing
To know they won, and hear these shouts of praise.

[559]

CRIES

God save the King! God send him many days!
Philip the King, the conqueror of the sea!
St. James for Spain, King Philip, victory!
King Philip! Santiago!

PRINCESS
Father.

PHILIP
Wait!
Kings must not yield them at too cheap a rate.

VOICES

Philip the King! The English are destroyed!
God save him! Victory! We are overjoyed!
Let the bells ring! King Philip! Philip! King!
Ring the Cathedral bells—ay, let them ring!
St. James for Spain! King Philip! Clear the guns!
[*Guns shot off*]
King Philip, fire—fire all at once.
King Philip, fire! King Philip, fire! St. James!
Thank God, the King of kings, the Name of names!
Fire, King Philip! Santiago, fire!
Give thanks to God who gives us our desire!
Philip, God save and bless him!

PHILIP
[*Going to window*]

I will speak.

VOICES

Fire! He's there! King Philip!

PHILIP
                Man is weak.

VOICES

He's there!

PRINCESS
Oh, father, look!

PHILIP
                        Stand at my side.

VOICES

God bless and guard our blessed country's guide!
King Philip, fire! The King! [*The bells begin.*]

PRINCESS
                        Oh, bells of joy!
And now the monks are singing.

THE MONKS

Let us give thanks unto the Lord of lords,
Who saves His faithful from the Egyptian swords.

VOICES

Amen. God save the King.

THE MONKS

He made the Red Sea waters to divide,
And led our Israel through with Him for guide.

VOICES

Amen. God save the King! Philip the King!

[561]

Philip

O God, I thank Thee for this marvellous thing.

The Monks

He whelmed King Pharaoh's army in the sea,
And of His mercy gave us victory.

Voices

The famous kings are blown like chaff
Before Thy fiery car.
Thou smit'st th' ungodly with Thy staff . . .
Philip the King! God save our prudent King!

Philip

My subjects, whom God gave me for His ends . . .

Princess

Whatever pain you bore, this makes amends.

Voices

Speak to your loving hearts, your Majesty.

Philip

I do His will; to God the glory be.

The Monks

Praise Him, O sun and moon, morning and evening star!
The kings who mocked His word are broken in the war.
Praise Him with heart and soul! Praise Him with voice and
lute!

Voices

The King! God save the King! Silence! He speaks. Salute!

The Monks

In the dark night, ere dawn, we will arise and sing
Glory to God on high, the praises of our King.

Voices

The King is going to speak.   He makes a sign.
God bless your noble Grace and all your line!
God bless you, Sir, for all your thought for us!
The conquering King, Philip victorious!
Philip the great and good! Hush! Silence! Peace!
Philip! Attention! Bid the ringers cease.
The King is going to speak; he raised his hand.

Princess

Dear, to be loved as you are is most grand.
Speak to them, father; thank them for their love.

The Monks

I will exalt the Name of God above.

Voices

The bells are hushed.   Be quiet!   Silence all!

Philip

I thought I heard, far off, a funeral call;
As in your dream, a melancholy cry.

Princess

It was the fifes.

Philip

No; listen!

PRINCESS
That sound?

PHILIP
Ay.

PRINCESS
It was the crowd outside.   Now they are still.

PHILIP
No, it was singing coming up the hill—
Sad singing, too.

PRINCESS
I did not hear it.

PHILIP
There!

PRINCESS
The bells have left a trembling in the air.

PHILIP
No; it was voices.   I will speak one word
To these below.   There is the noise I heard

[RECALDE'S *men are heard singing*]

RECALDE'S MEN
Out of the deep, out of the deep, we come,
Preserved from death at sea to die at home.
Mercy of God alone preserved us thus;
In the waste sea Death laid his hand on us.

PRINCESS
The Black Monks in a penitential psalm.

[564]

VOICES

Philip the King!

PHILIP

I'll wait.

PRINCESS

Oh, speak!

PHILIP

Be calm!
I cannot cross God's word with words of mine.

VOICES

Quiet, you singers!

PRINCESS

They are men in line.

[RECALDE'S *men are heard singing*]

RECALDE'S MEN

We called the world too small with boastful lips;
Now we are ghosts crawled from the bones of ships.
We were most glorious at our setting sail;
Now our knees knock, our broken spirits fail.
Our banner is abased and all our pride:
A tale of ships that sank and men who died.

PRINCESS

Listen! Who are they?

PHILIP

What is it they sing?

VOICES

The King is speaking.   Silence for the King!

Let the King speak; be still. You ragged crew,
Have you no manners? Silence! Who are you?

RECALDE'S MEN

We are the beaten men, the men accursed,
Whose bitter glory 'tis t' have borne the worst.

PRINCESS

They are not monks.

PHILIP

Nor beggars.

PRINCESS

Now they stand.

VOICES

Yon navy's sweepings driven back to land.
Go to the hens and tunnies; beat them down
Back to the sea you ran from; back and drown.

RECALDE'S MEN

Pity our shame, you untried heroes here.
Defeat's not victory, but 'tis bought as dear.

PHILIP

They are sailors from the fleet.

PRINCESS

They come with news.
They are ragged to the skin, they have no shoes.

PHILIP

The crowd is still.

PRINCESS

Why do they come like this?

PHILIP

Listen; their Captain tells them what it is.

RECALDE'S MEN

Darken the bedrooms for us, people all,
And let us turn our faces to the wall,
And let the darkness and the silence make
A quiet time in which our hearts may break.

[*A murmur runs through the Court*]

PRINCESS

Father, what is it?

PHILIP

Child, the Act of One
Who chastens earthly kings, whose Will be done.

PRINCESS

It means that we are beaten?

PHILIP

Who can tell?

PRINCESS

Father.

PHILIP

Dear child, even defeat is well.

PRINCESS

I thought that we were happy.

[567]

PHILIP
                    Watch the square.
Now tell me calmly what is passing there.

PRINCESS
The Captain comes, the crowd is making way.

PHILIP
Who is it? Can you see?
                    PRINCESS
                    His hair is grey.
He walks bareheaded, slowly, and the crowd
Shrink as though Death were passing in his shroud.

PHILIP
Worse news has come. Who is the man?

PRINCESS
His face . . .
I seem to know him, but the air is strange.
He puts the touch of Death upon the place.
Nothing but Death could fashion such a change.
He carries something. Now the people kneel.
We are defeated, Father.
                    PHILIP
                    What I feel
I cover. Go within. Misfortune stuns
None but the tender. [*Exit* PRINCESS.]

VOICES
                    Give us back our sons.
Philip, give back our sons, our lovely sons.

[568]

The Palace Guard

Halt! Who comes there?

A Voice

Spain and the Empire.

The Guard

Pass,

Spain and the Empire.

Voices

They are drowned. Alas!
Philip, give back our sons, our lovely sons.

[*Enter* Messenger, *carrying an Admiral's chain*]

Philip

What brings you to me, Captain?

Messenger

This gold chain . . .
Bears the twelve badges of the strength of Spain
Once linked in glory, Philip, but now loosed.

[*Detaching link from link*]

Castilla, Leon, Aragon, and these,
Palestine, Portugal, the Sicilies,
Navarre, Granada, the Valencian State,
The Indies, East and West, the Archducate,
The Western Mainland in the Ocean Sea.
Those who upheld their strength have ceased to be.
I, who am dying, King, have seen their graves.
Philip, your Navy is beneath the waves.

PHILIP THE KING

PHILIP

He who in bounty gives in wisdom takes.

MESSENGER

O King, forgive me, for my spirit breaks;
I saw those beaches where the Grange descends
White with unburied corpses of stripped friends.

PHILIP

I grieve that Spain's disaster brings such loss.

MESSENGER

From Pentland to the Groyne the tempests toss
Unshriven Spaniards driving with the tide.
They were my lovely friends and they have died,
Far from wind-broken Biscay, far from home,
With no anointing chrism but the foam.

PHILIP

The dead will rise from unsuspected slime;
God's chosen will be gathered in God's time.

MESSENGER

King, they died helpless; our unwieldy fleet
Made such a target to the English guns
That we were riddled through like sifted wheat.
We never came to grappling with them once.
They raked us from a distance, and then ran.
Each village throughout Spain has lost a man;
The widows in the seaports fill the streets.

PHILIP

Uncertain chance decides the fate of fleets.

MESSENGER

Now the North Sea is haunted for all time
By miserable souls whose dying words
Cursed the too proud adventure as a crime.
Our broken galleons house the gannet-birds.
The Irish burn our Captain's bones for lime.
O misery that the might of England wrought!

PHILIP

Christ is the only remedy for thought
When the mind sickens. We are pieces played,
Not moving as we will, but as we are made;
Beaten and spurred at times like stubborn steeds,
That we may go God's way. Your spirit bleeds,
Having been proved in trouble past her strength.
Give me the roll in all its ghastly length.
Which of my friends survive, if any live?

MESSENGER

Some have survived, but all are fugitive.
Your Admiral in command is living still;
Michael Oquendo too, though he is ill,
Dying of broken heart and bitter shame.
Valdes is prisoner, Manrique the same.

PHILIP

God willed the matter; they are not to blame.
Thank God that they are living. Name the rest.

MESSENGER

They are all dead . . . with him you loved the best.

PHILIP

I dreamed De Leyva died, so it is true?

MESSENGER

Drowned on the Irish coast with all his crew.
After enduring dying many days
The sea has given him quiet. Many ways
Lead men to death, and he a hard one trod,
Bearing much misery, like a knight of God.

PHILIP

Amen. Go on.

MESSENGER

Hugh de Monçada died,
Shot in his burning ship by Calais side,
Cheering his men to save her. Pimentel
Sank in a galleon shambled like a hell
Rather than yield, and in a whirl of flames
Pedro Mendoza, Captain of St. James,
Stood with Don Philip thrusting boarders back
Till their Toledan armour was burnt black,
And both their helms ran blood. And there they fell,
Shot down to bleed to death. They perished well,
Happy to die in battle for their King
Before defeat had fallen on their friends;
Happier than most, for where the merrows sing
Paredes and his brother met their ends,
And Don Alarcon, cast alive ashore,
Was killed and stripped and hanged upon a tree.
And young Mendoza, whom the flagship bore,
Died of starvation and of misery.

But hundreds perished, King; why mention these?
Battle and hunger, heart-break, and the seas
Have overwhelmed the chivalry of Spain.

PHILIP

Misfortune, after effort, brings no stain.
Perhaps I underjudged the English fleet.
How was it that the Spaniards met defeat?
What evil fortune brought about our fall?

MESSENGER

Their sailors and their cannon did it all.

PHILIP

Yet when the fleet reached Calais all went well.

MESSENGER

Our woes began there.

PHILIP

Tell me what befell.

MESSENGER

We were to ship the troops in Calais Road;
They lay encamped, prepared to go aboard.
To windward still the English fleet abode—
Still as in port when peace has been restored.

The wind and sea were fair,
We lay at anchor there;
The stars burned in the air,
The men were sleeping,
When in the midnight dark
Our watchman saw a spark

[573]

Suddenly light a bark
With long flames leaping.

Then, as they stood amazed,
Others and others blazed;
Then terror set them crazed,
They ran down screaming:
"Fire-ships are coming! Wake
Cast loose, for Jesus' sake!
Eight fire-ships come from Drake—
Look at their gleaming!"

Roused in the dark from bed,
We saw the fire show red,
And instant panic spread
Through troops and sailors;
They swarmed on deck unclad,
They did what terror bade,
King, they were like the mad
Escaped from jailers.

Some prayed for mercy, some
Rang bells or beat the drum,
As though despair had come
At hell's contriving;
Captains with terror pale
Screamed through the dark their hail,
"Cut cable, loose the sail,
And set all driving!"

Heading all ways at once,
Grinding each other's guns,
Our blundering galleons
Athwart-hawse galleys,

Timbers and plankings cleft,
And half our tackling reft,
Your grand Armada left
The roads of Calais.

Weary and overwrought
We strove to make all taut;
But when the morning brought
The dawn to light us,
Drake, with the weather gage,
Made signal to engage,
And, like a pard in rage,
Bore down to fight us.

Nobly the English line
Trampled the bubbled brine;
We heard the gun-trucks whine
To the taut laniard.
Onwards we saw them forge,
White billowing at the gorge.
"On, on!" they cried, "St. George!
Down with the Spaniard!"

From their van squadron broke
A withering battle-stroke,
Tearing our plankèd oak
By straiks asunder,
Blasting the wood like rot
With such a hail of shot,
So constant and so hot
It beat us under.

The English would not close;
They fought us as they chose,

Dealing us deadly blows
For seven hours.
Lords of our chiefest rank
The bitter billow drank,
For there the English sank
Three ships of ours.

*　　　*　　　*　　　*　　　*

Then the wind forced us northward from the fight;
We could not ship the army nor return;
We held the sea in trouble through the night,
Watching the English signals blink and burn.
The English in a dim cloud kept astern;
All night they signalled, while our shattered ships
Huddled like beasts beneath the drovers' whips.

*　　　*　　　*　　　*　　　*

At dawn the same wind held; we could not strive.
The English drove us north as herdsmen drive.

*　　　*　　　*　　　*　　　*

Under our tattered flags,
With rigging cut to rags,
Our ships like stricken stags
Were heaped and hounded.
Caught by the unknown tide,
With neither chart nor guide,
We fouled the Holland side,
Where four more grounded.

Our water-casks were burst,
The horses died of thirst,

The wounded raved and curst,
Uncared, untended.
All night we heard the crying
Of lonely shipmates dying;
We had to leave them lying.
So the fight ended.

PHILIP

God gives His victory as He wills.   But this
Was not complete destruction.   What thing worse
Came to destroy you?

MESSENGER

An avenging curse,
Due for old sins, destroyed us.

PHILIP

Tell the tale.

MESSENGER

O King, when morning dawned it blew a gale,
But still the English followed, and we fled
Till breakers made the dirty waters pale.
We saw the Zealand sandbanks right ahead,
Blind in a whirling spray that gave us dread;
For we were blown there, and the water shoaled.
The crying of the leadsmen at the lead,
Calling the soundings, were our death-bells tolled.

We drifted down to death upon the sands—
The English drew away to watch us drown;
We saw the bitter breakers with gery hands
Tear the dead body of the sandbank brown.

We could do nothing, so we drifted down
Singing the psalms for death—we who had been
Lords of the sea and knights of great renown,
Doomed to be strangled by a death unclean.

PHILIP
So there the ships were wrecked?

MESSENGER
Time had not struck.
O King, we learned how blessed mercy saves:
Even as our forefoot grounded on the muck,
Tripping us up to drown us in the waves,
A sudden windshift snatched us from our graves
And drove us north; and now another woe,
Tempest unending, beat our ships to staves—
A never-dying gale with frost and snow.

Now our hearts failed, for food and water failed;
The men fell sick by troops, the wounded died.
They washed about the wet decks as we sailed
For want of strength to lift them overside.
Desolate seas we sailed, so grim, so wide,
That ship by ship our comrades disappeared.
With neither sun nor star to be a guide,
LIke spirits of the wretched dead we steered.

Till, having beaten through the Pentland Pass,
We saw the Irish surf, with mists of spray
Blowing far inland, blasting trees and grass,
And gave God thanks, for we espied a bay
Safe, with bright water running down the clay—
A running brook where we could drink and drink.

But drawing near, our ships were cast away,
Bilged on the rocks; we saw our comrades sink . . .

Or worse: for those the breakers cast ashore
The Irish killed and stripped; their bodies white
Lay naked to the wolves—yea, sixty score—
All down the windy beach, a piteous sight.
The savage Irish watched by bonfire light
Lest more should come ashore; we heard them there
Screaming the bloody news of their delight.
Then we abandoned hope and new despair.

And now the fleet is sunken in the sea,
And all the seamen, all the might of Spain,
Are dead, O King, and out of misery,
Never to drag at frozen ropes again—
Never to know defeat, nor feel the pain
Of watching dear companions sink and die.
Death's everlasting armistice to the brain
Gives their poor griefs quietus; let them lie.

I, like a ghost returning from the grave,
Come from a stricken ship to tell the news
Of Spanish honour which we could not save,
Nor win again, nor even die to lose;
And since God's hidden wisdom loves to bruise
Those whom he loves, we, trembling in despair,
Will watch our griefs to see God's finger there,
And make His will our solace and excuse.

Defeat is bitter and the truth is hard—
Spain is defeated, England has prevailed;
This is the banner which I could not guard,

And this the consecrated sword which failed.
Do with your dying Captain as you will.

[He lays down sword and banner]

PHILIP

I, from my heart, thank God, from whose great hand
I am so helped with power, I can still
Set out another fleet against that land.
Nor do I think it ill
If all the running water takes its course
While there are unspent fountains at the source.

He sendeth out His word and melteth them.
Take back your standard, Captain.   As you go,
Bid the bells toll and let the clergy come.
Then in the city by the strike of drum
Proclaim a general fast.   In bitter days
The soul finds God, God us.

[Exit CAPTAIN]

PHILIP
[Alone]
                    De Leyva, friend,
Whom I shall never see, never again,
This misery that I feel is over Spain.
O God, beloved God, in pity send
That blessed rose among the thorns—an end:
Give a bruised spirit peace.

[He kneels.   A muffled march of the drums]

CURTAIN

GOOD FRIDAY

A DRAMATIC POEM

PERSONS

PONTIUS PILATE, Procurator of Judæa
PROCULA, His Wife.
LONGINUS, A Centurion.
A JEW, Leader of the Rabble.
A MADMAN.
A SENTRY.
JOSEPH OF RAMAH.
HEROD.
SOLDIERS, SERVANTS, THE JEWISH RABBLE, LOITERERS,
    IDLERS.

THE SCENE

The Pavement, or Paved Court, outside the Roman Citadel in Jerusalem. At the back is the barrack wall, pierced in the centre with a double bronze door, weathered to a green color. On the right and left sides of the stage are battlemented parapets overlooking the city. The stage or pavement is approached by stone steps from the front, and by narrow stone staircases in the wings, one on each side, well forward. These steps are to suggest that the citadel is high up above the town, and that the main barrack gate is below. THE CHIEF CITIZEN, THE RABBLE, JOSEPH, THE MADMAN, HEROD, *and* THE LOITERERS, *etc., enter by these steps.* PILATE, PROCULA, LONGINUS, THE SOLDIERS *and* SERVANTS *enter by the bronze doors.*

GOOD FRIDAY

A DRAMATIC POEM

PILATE

Longinus

LONGINUS

   Lord.

PILATE

[*Giving scroll.*] Your warrant. Take the key.
Go to Barabbas' cell and set him free,
The mob has chosen him.

LONGINUS

And Jesus?

PILATE

Wait.

He can be scourged and put outside the gate,
With warning not to make more trouble here.
See that the sergeant be not too severe.
I want to spare him.

LONGINUS

And the Jew, the Priest,

Outside?

PILATE

I'll see him now.

LONGINUS

Passover Feast.

Always brings trouble, Lord. All shall be done.
Dismiss?

[585]

PILATE

Dismiss. [*Exit* LONGINUS.]
   There's blood about the sun,
This earthquake weather presses on the brain.

[*Enter* PROCULA]

You?

PROCULA

Dear, forgive me, if I come again
About this Jesus, but I long to know
What Herod said. Did he dismiss him?

PILATE

       No.

He sent him back for me to try,
The charge being local.

PROCULA

    Have you tried him?

PILATE

        Ay,

Henceforth he will be kept outside the walls,
Now, listen, wife: whatever dream befalls,
Never again send word to me in Court
To interrupt a case. The Jews made sport
Of what you dreamed and what you bade me fear
About this Jesus man. The laws are clear.
I must apply them, asking nothing more
Than the proved truth. Now tell me of your dream:
What was it? Tell me then.

PROCULA

     I saw a gleam
Reddening the world out of a blackened sky,

[586]

Then in the horror came a hurt thing's cry
Protesting to the death what no one heard.

PILATE

What did it say?

PROCULA

A cry, no spoken word

But crying, and a horror, and a sense
Of one poor man's naked intelligence,
Pitted against the world and being crushed.
Then, waking, there was noise; a rabble rushed
Following this Jesus here, crying for blood,
Like beasts half-reptile in a jungle mud.
And all the horror threatening in the dim,
In what I dreamed of, seemed to threaten him. . . .
So in my terror I sent word to you,
Begging you dearly to have nought to do
With that wise man.

PILATE

I grant he says wise things.
Too wise by half, and too much wisdom brings
Trouble, I find.   It disagrees with men.
We must protect him from his wisdom then.

PROCULA

What have you done to him?

PILATE

Made it more hard

For him to wrangle in the Temple yard
Henceforth, I hope.

[Enter LONGINUS]

[587]

PROCULA

You have not punished him?

PILATE

Warned him.

LONGINUS

The envoy from the Sanhedrim
Is here, my lord.

PILATE

Go. I must see him. Stay.
You and your women, keep within to-day.
It is the Jewish Feast and blood runs high
Against us Romans when the zealots cry
Songs of their old Deliverance through the land.
Stay, yet. Lord Herod says that he has planned
To visit us to-night, have all prepared.

PROCULA

I would have gone to Herod had I dared,
To plead for this man Jesus. All shall be
Made ready. Dear, my dream oppresses me. [*Exit.*]

PILATE

It is this earthquake weather: it will end
After a shock. Farewell.

[*Enter* CHIEF CITIZEN]

CHIEF CIT.

Hail, Lord and friend.
I come about a man in bonds with you,
One Jesus, leader of a perverse crew
That haunts the Temple.

[588]

PILATE

Yes, the man is here.

CHIEF CIT.

Charged with sedition?

PILATE

It did not appear
That he had been seditious. It was proved
That he had mocked at rites which people loved.
No more than that. I have just dealt with him.
You wish to see him?

CHIEF CIT.

No, the Sanhedrim
Send me to tell you of his proved intent.
You know how, not long since, a prophet went
Through all Judæa turning people's brains
With talk of One coming to loose their chains?

PILATE

John the Baptiser whom old Herod killed.

CHIEF CIT.

The Jews expect that word to be fulfilled,
They think that One will come. This Jesus claims
To be that Man, Son of the Name of Names,
The Anointed King who will arise and seize
Israel from Rome and you. Such claims as these
Might be held mad in other times than ours.

PILATE

He is not mad.

GOOD FRIDAY

Chief Cit.

But when rebellion lowers
As now, from every hamlet, every farm,
One word so uttered does unreckoned harm.

Pilate

How do you know this?

Chief Cit.

From a man, his friend,
Frightened by thought of where such claims would end.
There had been rumors, yet we only heard
The fact but now. We send you instant word.

Pilate

Yes. This is serious news. Would I had known.
But none the less, this Jesus is alone.
A common country preacher, as men say,
No more than that, he leads no big array;
No one believes his claim?

Chief Cit.

At present, no.
He had more friends a little while ago,
Before he made these claims of being King.

Pilate

You know about him then?

Chief Cit.

His ministering
Was known to us, of course.

Pilate

And disapproved?

CHIEF CIT.

Not wholly, no; some, truly; some we loved.
At first he only preached. He preaches well.

PILATE

What of?

CHIEF CIT.

Of men, and of escape from hell
By good deeds done. But when he learned his power
And flatterers came, then, in an evil hour,
As far as I can judge, his head was turned.
A few days past, from all that we have learned
He made this claim, and since persists therein.
Deluders are best checked when they begin.
So, when we heard it from this frightened friend,
We took this course to bring it to an end.

PILATE

Rightly. I thank you. Do I understand
That friends have fallen from him since he planned
To be this King?

CHIEF CIT.

They have, the most part.

PILATE

Why?

What makes them turn?

CHIEF CIT.

The claim is blasphemy
Punished by death under the Jewish laws.

[591]

GOOD FRIDAY

PILATE

And under ours, if sufficient cause
Appear, and yet, if all the Jews despise
This claimant's folly, would it nor be wise
To pay no heed, not make important one
Whom all contemn?

CHIEF CIT.

His evil is not done.
His claim persists, the rabble's mind will turn.
Better prevent him, Lord, by being stern.
The man has power.

PILATE

That is true, he has.

CHIEF CITIZEN

His is the first claim since the Baptist was,
Better not let it thrive.

PILATE

It does not thrive.

CHIEF CIT.

All ill weeds prosper, Lord, if left alive.
The soil is ripe for such a weed as this.
The Jews await a message such as his,
The Anointed Man, of whom our Holy Books
Prophesy much.   The Jewish people looks
For Him to come.

PILATE

These ancient prophecies
Are drugs to keep crude souls from being wise.

Time and again Rome proves herself your friend,
Then some mad writing brings it to an end.
Time and again, until my heart is sick.
Dead prophets spreading madness in the quick.
And now this Jesus whom I hoped to save.
Have you the depositions?

CHIEF CIT.
Yes, I have.

PILATE

Give me.

CHIEF CIT.
This is the docquet.

PILATE
This is grave.

CHIEF CIT.
I thought that you would think so.

PILATE
I will learn
What he can say to this and than return.
Wait. I must speak. Although I shall not spare
Anyone, man or woman, who may dare
To make a claim that threatens Roman rule,
I do not plan to be a priestly tool.
I know your Temple plots; pretend not here
That you, the priest, hold me, the Roman, dear.
You, like the other Jews, await this King
Who is to set you free, who is to ding
Rome down to death, as your priests' brains suppose.

This case of Jesus shows it, plainly shows.
He and his claim were not at once disowned;
You waited, while you thought "He shall be throned,
We will support him, if he wins the crowd."
You would have, too. He would have been endowed
With all your power to support his claim
Had he but pleased the rabble as at first.
But, since he will not back the priestly aim,
Nor stoop to lure the multitude, you thirst
To win my favor by denouncing him.
This rebel does not suit the Sanhedrim.
I know. . . . The next one may.

CHIEF CIT.

You wrong us, Sire.

PILATE

Unless he blench, you 'complish your desite
With Jesus, though; there is no king save Rome
Here, while I hold the reins. Wait till I come.

[Exit PILATE]

THE MADMAN

Only a penny, a penny,
Lilies brighter than any
White lilies picked for the Feast.

[He enters, tapping with his stick]

I am a poor old man who cannot see,
Will the great noble present tell to me
If this is the Paved Court?

CHIEF CIT.

It is.

[594]

MADMAN
                    Where men
Beg for a prisoner's freedom?

                    CHIEF CIT.
                    Yes. What then?

MADMAN
I come to help the choosing.

                    CHIEF CIT.
                        You can go.

MADMAN
Where, lord?

                    CHIEF CIT.
Why, home. You hear that noise below,
Or are you deaf?

                    MADMAN
                    No, lordship, only blind.

                    CHIEF CIT.
Come this-day-next-year if you have the mind.
This year you come too late, go home again.

                    MADMAN
Lord. Is the prisoner loosed?

                    CHIEF CIT.
                        Yes, in the lane.
Can you not hear them cry "Barabbas" there?

                    MADMAN
Barabbas, Lord?

GOOD FRIDAY

CHIEF CIT.
The prisoner whom they bear
In triumph home.

MADMAN
Barabbas?

CHIEF CIT.
Even he.

MADMAN
Are not you wrong, my Lord?

CHIEF CIT.
Why should I be?

MADMAN
There was another man in bonds, most kind
To me, of old, who suffer, being blind.
Surely they called for him? One Jesus? No?

CHIEF CIT.
The choice was made a little while ago.
Barabbas is set free, the man you name
Is not to be released.

MADMAN
And yet I came
Hoping to see him loosed.

CHIEF CIT.
He waits within
Till the just pain is fitted to his sin.
It will go hard with him, or I mistake.
Pray God it may.

GOOD FRIDAY

MADMAN

I sorrow for his sake.

CHIEF CIT.

God's scathe.

[*Enter more* JEWS]

MADMAN

A penny for the love of Heaven.
A given penny is a sin forgiven.
Only a penny, friends.

FIRST CIT.

The case was proved.   He uttered blasphemy.
Yet Pilate gives him stripes: the man should die.

THIRD CIT.

Wait here awhile.   It is not over yet.
This is the door, the man shall pay his debt.
After the beating they will let him go
And we shall catch him.

SECOND CIT.

We will treat him so
That he will not be eager to blaspheme
So glibly, soon.

THIRD CIT.

We will.

FIRST CIT.

Did Pilate seem
To you, to try to spare him?

SECOND CIT.

Ay, he did,
The Roman dog.

THIRD CIT.
We will not.

SECOND CIT.
                    God forbid.

FIRST CIT.
Well, we'll stay here.

SECOND CIT.
We will anoint this King.

CHIEF CIT.
You talk of Jesus?

FIRST CIT.
          Yes.

CHIEF CIT.
              I had to bring
News from the Temple but a minute past,
To-day is like to be King Jesus' last.

FIRST CIT.
So?

CHIEF CIT.
It is sure. Wait here a little while.

FIRST CIT.
We mean to, Lord. His tongue shall not defile
Our Lord again, by God.

CHIEF CIT.
                    By a happy chance
There came a hang-dog man with looks askance,
Troubled in mind, who wished to speak with us.
He said that he had heard the man speak thus
That he was the Messiah, God in man.

[598]

He had believed this, but his doubts began
When Jesus, not content, claimed further things;
To be a yoke upon the necks of Kings,
Emperor and Priest.   Then, though he found him kind
In friendship, he was troubled.   With bowed mind
He came to us and swore what Jesus claimed.
This Emperor over Kings will now be tamed.

VOICES

Will Pilate back the priests?

CHIEF CIT.

He cannot fail.
It threatens Roman power.

A VOICE

Listen, friends,
Pilate is coming; hark! the sitting ends.
No.   'Tis the Bench.

[*The bench is set by* SLAVES]

What will Lord Pilate do?

[THE SLAVES *do not answer*]

You Nubian eunuchs answer to the Jew.
Is the man cast?

A SLAVE

The circumcised will see
When Rome is ready.

[*Goes in and shuts the door*]

A VOICE

There.   They nail a tree.
They make a cross, for those are spikes being driven.
He's damned.

[599]

A Voice

Not so, he still may be forgiven.
The cross may be for one of those two thieves.

A Voice

I had forgotten them.

A Voice

This man believes
That Pilate was inclined to let him go.

Second Cit.

That was before this charge came.

A Voice

Even so
This Roman swine is fond of swine like these.

A Voice

Come, Pilate, come.

A Voice

He will not have much ease
This Paschal Feast, if Jesus is not cast.

A Voice

There is the door. Lord Pilate comes at last.
No. 'Tis the trumpet.

[A Trumpeter *comes out*]

Voices

Blow the trumpet, friend.

A Voice

Roman. Recruit. When will the sitting end?

GOOD FRIDAY

Voices
Fling something at him.   Roman.

A Voice
               O, have done.
He will not hang until the midday sun.
And we shall lose our sleeps.   Let sentence pass.

A Voice
[*Singing*.]   As I came by the market I heard a woman sing:
"My love did truly promise to wed me with a ring,
But, oh, my love deceived me and left me here forlorn
With my spirit full of sorrow, and my baby to be born."

A Voice
Why are you standing here?

A Voice
               I came to see.

A Voice
O, did you so?

A Voice
           Why do you look at me?

A Voice
You were his friend: you come from Galilee.

A Voice
I do not.

A Voice
       Yes, you do.

A VOICE
I tell you, No.

A VOICE
You know this man quite well.

A VOICE
                    I do not know
One thing about him.

A VOICE
Does he know the cur?

A VOICE
Ay, but denies.   He was his follower.

A VOICE
I was not.

A VOICE
          Why, I saw you in the hall,
I watched you.

A VOICE
I was never there at all.

A VOICE
So he would be a King.

A VOICE
That was the plan.

A VOICE
I swear to God I never saw the man.

A VOICE
He did; you liar; fling him down the stair.

GOOD FRIDAY

A VOICE

I did not, friends. I hate the man, I swear.

VOICES

You swear too much for truth, down with him, sons.
Leave him, here's Pilate.

[*Enter* LONGINUS *and* SOLDIERS]

LONGINUS

Stand back. Keep further back. Get down the stair,
Stop all this wrangling. Make less babble there.
Keep back yet further. See you keep that line.
Silence. These Jewish pigs.

THE JEWS

The Roman swine.

[*Enter* PILATE]

PILATE

Longinus.

LONGINUS

Lord.

PILATE

No Jew here thinks him King.
They want his blood.

LONGINUS

They would want anything
That would beguile the hours until the Feast.

PILATE

I would be glad to disappoint the priest.

GOOD FRIDAY

I like this Jesus man.   A man so wise
Ought not to end through crazy prophecies.
Still, he persists.

LONGINUS

They are a stubborn breed.
The medicine Cross is what they mostly need.

PILATE

Still, this man is, in fact, a kind of king,
A God beside these beasts who spit and sting,
The best Jew I have known.

LONGINUS

He had his chance.

PILATE

O, yes, he had.   We'll let the Jews advance
Into the court.   I tried to set him free.
Still, if he will persist, the thing must be.
And yet I am sorry.

LONGINUS

I am sorry, too.
He seemed a good brave fellow, for a Jew.
Still, when a man is mad there is no cure
But death, like this.

PILATE

I fear so.

LONGINUS

I am sure.

Shall I begin?

PILATE

Yes.

LONGINUS

Sound the Assembly. [*Trumpet.*]
      Sound
The Imperial call. [*Trumpet.*]

PILATE

      You people, gathered round,
Behold your King.

VOICES

      Our King. I see him. Where?
That heap of clothes behind the soldiers there.
He has been soundly beaten. Look, he bleeds.
A cross on Old Skull Hill is what he needs.

PILATE

What would you, then, that I should do to him?

VOICES

Stone the blasphemer, tear him limb from limb,
Kill him with stones, he uttered blasphemy,
Give him to us, for us to crucify.
Crucify!

PILATE

Would you crucify your King?

VOICES

He is no King of ours; we have no King
But Cæsar. Crucify!

PILATE

      Bring pen and ink.

LONGINUS

Hold up the prisoner, Lucius; give him drink.

PILATE

I come to sentence.

SERVANT

Writing things, my lord.

PILATE

Fasten the parchment to the piece of board.
So.   I will write.

VOICES

What does his writing mean?
It is the sentence of this Nazarene,
Condemning him to death.   A little while
And he'll be ours.   See Lord Pilate smile.
Why does he smile?

PILATE

Longinus.

LONGINUS

Lord.

PILATE

Come here.

Go to that man, that upland targeteer,
I want this writ in Hebrew.   Bid him write
Big easy letters that will catch the sight.

LONGINUS

I will, my lord.   Make way.

[*Exit* LONGINUS]

GOOD FRIDAY

A Voice
                    What's on the scroll?

A Voice
It gives the prisoner into his control
To nail to death, the foul blaspheming beast.

A Voice
D'you think he will be dead before the Feast?

A Voice
They'll spear him if he lingers until dark.

A Voice
When Feast begins he will be stiff and stark.
There's little life in him as it is.

Voices
We'll hammer iron through those hands of his,
And through his feet, and when the cross is set
Jolt it; remember.   I will not forget.

A Voice
Here comes the sentence.
                    [*Enter* Longinus]

A Voice
                    Wait; it is not signed.

A Voice
Come to the hill, you will be left behind.
I want a good place at the cross's foot.

GOOD FRIDAY

A Voice
I've got a stone for when they move the brute.
Besides, I mean to bait him on the way.
I'll spatter him with filth.

A Voice
No, come away.

Pilate
Imperial finding in the High Priest's suit.
In the name of Cæsar and of Rome. . . .

Longinus
Salute.

Pilate
I, Procurator of Judæa, say
That Jesus, called the King, be led away
To death by crucifixion, here and now.
In the name of Cæsar and of Rome. . . .

Longinus
We bow
To the sentence of the court.

Pilate
See sentence done.
This is your warrant.

Longinus
Sentence shall be done.

Voices
Away, friends, hurry. Keep a place for me.
Get there before they come, then we shall see
All of the nailing and the fixing on.

PILATE

Longinus.

LONGINUS

Lord.

PILATE

Display this scroll upon
The head of Jesus' cross, that men may read.
Wait; I'll declare it publicly. Take heed. . . .
I add this word, that over Jesus' head
This scroll shall be displayed till he is dead.
Show it, Longinus. Read it if you choose.

VOICES

"Jesus of Nazareth, the King of the Jews."
We'll make him King, we'll set him up in state.
At Golgotha. Come; drag him through the gate.
Give him his cross. Come, soldiers.

CHIEF CIT.

Israel, wait.

Wait. I must speak. Lord Pilate.

VOICES

Stand aside. . . .

Are we to miss his being crucified?

CHIEF CIT.

Wait. Only wait. One word.

MADMAN

Lord Pilate. Lord.

SENTRY

Stand back.

MADMAN

I'll speak.

SENTRY

I'll tame you with the sword.

MADMAN

Lord Pilate, Jesus is an upright man,
I heard his teaching since it first began.
You are mistaken, Lord, you are misled.
Spare him, great King.

SENTRY

Get down.

MADMAN

Kill me instead.

He never said this thing. [*He is beaten aside.*]

LONGINUS

The company,
Attention. Front. Take up the prisoner. By
The left, quick wheel. Down to the courtyard, wheel.

[THE TROOPS *go out by the doors, into the barracks, so as to
reach the main gate from within. The* PRISONER *is not
shown, but only suggested.*]

A VOICE

He cannot lift his cross, I saw him reel.

A VOICE

We'll find a man to bring it. Hurry, friends.
Three to be nailed.

[610]

A Voice

The thieves will make good ends;
They always do. This fellow will die soon.

A Voice

The troops will spear them all before full moon.
Come; watch them march them out.

Get mud to fling.

[*They hurry down the staircase O. P. side*]

Chief Cit.

[*To* Pilate.] Lord Pilate, do not write "Jesus the King,"
But that "He called himself, 'Jesus the King.'"

Pilate

Empty this water here. [Servant *does*]

Remove this board.

Take in the bench.

Chief Cit.

I have to ask, my lord,
That you will change the wording of your scroll,
My lord, it cuts my people to the soul.

Pilate

Tell Caius Scirrus that I want him. [*Exit* Servant.]
So. [*To* Chief Citizen.]
What I have written, I have written. Go.

[*Exit* Chief Citizen. Pilate *watches him. A yell below as
the* Troops *march out from the main gate.* Longinus'
voice is heard shouting.]

GOOD FRIDAY

Longinus

Right wheel.   Quick march.
Close up.   Keep your files close.

[*A march is played, oboe and trumpet.* Pilate *goes in, the* Troops *salute, the bronze doors are closed, but a* Sentry *stands outside them.* The Madman *remains.*

Madman

They cut my face, there's blood upon my brow.
So, let it run, I am an old man now,
An old, blind beggar picking filth for bread.
Once I wore silk, drank wine,
Spent gold on women, feasted, all was mine;
But this uneasy current in my head
Burst, one full moon, and cleansed me, then I saw
Truth like a perfect crystal, life its flaw,
I told the world, but I was mad, they said.

I had a valley farm above a brook,
My sheep bells there were sweet,
And in the summer heat
My mill wheels turned, yet all these things they took;
Ah, and I gave them, all things I forsook
But that green blade of wheat,
My own soul's courage, that they did not take.

I will go on, although my old heart ache.
Not long, not long.
Soon I shall pass behind
This changing veil to that which does not change,
My tired feet will range

In some green valley of eternal mind
Where Truth is daily like the water's song.

[*Enter the* CHIEF CITIZEN]

CHIEF CIT.

Where is Lord Pilate?

MADMAN

Gone within.

CHIEF CIT.

You heard
The way he spoke to me?

MADMAN

No, not a word.
The dogs so bayed for blood, I could not hear.
Ask the tall sentry yonder with the spear.

CHIEF CIT.

I wish to see Lord Pilate.

SENTRY

Stand aside.

CHIEF CIT.

Send word to him; I cannot be denied.
I have to see him; it concerns the State
Urgently, too, I tell you.

SENTRY

It can wait.

CHIEF CIT.

It may mean bloodshed.

[613]

GOOD FRIDAY

SENTRY
Bloodshed is my trade.
A sentry's orders have to be obeyed
The same as God's, that you were talking of.

CHIEF CIT.
I tell you, I must see him.

SENTRY
That's enough.
You cannot now.

MADMAN
The soldier's words are true.

CHIEF CIT.
Could you send word?

SENTRY
Sir, I have answered you.

CHIEF CIT.
Those words that Pilate wrote, the Hebrew screed,
May cause a riot.

MADMAN
Yes?

CHIEF CIT.
And death.

SENTRY
Indeed.
You got the poor man's life, what would you more?

CHIEF CIT.
Means to see Pilate.

SENTRY

As I said before,
You cannot. Stand away. A man like you
Ought to know better than to lead a crew
To yell for a man's blood. God stop my breath,
What does a man like you with blood and death?
Go to.

CHIEF CIT.

You will not send?

SENTRY
I will not send.

CHIEF CIT.
[*Going.*] You shall regret this.

SENTRY
Right. Goodbye, my friend.

CHIEF CIT.
Means will be found. [*Exit.*]

SENTRY
These priests, these preaching folk. [*Pause. Sings.*]
"Upon a summer morning, I bade my love goodbye,
In the old green glen so far away,
To go to be a soldier on biscuits made of rye."

It is darker than it was.

MADMAN
It is falling dark.

SENTRY
It feels like earthquake weather. Listen.

[615]

GOOD FRIDAY

MADMAN
                                Hark.

SENTRY
It sounded like a shock inside the walls.

MADMAN
God celebrates the madman's funerals.

SENTRY
The shouts came from the Temple.

MADMAN
                                Yes, they sing
Glory to God there, having killed their King.

SENTRY
You knew that man they are hanging?

MADMAN
                                Yes. Did you?

SENTRY
Not till I saw him scourged. Was he a Jew?

MADMAN
No. Wisdom comes from God, and he was wise.
I have touched wisdom since they took my eyes.

SENTRY
So you were blinded? Why?

MADMAN
                                Thinking aloud,
One Passover.

GOOD FRIDAY

SENTRY

How so?

MADMAN

                I told the crowd
That only a bloody God would care for blood.
The crowd kill kids and smear the lintel wood,
To honor God, who lives in the pure stars.

SENTRY

You must have suffered; they are angry scars.

MADMAN

There is no scar inside.

SENTRY

                That may be so;
Still, it was mad; men do not wish to know
The truth about their customs, nor aught else.   [*Cries off.*]

MADMAN

They have nailed the teacher Jesus by those yells.

SENTRY

It is darker. There'll be earthquake before night.
What sort of man was he?

MADMAN

                He knew the right
And followed her, a stony road, to this.

SENTRY

I find sufficient trouble in what is
Without my seeking what is right or wrong.

MADMAN

All have to seek her, and the search is long.

SENTRY

Maybe.

MADMAN

And hard.

SENTRY

Maybe. [*Pause. Sings.*]
"I mean to be a captain before I do return,
Though the winters they may freeze and the summers they
    may burn,
I mean to be a captain and command a hundred men
And the women who . . ." [*A bugle call off.*]
There is recall.

[*The doors are opened and the* SENTRY *goes*]

MADMAN

The wild-duck, stringing through the sky,
Are south away.
Their green necks glitter as they fly,
The lake is gray,
So still, so lone, the fowler never heeds.
The wind goes rustle, rustle, through the reeds.

*   *   *   *   *   *

There they find peace to have their own wild souls.
In that still lake,
Only the moonrise or the wind controls
The way they take,

[618]

Through the gray reeds, the cocking moorhen's lair,
Rippling the pool, or over leagues of air.

      *   *   *   *   *

Not thus, not thus are the wild souls of men.
No peace for those
Who step beyond the blindness of the pen
To where the skies unclose.
For them the spitting mob, the cross, the crown of thorns,
The bull gone mad, the saviour on his horns.

      *   *   *   *   *

         Beauty and Peace have made
         No peace, no still retreat,
         No solace, none.
         Only the unafraid
         Before life's roaring street
         Touch Beauty's feet,
         Know Truth, do as God bade,
         Become God's son.   *[Pause.]*

Darkness come down, cover a brave man's pain.
Let the bright soul go back to God again.
Cover that tortured flesh, it only serves
To hold that thing which other power nerves.
Darkness, come down, let it be midnight here,
In the dark night the untroubled soul sings clear. *[It darkens.]*

I have been scourged, blinded and crucified,
My blood burns on the stones of every street
In every town; wherever people meet
I have been hounded down, in anguish died. *[It darkens.]*
The creaking door of flesh rolls slowly back.

Nerve by red nerve the links of living crack,
Loosing the soul to tread another track.

Beyond the pain, beyond the broken clay,
A glimmering country lies
Where life is being wise,
All of the beauty seen by truthful eyes
Are lilies there, growing beside the way.
Those golden ones will loose the torted hands,
Smooth the scarred brow, gather the breaking soul,
Whose earthly moments drop like falling sands
To leave the spirit whole.
Now darkness is upon the face of the earth. [*He goes.*]

[PILATE *entering, as the darkness reddens to a glare*]

PILATE

This monstrous day is in the pangs of birth.
There was a shock. I wish the troops were back
From Golgotha. The heavens are more black
Than in the great shock in my first year's rule.
Please God these zealot pilgrims will keep cool
Nor think this done by God for any cause.
The lightning jags the heaven in bloody scraws
Like chronicles of judgment. Now it breaks.
Now rain.

PROCULA

[*Entering.*]   O Pilate.

PILATE

What?

PROCULA

For all our sakes
Speak. Where is Jesus?

PILATE

He is crucified.

PROCULA

Crucified?

PILATE

Put to death. My wife, I tried
To save him, but such men cannot be saved.
Truth to himself till death was all he craved.
He has his will.

PROCULA

So what they said is true.
O God, my God. But when I spoke to you
You said that you had warned him.

PILATE

That is so.
Another charge was brought some hours ago,
That he was claiming to be that great King
Foretold by prophets, who shall free the Jews.
This he persisted in. I could not choose
But end a zealot claiming such a thing.

PROCULA

He was no zealot.

PILATE

Yes, on this one point.
Had he recanted, well. But he was firm.
So he was cast.

PROCULA

The gouts of gore anoint
That temple to the service of the worm.

[621]

GOOD FRIDAY

It is a desecration of our power.
A rude poor man who pitted his pure sense
Against what holds the world its little hour,
Blind force and fraud, priests' mummery and pretence,
Could you not see that this is what he did?

PILATE

Most clearly, wife. But Roman laws forbid
That I should weigh, like God, the worth of souls.
I act for Rome, and Rome is better rid
Of these rare spirits whom no law controls.
He broke a statute, knowing from the first
Whither his act would lead, he was not blind.

PROCULA

No, friend, he followed hungry and athirst
The lonely exaltation of his mind.
So Rome, our mother, profits by his death,
You think so?

PILATE

                    Ay.

PROCULA

                    We draw securer breath,
We Romans, from his gasping on the cross?

PILATE

Some few will be the calmer for his loss.
Many, perhaps; he made a dangerous claim.
Even had I spared it would have been the same
A year, or two, from now. Forget him, friend.

PROCULA

I have no part nor parcel in his end.
Rather than have it thought I buy my ease,
My body's safety, honor, dignities,
Life and the rest at such a price of pain
There [*she stabs her arm with her dagger*] is my blood, to wash
    away the stain.
There. There once more. It fetched too dear a price.
O God, receive that soul in paradise.

PILATE

What have you done?

PROCULA

          No matter; it atones.
His blood will clamor from the city stones.

PILATE

Go in. No, let me bind it.

PROCULA

          Someone comes.
A councillor, I think. Ask what he wants.

[*Enter* JOSEPH]

JOSEPH

Greetings, Lord Pilate.

PILATE

        And to you.

JOSEPH

[*To* PROCULA.]   And you.
[*To* PILATE.] I have a boon to ask.

PROCULA
                              What can we do?

JOSEPH

Lord Pilate, may I speak?

PILATE

[*To* PROCULA.]   Go in.   [*She goes in.*]   Go on [*to* JOSEPH].

JOSEPH

The man called Christ, the follower of John,
Was crucified to-day by your decree.
[PILATE *bows.*]   He was my master, very dear to me.
I will not speak of that.   I only crave
Leave to prepare his body for the grave,
And then to bury him.   May I have leave?

PILATE

Yes, you may have him when the guards give leave.
Wait.   In a case like this, men may believe
That the dead master is not really dead.
This preaching man, this King, has been the head
Of men who may be good and mean no harm,
Whose tenets, none the less, have caused alarm
First to the priests, and through the priests to me.
I wish this preacher's followers to see
That teaching of this kind is to be curbed.
I mean, established truths may be disturbed,
But not the Jews, nor Rome.   You understand?

JOSEPH

I follow; yes.

GOOD FRIDAY

PILATE
A riot might be fanned,
Such things have been, over the martyr's grave.

JOSEPH
His broken corpse is all his followers crave.

PILATE
Why, very well then.

JOSEPH
Will you give your seal?

PILATE
My seal? What for?

JOSEPH
That I may show the guard
And have the body.

PILATE
Gladly; but I feel . . .
Not yet; not until dark.

JOSEPH
It will be hard
To bury him to-night . . . the feast begins.

PILATE
I know, but still, when men are crucified . . .

JOSEPH
There is no hope of that. The man has died.

PILATE
Died? Dead already?

JOSEPH

Yes.

PILATE

'Tis passing soon.

JOSEPH

God broke that bright soul's body as a boon.
He died at the ninth hour.

PILATE

Are you sure?

JOSEPH

I saw him, Lord.

PILATE

I thought he would endure
Longer than that; he had a constant mind.

JOSEPH

The great soul burns the body to a rind.

PILATE

But dead, already; strange; strange. [*Calling.*]
You in the court,
Send me Longinus here with his report.

A VOICE

I will, my lord.

PILATE

This teacher was your friend?

GOOD FRIDAY

JOSEPH

Was, is, and will be, till the great world end;
Which God grant may be soon.

PILATE

                I disagree
With teachers of new truth.   For men like me
There is but one religion, which is Rome.
No easy one to practise, far from home.
You come from Ramah?

JOSEPH
Yes.

PILATE
                What chance is there
Of olives being good?

JOSEPH
         They should be fair.

PILATE

You will not use Italian presses?   No?

JOSEPH

Man likes his own, my lord, however slow;
What the land made, we say, it ought to use.

PILATE

Your presses waste; oil is too good to lose.
But I shall not persuade.

SERVANT
       Longinus, lord.

GOOD FRIDAY

PILATE

Make your report, centurion. Where's your sword?
What makes you come thus jangled? Are you ill?

LONGINUS

There was a shock of earthquake up the hill.
I have been shaken. I had meant to come
Before; but I was whirled . . . was stricken dumb.
I left my sword within. . . .

PILATE

                    Leave it. Attend.
Is the man, Jesus, dead? This is his friend
Who wants to bury him, he says he is.

LONGINUS

Jesus is out of all his miseries.
Yes, he is dead, my lord.

PILATE

            Already?

LONGINUS

                      Yes.
The men who suffer most endure the less.
He died without our help.

JOSEPH

              Then may I have
His body, Lord, to lay it in the grave?

PILATE

A sentry's there?

GOOD FRIDAY

Longinus

Yes, Lord.

Pilate

                   Have you a scroll?
[*Takes paper.*] Right. Now some wax. [*Writes.*]
                              Give into his control
The body of the teacher; see it laid
Inside the tomb and see the doorway made
Secure with stones and sealed, then bring me word.
This privilege of burial is conferred
On the conditions I have named to you.
See you observe them strictly.

Joseph

                       I will do
All that himself would ask to show my sense
Of this last kindness. I shall go from hence
Soon, perhaps far; I give you thanks, my lord.
Now the last joy the niggard fates afford;
One little service more, and then an end
Of that divineness touched at through our friend. [*Exit.*]

Pilate

See that the tomb is sealed by dark to-night.
Where were you hurt, Longinus? You are white.
What happened at the cross?

Longinus

                       We nailed him there
Aloft, between the thieves, in the bright air.

[629]

GOOD FRIDAY

The rabble and the readers mocked with oaths,
The hangman's squad were dicing for his clothes.
The two thieves jeered at him. Then it grew dark,
Till the noon sun was dwindled to a spark,
And one by one the mocking mouths fell still.
We were alone on the accursed hill
And we were still, not even the dice clicked,
Only the heavy blood-gouts dropped and ticked
On to the stone; the hill is all bald stone.
And now and then the hangers gave a groan.
Up in the dark, three shapes with arms outspread.
The blood-drops spat to show how slow they bled.
They rose up black against the ghastly sky,
God, Lord, it is a slow way to make die
A man, a strong man, who can beget men.
Then there would come another groan, and then
One of those thieves (tough cameleers those two)
Would curse the teacher from lips bitten through
And the other bid him let the teacher be.
I have stood much, but this thing daunted me,
The dark, the livid light, and long long groans
One on another, coming from their bones.
And it got darker and a glare began
Like the sky burning up above the man.
The hangman's squad stood easy on their spears
And the air moaned, and women were in tears,
While still between his groans the robber cursed.
The sky was grim: it seemed about to burst.
Hours had passed: they seemed like awful days.
Then . . . what was that?

PILATE

What? Where?

[630]

LONGINUS

A kind of blaze,
Fire descending.

PILATE

No.

LONGINUS

I saw it.

PILATE

Yes?
What was it that you saw?

LONGINUS

A fiery tress
Making red letters all across the heaven.
Lord Pilate, pray to God we be forgiven.

PILATE

"The sky was grim," you said, there at the cross.
What happened next?

LONGINUS

The towers bent like moss
Under the fiery figures from the sky.
Horses were in the air, there came a cry.
Jesus was calling God: it struck us dumb.
One said "He is calling God. Wait. Will God come?
Wait." And we listened in the glare. O sir,
He was God's son, that man, that minister,
For as he called, fire tore the sky in two,
The sick earth shook and tossed the cross askew,
The earthquake ran like thunder, the earth's bones
Broke, the graves opened, there were falling stones.

[631]

GOOD FRIDAY

PILATE

I felt the shock even here.   So?

LONGINUS

Jesus cried
Once more and drooped, I saw that he had died.
Lord, in the earthquake God had come for him.
The thought of 't shakes me sick, my eyes are dim.

PILATE

Tell Scirrus to relieve you.

LONGINUS

Lord. . . .

PILATE

Dismiss.

Lie down and try to sleep; forget all this.
Tell Scirrus I command it.   Rest to-night.
Go in, Longinus, go.

LONGINUS

Thank you, Lord Pilate.

[*Exit* LONGINUS]

PILATE

[*Alone.*]   No man can stand an earthquake.   Men can bear
Tumults of water and of fire and air,
But not of earth, man's grave and standing ground;
When that begins to heave the will goes round.
Longinus, too.   [*Noise below.*]   Listen.

Does Herod come?

I heard his fifes.

GOOD FRIDAY

[*The doors open.* SERVANTS *enter*]

SERVANT
Lord Herod is at hand;
Will it please your Lordship robe?

PILATE
Sprinkle fresh sand,
For blood was shed to-day, here, under foot. [*He robes.*]
Well, that; the other clasp. [*Music off.*]

A VOICE
Cohort. Salute.

PILATE
Leave torches at the door. Dismiss. [SERVANTS *go.*]
He comes
Welcomed by everyone; the city hums
With joy when Herod passes. Ah, not thus
Do I go through the town. They welcome us
With looks of hate, with mutterings, curses, stones.

[*Enter* PROCULA]

Come, stand with me. Welcome Lord Herod here.
Welcome must make amends for barrack cheer.

[THE NUBIANS *hold torches at the door*]

HEROD *enters*
Come in, good welcome, Herod.

PROCULA
Welcome, sir.

GOOD FRIDAY

Herod

To Rome, to Pilate, and to Beauty, greeting;
Give me your hands. What joy is in this meeting.
Pilate, again. You, you have hurt your hand?

Pilate

It is nothing, sir.

Herod

Beauty has touched this land,
A wound has followed.

Procula

What you please to call
Beauty, my lord, did nothing of the kind.
An earthen vessel tilted with a wall.

Herod

May it soon mend. Now let me speak my mind.
Pilate, since you have ruled here, there have been
Moments of . . . discord, shall we say? between
Your government and mine. I am afraid
That I, the native here, have seldom made
Efforts for friendship with you.

Pilate
Come.

Herod

I should
Have done more than I have, done all I could,
Healed the raw wound between the land and Rome,
Helped you to make this hellish town a home,
Not left it, as I fear it has been, hell
To you and yours cooped in a citadel

Above rebellion brewing. For the past
I offer deep regret, grief that will last,
And shame; your generous mind leaves me ashamed.

PILATE

Really, my lord.

PROCULA

These things must not be named.

PILATE

It is generous of you to speak like this,
But, Herod, hark.

PROCULA

If things have been amiss,
The fault was ours.

HEROD

No, the fault was mine.
Your generous act this morning was a sign
Of scrupulous justice done to me by you
For all these years, unnoticed hitherto,
Unrecognized, unthanked. I thank you now.
Give me your hand . . . so . . . thus.

PILATE

Herod, I bow
To what you say. To think that I have done
Something (I know not what) that has begun
A kindlier bond between us, touches home.
I have long grieved lest I have injured Rome
By failing towards yourself, where other men
Might have been wiser. . . . That is over, then?

[635]

Our differences henceforth may be discussed
In friendly talk together;

HEROD

So I trust.

PILATE

Give me your hand; I have long hoped for this.
I need your help, and you, perhaps, need mine.
The tribes are restless on the border-line,
The whole land seethes: the news from Rome is bad.
But this atones.

PROCULA

O, fully.

HEROD

I am glad.

PILATE

Let us go in.

HEROD

You lead.

PROCULA

A moment, one. . . .

You named a generous act that he had done. . . . ?

HEROD

This morning, yes; you sent that man to me
Because his crime was laid in Galilee.
A little thing, but still it touched me close;
It made me think how our disputes arose
When thieves out of your province brought to me
Were punished with a fine, perhaps set free,

[636]

Not sent to you to judge, as you sent him.
In future you will find me more a friend.
Or so I hope.

PILATE

Thanks.   May the gods so send
That this may lead to happier days for us.

VOICES OF THE CROWD

[*Who are now flocking in, among them* THE MADMAN.]   Herod
    the good, Herod the glorious.
Long life to Herod.

PILATE

Come, the crowd begin. . . .

VOICES

Herod for ever.

PILATE

Let us go within. . . .

HEROD

Yes.   By the by, what happened to the man?
I sent him back to you; a rumor ran
That he was crucified.

PILATE

He was.

HEROD

The priests
Rage upon points of doctrine at the feasts.

VOICES

God bless you, Herod; give you length of days, Herod.

[637]

GOOD FRIDAY

HEROD

[*To the* CROWD]. Go home. To God alone give praise.
This is Deliverance Night; go home, for soon
Over the dusty hill will come the moon,
And you must feast, with prayer to the Adored.
[*To* PILATE.] He well deserved his death.

VOICES

God bless you, Lord.

PILATE

I'll lead the way. . . .

VOICES

Herod.

HEROD

[*To* PROCULA.] Lady, your hand.

PROCULA

There is a just man's blood upon the sand.
Mind how you tread.

[*They go in. The bronze doors are closed. The* CROWD *remains
for an instant watching the doors.*]

A VOICE

Herod the Fox makes friends with Pilate. Why?

A VOICE

He needs a Roman loan.

A VOICE

Look at the sky,
The Paschal moon has risen.

GOOD FRIDAY

A Voice
God is great.
Why did I linger here? I shall be late. [*Going.*]

A Voice
Good night and blessing.

A Voice
[*Going.*]   Pilate's color changed
When we cheered Herod.

A Voice
They have been estranged
A long while now; but now they will be friends. [*Going.*]

A Voice
What joy it is when Preparation ends.
Now to our Feast. Do you go down the stair?

A Voice
Yes, past the pools; will you come with me there?

A Voice
I love to walk by moonlight; let us go. [*They go.*]

A Voice
[*Singing.*] Friends, out of Egypt, long ago,
Our wandering fathers came,
Treading the paths that God did show
By pointing cloud and flame.
By land and sea His darkness and His light
Led us into His peace. . . . [*The voice dies away.*]

GOOD FRIDAY

A Voice

[*Off.*]   Good-night.

[*Only* The Madman *remains. He takes lilies from a box and begins to tie them in bunches.*]

Madman

Only a penny, a penny,
Lilies brighter than any,
Lilies whiter than snow. [*He feels that he is alone.*]
Beautiful lilies grow
Wherever the truth so sweet
Has trodden with bloody feet,
Has stood with a bloody brow.
Friend, it is over now,
The passion, the sweat, the pains,
Only the truth remains. [*He lays lilies down.*]

* * * * * *

I cannot see what others see;
Wisdom alone is kind to me,
Wisdom that comes from Agony.

* * * * * *

Wisdom that lives in the pure skies,
The untouched star, the spirit's eyes;
O Beauty, touch me, make me wise.

Curtain

Printed in the United States of America

THE WORKS OF JOHN MASEFIELD

A Mainsail Haul

Cloth, 12mo, $1.25. Leather, $1.75

As a sailor before the mast Masefield has traveled the world over. Many of the tales in this volume are his own experiences written with the same dramatic fidelity displayed in " Dauber."

Multitude and Solitude

$1.35

" This is material of the best kind for a story of adventure, and Mr. Masefield uses it to the best advantage. He has the gift of direct and simple narrative, and it need hardly be said that he knows the *human heart.*"— *Argonaut.*

Captain Margaret

Cloth, $1.50

" Worthy to rank high among books of its class. The story has quality, charm, and spirited narrative."— *Outlook.*

Lost Endeavour

$1.50

A stirring story of adventure, dealing with pirates and buccaneers, and life on the seas in a day when an ocean trip was beset with all kinds of dangers and excitements. Those who have enjoyed " Captain Margaret " and " Multitude and Solitude " will find this tale equally exhilarating.

THE MACMILLAN COMPANY

Publishers   64–66 Fifth Avenue   New York